AF837068

The Trial of Hissein Habré

The Trial of Hissein Habré

The International Crimes of a Former Head of State

Emmanuel Guematcha

LEXINGTON BOOKS
Lanham • Boulder • New York • London

Published by Lexington Books
An imprint of The Rowman & Littlefield Publishing Group, Inc.
4501 Forbes Boulevard, Suite 200, Lanham, Maryland 20706
www.rowman.com

86-90 Paul Street, London EC2A 4NE

Copyright © 2022 by The Rowman & Littlefield Publishing Group, Inc.

All rights reserved. No part of this book may be reproduced in any form or by any electronic or mechanical means, including information storage and retrieval systems, without written permission from the publisher, except by a reviewer who may quote passages in a review.

British Library Cataloguing in Publication information available

Library of Congress Cataloging-in-Publication Data available

ISBN 9781666903911 (hardcover) | ISBN 9781666903928 (epub)

Contents

Acknowledgments

My special thanks go to Professor Sandra Szurek. Without her, this project would not have been possible. The discussions I had with her enriched the topics developed in this book. I am also indebted to those who provided helpful comments or support during the writing and finalization of the book, especially the anonymous reviewers at Lexington Books, Mustapha Ka, Beth McAuley, Patricia Kela, and my editors at Lexington Books, Shelby Russell and Sydney Wedbush. Finally, I am grateful to Monika Jagadeesh and Monica Sukumar at Deanta for their assistance. Any errors or mistakes remain my own.

Disclaimer

The author of the following pages was a legal assistant in the office of the prosecutor of the Extraordinary African Chambers, the tribunal that tried Hissein Habré, the former head of state of Chad. The author attended some of the trial sessions and witnessed some of the facts presented here. He met and collaborated with some of the personnel of the Extraordinary African Chambers. However, the majority of the material gathered to write these pages comes from post-trial research. The sources relied upon by the author include official legal documents, official archives, reports, videos broadcasts made during the trial, and books and published articles. Videos of the trial have been released and transcripts of the hearings are cited in the judgments of the Extraordinary African Chambers. The majority of the sources used, including excerpts and quotations from the hearings, are in French and have been translated into English by the author. The author's personal account of the trial, its analysis, and the conclusions reached are solely his own. In particular, this account does not place any responsibility on the Extraordinary African Chambers or the organizations for which he has worked or is working.

Key Abbreviations

	French	English
AVCPR	Association des victimes des crimes et répressions politiques	Association of Victims of Crimes and Political Repressions
BSIR	Brigade spéciale d'intervention rapide	Special Rapid Intervention Brigade
CAE/EAC	Chambres africaines extraordinaires	Extraordinary African Chambers
CEDEAO/ECOWAS	Communauté économique des Etats de l'Afrique de l'Ouest	Economic Community of West African States
CIJ/ICJ	Cour internationale de justice	International Court of Justice
CPI/ICC	Cour pénale internationale	International Criminal Court
CrADHP/ACtHPR	Cour africaine des droits de l'homme et des peuples	African Court of Human and Peoples' Rights
DDS	Direction de la documentation et de la sécurité	Directorate of Documentation and Security
FIDH	Fédération internationale des droits de l'Homme	International Federation for Human Rights
GUNT	Gouvernement d'Union Nationale du Tchad	Government of National Unity of Chad
MOSANAT	Mouvement pour le Salut National du Tchad	Movement for the National Salvation of Chad
ONG/NGOs	Organisations non gouvernementales	nongovernmental organizations
ONU/UN	Organisation des Nations Unies	United Nations
RADHT	Réseau des associations des droits de l'homme du Tchad	Network of Human Rights Associations of Chad
TSL/STL	Tribunal spécial pour le Liban	Special Tribunal for Lebanon
TPIR/ICTR	Tribunal pénal international pour le Rwanda	International Criminal Tribunal for Rwanda
TPIY/ICTY	Tribunal pénal international pour l'ex Yougoslavie	International Criminal Tribunal for the former Yugoslavia
TSSL/SCSL	Tribunal spécial pour la Sierra Leone	Special Court for Sierra Leone
UA/AU	Union africaine	African Union

Introduction

SEPTEMBER 7, 2015, COURTROOM NO. 4, PALAIS DE JUSTICE, DAKAR, SENEGAL

It's obviously a big day.[1] The room is not full but crowded: there are men in dark jackets; well-dressed women; journalists armed with cameras, computers, and notebooks; representatives of nongovernmental and international organizations; lawyers in black robes; and people interested in the trial. Framing this crowd are the security forces personnel, who are standing in the corners of the room, young, bare heads, watchful eyes, clenched teeth, and serious faces. In spite of the slight rattling sound of the devices in the hands of the press, the footsteps of people who are entering, whispering, sitting down, getting up, coming and going, there is a precarious calm, like the quiet before a storm. The atmosphere is overheated and tense. Similar to spectators in a theater waiting for the curtain to go up, the crowd often look toward the stage of the courtroom where the judges of the Extraordinary African Assize Chamber should soon appear for the beginning of the trial of Hissein Habré, the former head of the state of Chad, a landlocked country located in the center of the African continent.

With shiny and serious faces, they finally arrive, wrapped in their bright reddish-black robes. Everyone in the courtroom is standing up. The judges sit down. So does the courtroom audience. The president of the Extraordinary African Assize Chamber, Gustave Kam, a judge from Burkina Faso and former judge of the International Criminal Tribunal for Rwanda, declares the trial open. The defendant, Hissein Habré, is absent. The president of the Assize Chamber exchanges words with the other judges, the general prosecutor, the lawyers of the civil parties, and the defense lawyers. The public is informed that the accused, Hissein Habré, is in the basement of the courtroom and refuses to appear before the Chamber. After further exchanges and a recess, the judges give the order to bring the accused by force. The courtroom is holding its breath.

The public hear noises in the distance. What the noises are becomes clearer when two black-clad prison guards appear through the door next to the judges' dais. The two prison guards, followed by three others, are carrying a white-clad, turbaned person firmly in their arms. The person is the accused. Appearing for a moment motionless in the arms of his jailers, the accused suddenly begins to gesticulate. He lifts his feet, raises his arms, shakes his head, twists his head, contorts himself suddenly, defies the prison guards, and refuses to advance toward the courtroom. For a second, the prison guards seem distraught by the former head of state's attitude. After a quick pause, as if to catch their breath and organize themselves better, they grasp the accused and hold him firmly by the waist. In a brief and sharp movement, they bring his two legs together in a single block, lock him with their muscular arms, lift him up, and drag him to a reserved seat in the courtroom.

While the prison guards are busy with this inelegant task, adding to the confusion and chaos that seem to be brewing, young men in the audience suddenly stand up, rush to the front of the courtroom, and shout their support for the accused. The security forces personnel leap from their position and seize the young men in a concert of screams, noises, and breathless voices. In a perfectly executed movement, they surround them and push them out of the courtroom through a side door.

The accused, now seated in a comfortable chair in front of the judges, gesticulates vigorously. He is surrounded by four prison guards. Three keep him sitting on the seat while a fourth talks to him, apparently trying to convince him to calm down. The defendant shouts: "Mercenaries! You don't belong here."[2]

A few long seconds later, when the precarious calm returns, the president of the Assize Chamber starts to speak. The accused interrupts him: "Shut up!" he says. He shouts and gesticulates as his guards again try to glue him to his seat and prevent him from moving. "Mr. Hissein Habré, it is the Tribunal that ordered that you be brought before it," continues the president. "Which Tribunal?!" the accused shouts back in a hoarse, deep, and strong voice. The president indicates that the tribunal will not compromise and the accused will be brought to trial and tried either by force or willingly, and the accused replies, "An illegal organization, outlawed . . . a free and independent Africa, down with the imperialists!"

This dialogue of the deaf remains the only one between the president of the Assize Chamber and the accused. A few minutes after the start of his trial, Hissein Habré stops gesticulating and falls into silence.

MAY 30, 2016, COURTROOM NO. 4, PALAIS DE JUSTICE, DAKAR, SENEGAL

Draped in a large and wide white *boubou* (an elegant full-length robe), turbaned, and sheltered behind sunglasses and surrounded by prison guards dressed in black clothes, Hissein Habré sits impassively in his seat.[3] The judges of the Extraordinary African Assize Chamber have just pronounced a judgment that sentences him to life imprisonment.

As after each hearing since the beginning of the trial, the public rises as the judges, prosecutors, and clerks leave the courtroom. In the courtroom, victims exult and form the "V for victory" with their fingers. Some jump for joy, some cry. Hissein Habré stands up and prison guards escort him to a convicted offenders' exit. His relatives and supporters, present in the room and having assiduously attended the trial, applaud, shout, and express support for the former head of state. Hissein Habré turns toward them. In a gesture he repeated after many hearing days,[4] he raises his arms and brandishes his right fist toward them. Accompanied by the applause of his supporters, he returns to jail.

On April 27, 2017, the Extraordinary African Assize Appeals Chamber confirms Hissein Habré's sentence to life imprisonment.

How was Hissein Habré, former head of the state of Chad, brought to justice in a trial that began on September 7, 2015, and concluded less than two years later, and why was he sentenced to life imprisonment? This book proposes to discover the answers while analyzing the prosecution of Hissein Habré and the impact and significance of his trial.

Chapters 1 and 2 present the legal history and background of Hissein Habré's trial and the characteristics and proceedings of the court that tried him. Chapter 3 examines the investigation phase that preceded his trial. Chapter 4 presents the beginning of the trial in courtroom. Chapter 5 explores the historical context of the commission of the crimes in Chad as outlined at the beginning of the trial by a Chadian historian, and later by victims and witnesses. Chapters 6–11 examine various aspects of the crimes perpetrated in Chad, the machinery of repression, the tragic experiences of victims, the sequels of the crimes, the verdict of Hissein Habré's trial, and the appeal phase. Chapters 4–11, which describe the trial and the appeal, are based on the oral and public proceedings. They place particular emphasis on individual experiences of international crimes and present the crimes committed through the excerpts of the testimonies of victims, witnesses, experts, and their exchanges with lawyers, prosecutors, and judges during the trial. Chapter 12 measures the impact of the trial on reconciliation in Chad, and chapter 13 measures the trial's significance in the global fight against impunity in Africa.

The conclusion argues that the criminal proceedings in the Habré case must be positioned within the framework of human criminal justice.

NOTES

1. About what happened that day, see EAC, 07-09-2015, in Online Playlist of the *Forum interactif sur les CAE*: https://www.youtube.com/channel/UCgING8GqD65mKzs8NALpd2g/playlists; TrustAfrica, *Ministère public contre la défense de Habré, Rapport de l'audience numéro 3 du jeudi 7 septembre 2015*: https://www.trustafrica.org/images/ICJ_reports/fr/CAE%20-%20Audience%20du%207%20septembre%202015.pdf; Human Rights Watch, *Blog, Le procès de Hissène Habré*, September 7, 2015, https://www.hrw.org/fr/content/280858. Websites accessed 10/28/2021.

2. The excerpts and quotations of the trial are in French and have been translated to English by the author.

3. About what happened that day, see EAC, Video Verdict Procès Hissene Habré, May 30, 2016, Online Playlist of the *Forum interactif sur les CAE*, op. cit., note 1; Martien Schotsmans, "Editorial," in *Le procès Habré*, RCN Justice & Démocratie, Le Bulletin n°48, July–August 2016, 3.

4. For example, EAC, Hearing of Souleymane Abdoulaye Taher, November 10, 2015, in Online Playlist of the *Forum interactif sur les CAE*, ibid.; TV5-Monde, *Tchad: En quoi le procès et la condamnation de Hissène Habré ont été un tournant en Afrique?*, August 28, 2021, https://information.tv5monde.com/afrique/tchad-en-quoi-le-proces-et-la-condamnation-de-hissene-habre-ont-ete-un-tournant-en-afrique, accessed 10/28/2021.

Chapter 1

The Tortuous Paths to the Trial of Hissein Habré

Hissein Habré was widely known.[1] He was born in 1942 in Faya-Largeau, a town in northern Chad. After primary and secondary schooling in his country, he went to France in the 1960s and attended the prestigious Institut d'Etudes Politiques de Paris.

Hissein Habré returned to Chad in the early 1970s and worked for his country. Later, he joined the armed struggle against the regime of the then Chadian president François Tombalbaye. He agreed to participate in political life a few years after the collapse of that regime and the accession of Félix Malloum to the presidency of the Republic of Chad. He was appointed prime minister in 1978 before breaking with the new regime that was overthrown in the late 1970s. Goukouni Weddeye, a former ally of Hissein Habré, became president of Chad in 1979. Hissein Habré held high official positions in the Goukouni Weddeye government. Not for long, though. Hissein Habré broke ranks with Goukouni Weddeye a few months later and engaged in an armed confrontation against him. After suffering setbacks, he finally ousted his former ally from power on June 7, 1982. Hissein Habré then took power in Chad, which he led until the beginning of December 1990. He was overthrown by Idriss Déby Itno, his former army chief of staff and adviser, with whom he had fallen out.

From eastern Chad, armed rebels led by Idriss Déby Itno launched a lightning attack on N'Djamena, the capital of Chad. Hissein Habré, understanding the impossibility of a counterattack against the rebels, fled Chad. After a brief stay in Cameroon, he went into exile in Senegal where, surrounded by many relatives, he settled down.[2]

THE STARTING POINT

Far from the political arena, any immediate prospect of a return to power proved unrealistic after the defeat of his supporters; more than likely, Hissein Habré probably wanted to live a peaceful exile in Senegal. However, two forces with converging interests on the need to establish his responsibility for alleged heinous crimes committed during his presidency disturbed his peace.

First, the new government in Chad intended to shed light on the crimes committed during the years of Hissein Habré's presidency and to cast shame on his deposed regime. By a decree of December 29, 1990, less than four weeks after the rebels took power, Idriss Déby Itno, the new Chadian president, set up a commission to investigate "the crimes and embezzlements of the former president, his co-authors and/or accomplices."[3] The National Commission of Inquiry issued a damning report in 1992.[4] It reported a macabre series of abuses and horrors committed under the Hissein Habré regime: massacres, assassinations, extrajudicial executions, arbitrary detentions, abysmal and chilling conditions of detention, atrocious acts of torture, and threats of all kinds. The report also mentioned economic crimes, seizures, arbitrary confiscation of property, and misappropriation of public funds. The commission attributed primary responsibility for the crimes committed to the former president Hissein Habré and accused him of embezzling public funds during the last days of his regime and taking about 4 billion CFA francs from the public treasury before fleeing Chad. Attaching strong images to the written report, the commission produced and published a video on its fieldwork and conclusions.[5] The video showed dozens of skulls and human bones, carefully unearthed from mass graves, arranged and lined up in a vast courtyard. It displayed prisoners and survivors freed from the jails of the Hissein Habré regime, skin on bones, emaciated faces, sad and empty eyes. These images of the prisoners were not too far from those images of the prisoners of the Nazi concentration camps released during liberation in 1945. In its report, the commission recommended that the perpetrators of the crimes be prosecuted. This recommendation remained a dead letter, as the new government was more concerned with consolidating the power it had acquired, in particular by integrating former agents of the previous regime into its apparatus. However, the commission's report became a milestone achievement in the attempt to hold Hissein Habré responsible.

Second, Chadians, claiming to be victims of Hissein Habré's regime, began to organize. Undoubtedly strengthened by the activities of the Chadian National Commission of Inquiry, whose work will be used in the criminal proceedings they will initiate, victims of the Hissein Habré regime created the Association des victimes des crimes et des répressions politiques (AVCPR—Association of Victims of Crimes and Political Repressions in Chad) in 1991.

Souleymane Guengueng, a survivor of the Habré regime's jails and a leading figure in the efforts to hold Hissein Habré accountable, was the first president of this organization that aimed to bring perpetrators to justice. In a book he published in 2012, he related his experiences in the jails and described the conditions that created the organization and his accession to its head.[6]

The victims decided to go after Hissein Habré, determined to have their status as victims recognized and to bring about his criminal accountability. In January 2000, several victims filed a complaint against Hissein Habré with the Senegalese courts.[7] They accused him of crimes against humanity, barbarism, and torture committed during his presidency. More than nine years elapsed between the fall of Hissein Habré and the filing of the complaint in Senegal. This duration can be explained.

Before the beginning of the year 2000, some victims with an embryonic organization wanted to take legal action against the former head of state. In his book, Souleymane Guengueng explains that the new regime's retention of former collaborators of Hissein Habré's regime in the Chadian state security apparatus frightened the victims.[8] This retention clearly indicated that the new government had no intention to prosecute past crimes of the former regime. Moreover, the victims residing in Chad could not engage in a difficult, distant, and costly battle against a former head of state who was welcomed and now well settled in Dakar, Senegal.

The decisive trigger came from outside and from nongovernmental organizations. In the late 1990s, Human Rights Watch and Reed Brody met with Delphine Djiraibe, who along with Jacqueline Moudeina was one of the lead lawyers for victims in the Habré case.[9] Delphine Djiraibe asked for their help and Human Rights Watch decided to support their commitment to bring the former Chadian head of state to justice.[10] In particular, Reed Brody was interested in the Habré case. The latter could not have fallen on a tougher opponent.

Reed Brody is an American, a former assistant attorney general, a lawyer, and a particularly pugnacious human rights activist. At the end of the 1990s, he had played a role in the proceedings in Spain and the UK to try the former Chilean head of state Augusto Pinochet.[11] A few years earlier, in 1985, Reed Brody had denounced the crimes committed in Nicaragua by the contras, an organization supported by the American administration that fought against the Sandinista government, which had close ties to Cuba. He had conducted an independent investigation, and written and published a report outlining the crimes committed.[12] At the height of the Cold War, this report, presented and commented on in the prestigious *New York Times*,[13] earned him the wrath of the administration of Ronald Reagan, the president of the United States. In a thinly veiled allusion to Reed Brody, Ronald Reagan attacked him in a speech on April 15, 1985.[14] He considered that "the so-called independent investigation was the work of one of dictator Ortega's supporters, a sympathizer who has openly embraced Sandinismo and who was shepherded through Nicaragua by Sandinista operatives." On April 17, 1985, Reed Brody's response to these attacks by the American president was scathing. Reed Brody insisted on the reality of the reported facts and the *New York Times* published his reply on April 26, 1985.[15]

Whether it was a historical coincidence or not, by seizing the Habré case and deciding to help Chadian victims in their quest for justice, Reed Brody aimed to bring to justice a former Chadian head of state who had been officially received in the United States in 1987 and was supported by the Reagan administration,[16] whose inappropriate behavior he denounced in Central America!

With an internationally known activist and nongovernmental organizations supporting them, the victims benefited from a network of human rights lawyers and defenders and were finally able to take Hissein Habré to court in Senegal in the early 2000s.[17]

After the complaint was filed, a Senegalese public prosecutor opened a judicial investigation against Hissein Habré.[18] The investigating judge, Demba Kandji, at the time the senior Senegalese investigating judge, heard the plaintiffs, examined the documents produced, and, on February 3, 2000, placed Hissein Habré under house arrest.[19] On the basis of the Senegalese Criminal Code, he charged Hissein Habré with complicity in crimes against humanity, which included acts of torture and barbarism committed during his presidency of Chad. Hissein Habré denied any wrongdoing. The indictment of Hissein Habré triggered a sense of relief and joy among the victims, while human rights nongovernmental organizations welcomed a significant step forward in the fight against impunity after the adoption of the Statute of the International Criminal Court (ICC) in 1998.[20] However, in early February 2000, no one suspected that the victims and their supporters had just embarked on a long and tedious journey.

THE JUDICIAL ODYSSEY (2000–2012)

Bringing Hissein Habré to justice was a judicial odyssey. Senegal, Belgium, the Committee against Torture, the African Union, the Court of the Economic Community of West African States (ECOWAS), and the International Court of Justice (ICJ) were the main steps of this uncertain odyssey. It was strewn with pitfalls, marked by slowdowns, accelerations, and numerous round trips before a trial was set in Senegal within the framework of the Extraordinary African Chambers (EAC).

The Case before the Senegalese Courts

At the beginning of 2000, when the struggle for a trial of Hissein Habré in Senegal began, the victims suffered their first defeats. Indeed, five months after the indictment of Hissein Habré, they were disillusioned. On July 4, 2000, the Indictment Chamber of the Dakar Court of Appeal overturned the indictment of Hissein Habré.[21] It ruled out the criminalization of crimes against humanity retained by the Investigative Chamber. On the basis of the principle of the legality of offences and penalties, it noted that crimes against humanity did not exist in Senegalese law. With respect to the crime of torture, the complaint against Hissein Habré stressed the applicability of the 1984 Convention against Torture and Other Cruel, Inhuman or Degrading Treatment or Punishment (hereafter the Convention against Torture), ratified by Senegal in 1986.[22] The states parties to this Convention have undertaken, under the terms of Article 5, paragraph 2, and Article 7, paragraph 1, to prosecute or extradite individuals accused of torture and present in any of their territories. However, the Indictment Chamber noted that the Senegalese legislature had not taken measures to give effect to the 1984 Convention. The Indictment Chamber insisted that, although Senegal had ratified the 1984 Convention, there was nothing in the Senegalese code of criminal procedure to establish the jurisdiction of Senegalese judges in cases of alleged torture committed abroad by a foreigner. The Indictment Chamber concluded that Senegalese judges were incompetent to try a foreigner who had committed the crime of torture abroad.

Although shocked by this ruling, the victims were not discouraged. They filed an appeal in cassation, hoping that the Senegalese Court of Cassation, which was the highest judiciary court in Senegal, would overrule the Indictment Chamber's decision. This did not happen. The Senegalese Court of Cassation dismissed the appeal on March 20, 2001, and confirmed the Indictment Chamber's ruling.[23] It concluded that no legal instrument established the universal jurisdiction of Senegalese courts for acts of torture committed abroad by a foreigner, which meant that Senegalese courts could not prosecute a foreigner accused of committing crimes of torture abroad. In 2001, this decision put an end to the possibility of trying Hissein Habré before the Senegalese courts. It inevitably raised a question: apart from legal arguments, why had Senegal and the Senegalese justice system refused to try Hissein Habré in the early 2000s? An impact of politics on the judiciary had sometimes been mentioned to answer that question.

While the Senegalese political authorities seemed to be standing outside the judicial process when the investigating judge indicted Hissein Habré on February 3, 2000, an event that took place the following month shook up the judicial agenda. In March 2000, Senegal elected a new president. Abdoulaye Wade, a long-time leading figure in the Senegalese political opposition, became president of the Republic of Senegal. Although it is difficult to find verifiable information about discussions that may have taken place between Hissein Habré's defenders and the new authorities, several people have analyzed a series of troubling decisions made by the new political authorities and raised questions about their connection to the failure of the case against Hissein Habré.[24]

First, the new Senegalese president chose as his special adviser the lawyer Madické Niang. Madické Niang was also, at the time of his appointment, Hissein Habré's counsel in the proceedings pending against him before the Senegalese courts, although later he would no longer represent Hissein Habré in court. Second, in a gesture that resembled a sanction, the Higher Council of the Judiciary of Senegal (Conseil supérieur de la magistrature),[25] chaired by the new Senegalese president, decided at the end of June 2000 to transfer the investigating judge Demba Kandji off the Habré case. Demba Kandji, who had indicted Hissein Habré, was relegated to the position of assistant to the prosecutor of the Dakar Court of Appeal. And third, the Higher Council of the Judiciary of Senegal appointed to the Senegalese Council of State (Conseil d'Etat), the highest administrative tribunal in Senegal at the time, the president of the Indictment Chamber of the Dakar Court of Appeal, where the Habré case was taking its course. This appointment looked like a decision aimed to facilitate the quashing of Hissein Habré's indictment by the Indictment Chamber of the Dakar Court of Appeal.

With the Senegalese courts having sealed the door to a trial of Hissein Habré, victims had a choice: giving up or seeking and activating new forums of justice. They made the second choice by taking their case to the Belgian courts and the United Nations Committee against Torture.

The Case before the Belgian Courts

The Belgian proceedings in the Habré case began in 2000. According to Souleymane Guengueng, victims "discreetly filed a complaint in Belgium against Hissein Habré" after the disappointing decision of the Indictment Chamber of the Dakar Court of Appeal.[26] The Belgian proceedings gained momentum by the end of 2001, after a particularly fruitful discovery by victims and NGOs. In May 2001, Reed Brody and Human Rights Watch researcher Olivier Bercault traveled to Chad where they obtained permission from the Chadian state to access the premises of the DDS, the Directorate of Documentation and Security (Direction de la documentation et de la sécurité), which was the former political police accused of being one of the most repressive organs of Hissein Habré's regime.[27] The DDS premises offered an unhoped-for opportunity to uncover the secrets of the repression of Hissein Habré's presidency when the investigators of Human Rights Watch discovered the archives of the DDS. There they found heaps of papers yellowed and blackened by time, files on people who had been arrested, interrogation reports, lists of people who had been arrested and the reasons for their arrests, notes of tailings, daily reports, and so on. This fortunate discovery was the starting point of a new and dynamic approach.

In the months that followed, Human Rights Watch, the International Federation for Human Rights (FIDH), and the AVCPR conducted investigations in Chad into crimes committed by the regime of Hissein Habré. Having access to the DDS premises, nongovernmental organizations and victims began to analyze and exploit the archives, adding these new documents to the testimonies of the witnesses and victims who had been interviewed and to the report of the National Commission of Inquiry and its minutes.[28] Armed with this veritable arsenal of evidence, several victims filed new complaints in Belgium against Hissein Habré in December 2001.[29]

Belgium offered several new advantages. The state was party to the 1984 Convention against Torture and the 1948 Convention on the Prevention and Punishment of the Crime of Genocide. It also had, at the time of the filing of complaints, a famous law on universal jurisdiction. Adopted in 1993,[30] and amended in particular in 1999,[31] this law provided unlimited universal jurisdiction over war crimes, crimes against humanity, and genocide. It allowed Belgium to prosecute these crimes wherever they were committed. The victims then relied on these legal instruments and on international custom to accuse Hissein Habré of crimes against humanity, genocide, war crimes, torture, and acts of barbarism.

After investigations and an assurance from the Chadian government that Hissein Habré's immunity from jurisdiction had been waived,[32] a Belgian investigating judge indicted the former Chadian president on September 19, 2005, for genocide, crimes against humanity, war crimes, acts of torture, and other violations of international humanitarian law.[33] The judge issued an international arrest warrant for Hissein Habré and asked Senegal for his extradition.[34]

When consulted for an opinion on the Belgian extradition request, the Dakar Court of Appeal stated that Hissein Habré was a former head of state and as such enjoyed immunity from jurisdiction even after he had ceased to hold office.[35] The court declared itself incompetent to rule on "the lawfulness of acts of pursuit and the validity of arrest warrant applying to a head of state."[36] Senegal refused to extradite Hissein Habré to Belgium. However, it decided to refer the matter to the African Union, to which it entrusted the fate of the former president.[37]

While the Belgian procedure was being implemented and dealing with the obstacle of Senegal's refusal to extradite Hissein Habré, another procedure initiated in 2001 was underway before the United Nations Committee against Torture.

The Case before the United Nations Committee against Torture

In 2001, following the decision of the Senegalese Court of Cassation confirming the incompetence of the Senegalese courts, victims, represented by Reed Brody, referred the matter to the Committee against Torture, the United Nations body responsible for monitoring compliance by states parties to the 1984 Convention against Torture. The complaint filed on April 18, 2001, accused Senegal of having violated Article 5, paragraph 2, of the Convention by failing to adopt legislative measures to give effect to the Convention, and Article 7, paragraph 1, of the Convention by refusing to try or extradite Hissein Habré.[38] The victims asked the Committee to take interim measures to prevent Hissein Habré from leaving Senegal and possibly taking refuge in a state not party to the Convention against Torture.[39] This request was motivated by recent circumstances. A few days earlier, Senegalese president Abdoulaye Wade had asked Hissein Habré to leave Senegal.[40] The Committee granted the victims' request. During the consideration of the complaint, Senegal was requested not to expel Hissein Habré unless the expulsion took place in the context of extradition proceedings.[41] The Committee against Torture rendered its decision on the merits on May 17, 2006. Taking into account the refusal to extradite the former president to Belgium, the Committee held that Senegal had violated Article 5, paragraph 2, and Article 7, paragraph 1, of the Convention against Torture.[42] The Committee called on Senegal to try or extradite Hissein Habré and to take steps to establish its jurisdiction over torture. After the ruling of the Committee, Senegal could no longer shirk its obligations. However, having surrendered the case of Hissein Habré to the African Union, it awaited the African Union's decision.

The African Union and Senegal

In order to respond to Senegal's request, the African Union established a Committee of Eminent African Jurists responsible for reflecting on and proposing solutions to the problems posed by the Habré case.[43] The Committee was composed of Judges Guibril Camara (Senegal) and Joseph S. Warioba (Tanzania); Professors Delphine Emmanuel (Republic of Congo), Henrietta J. A. N. Mensa-Bonsu (Ghana), and Michael Ayodele Ajomo (Nigeria); and lawyers Robert Dossou (Benin) and Anil Kumarsingh Gayan (Mauritius).[44]

The Committee of Eminent African Jurists issued its report on July 2, 2006. It argued for an "African solution" and recommended that Hissein Habré could be tried in Senegal, Chad, or any other African state.[45] It added that Hissein Habré could also be tried by an ad hoc African tribunal.[46] However, the Committee held that Senegal was the most appropriate state for a trial.[47] The African Union took note of the Committee's report and mandated Senegal to try Hissein Habré "on behalf of Africa."[48]

All eyes turned to Senegal, watching for the slightest sign of progress toward a trial. As a sign of its goodwill, Senegal issued a press release on November 2, 2006, in which it stated that it was preparing for the trial of Hissein Habré, adapting its legislation and taking various measures, in particular with regard to cooperation and witness protection.[49] However, the press release stressed the lack of financial means available to carry out such a trial.[50] Senegal noted that, despite the African Union's insistence on the need to provide international assistance for the organization of a trial, it had not received "one dollar or euro."[51] While the reference to the lack of funding gave rise to fears of a new obstacle on the way to a trial, Senegal did adopt new legislation in 2007.[52] The crime of genocide, crimes against humanity, war crimes, and other breaches of international humanitarian law were incorporated into the Senegalese Criminal Code.[53] The Senegalese Criminal Procedure Code provided for the possibility of prosecuting in Senegal a foreigner accused of committing these crimes abroad, when the foreigner or the victim lived in Senegal, or when the government of Senegal had obtained the foreigner's extradition.[54] It stated that there was no statute of limitations for these crimes.[55] This possibility of prosecuting a foreigner was extended to the crime of torture, which was already recognized as a crime in the Criminal Code.[56] Senegal also revised its Constitution, which now provided that there was no statute of limitations for crimes against humanity, genocide, and war crimes.[57]

Despite these changes in Senegalese law, the trial was still not on the agenda and other developments were worrying the victims. In April 2008, Madické Niang, Hissein Habré's former counsel and adviser to reelected president Abdoulaye Wade, was appointed minister of justice, a position which, because of his position as the superior of the prosecuting magistrates, was linked to the Habré case.[58]

However, the victims of the Hissein Habré regime did not give up. In September 2008, several of them filed new complaints in Senegal against Hissein Habré for crimes against humanity and torture.[59] In order to curb the new dynamic that gave rise to fears of a trial after Senegal's legislative changes regarding the prosecution of international crimes, Hissein Habré and his lawyers counterattacked. In October 2008, they brought the case before the ECOWAS the Court of Justice.

The Economic Community of West African States' Court of Justice and the African Court on Human and People's Rights

The ECOWAS Court of Justice is a West African subregional court with jurisdiction, inter alia, to examine allegations of human rights violations committed against individuals under the jurisdiction of ECOWAS member states. Before this court, Hissein Habré and his lawyers argued that, by attempting to reactivate the trial and relying on a solution from the African Union, Senegal had violated the rules of international human rights law.[60] They relied on the principle of res judicata, a principle that prohibits the re-examination of a dispute on which a final decision has been rendered. They claimed that the highest court in Senegal, the Senegalese Court of Cassation, had already issued a final decision in the Habré case. They also argued that Senegal had violated the principle of non-retroactivity of criminal law, a principle that prohibits the application of a new criminal law to acts that took place before the new law came into force. They accused Senegal of adopting new criminal laws to make it possible to hold a trial that could not have taken place under previous Senegalese criminal laws.

The ECOWAS Court of Justice considered their arguments and rendered its decision in 2010. Referring to the legal reforms undertaken by Senegal, it held that there was a likelihood that Hissein Habré's human rights would be violated.[61] It ordered Senegal to respect the principles of res judicata and non-retroactivity.[62] However, it did not close the door to a trial. It considered that the mandate given to Senegal by the African Union meant that Hissein Habré could be judged within the framework of a special ad hoc procedure as practiced in international law.[63] Thus, the possibility of organizing a trial of Hissein Habré within a specific framework to be defined was raised by the ECOWAS Court of Justice.

In 2008, an individual of Chadian nationality also filed a complaint against Senegal with the African Court on Human and Peoples' Rights, which is mandated, under certain conditions, to examine human rights violations committed by African states.[64] He presented arguments on Senegal's violation of the principle of non-retroactivity of criminal law in the Habré case.[65] The African Court rejected the complaint because Senegal had not made a declaration recognizing the possibility for individuals to file complaints, as required by Article 34, paragraph 6, of the protocol creating the court.[66]

During these courts' proceedings, the Habré case did not see any significant developments until Senegal came under unsustainable pressure.

Senegal under Pressure: Funding, the International Court of Justice, and the Election of Macky Sall

Because of Senegal's inaction, Belgium, which was still seeking the extradition of Hissein Habré without success, decided on February 19, 2009, to refer the case to the ICJ,[67] a court that settles disputes between states. Belgium argued that, by deciding neither to try Hissein Habré nor to extradite him to Belgium for the crime of torture and crimes against humanity, Senegal had violated international law.[68] The arguments of Belgium were based on the 1984 Convention against Torture.[69] Belgium also asked the ICJ to indicate provisional measures to prevent Hissein Habré from leaving Senegal until a decision was made.[70] Deciding on the request for provisional measures, the court did not grant Belgium's request but stated that Senegal had formally undertaken to keep Hissein Habré in its territory.[71]

At the end of 2010, responding to the recurring complaint of Senegal about the lack of funding for the trial, some states and donors met for a round table in November. The European Union, the African Union, Chad, France, the Netherlands, Germany, Luxembourg, and Belgium pledged nearly 8.6 million euros for the trial of Hissein Habré.[72] The Office of the United Nations High Commissioner for Human Rights offered technical support.[73]

Under pressure because of these new developments, Senegal seemed to be overwhelmed. Senegal's president Abdoulaye Wade expressed his annoyance. In 2011, while discussing with the African Union the establishment of an ad hoc international tribunal that could deal with crimes committed in Chad, he threatened first to hand over Hissein Habré to the African Union and then to send him back to Chad.[74] This second possibility sparked indignation because of its potential consequences, which were based on the events that took place three years earlier.

In February 2008, following an armed attack, rebels opposed to the then-Chadian president Idriss Déby Itno, arrived in N'Djamena, and determined to overthrow him.[75] Pushed back and weakened, Idriss Déby Itno managed at the very last moment, with the help of France, to save his regime and defeat the rebels.[76] The Chadian authorities saw in the attempted coup the hand of former president Hissein Habré. A Chadian criminal court tried Hissein Habré *in absentia* and sentenced him to death in August 2008 for his alleged involvement in this attempt to destabilize the Chadian "constitutional order."[77]

As a result of the 2008 attack and in the event of expulsion to Chad, Hissein Habré could, without having been held accountable for the crimes of which he was accused by thousands of victims, be executed under this death sentence in Chad. The UN High Commissioner for Human Rights and several human rights organizations were concerned about the possibility of expulsion to Chad and strongly opposed it.[78] Yielding to international pressure, Senegal finally gave up the expulsion.[79]

The African Union called on African states willing to try Hissein Habré.[80] Although Rwanda expressed its willingness,[81] this was not enough of a significant development to lead to the trial. At the beginning of 2012, the trial of the former Chadian head of state seemed doomed to fail. However, it was during this year that a succession of events accelerated the progress toward a trial.

The first event was undoubtedly the loss of the presidential election by Abdoulaye Wade in March 2012. Macky Sall, his main political opponent, became the head of state of Senegal. President Abdoulaye Wade's recurring reversals had cast doubt on his willingness to facilitate a trial. A few weeks after his election, the new President Macky Sall showed his willingness to have Hissein Habré tried in Senegal. A working group was set up to reflect on the subject.[82] Decisive negotiations were carried out with the African Union for the establishment of a tribunal.[83] Thus, while the election of Abdoulaye Wade in 2000 marked the beginning of obstacles to prevent the trial of Hissein Habré, in 2012, his failure in the presidential election paved the way for the trial.

The second event was certainly the condemnation of Senegal by the ICJ. On July 20, 2012, in the case between Belgium and Senegal, the ICJ ruled that by refusing to prosecute Hissein Habré or extradite him to Belgium for the acts of torture of which he was accused, Senegal had violated the 1984 Convention against Torture.[84] The ICJ ordered Senegal to prosecute Hissein Habré if it did not extradite him.[85]

Finally, on August 22, 2012, negotiations between Senegal and the African Union led to the establishment of the EAC,[86] an African criminal court to be financed, inter alia, by funds that had been pledged by donors in 2010.[87]

NOTES

1. For the background of Hissein Habré, see for example, Paul R. Bartrop, *A Biographical Encyclopedia of Contemporary Genocide Portraits of Evil and Good* (Santa-Barbara: ABC-CLIO, 2012), 115–117. Arthur S. Banks and Thomas C. Muller, eds., *Political Handbook of the World: 1998: Governments and Intergovernmental Organizations as of January 1, 1998* (New York: CSA Publications, 1998), 169–171. See also the biography on the official website of the former president of Chad, Hissein Habré: http://hisseinhabre.com/hissein-habre-resume-de-la-biographie-de-l-ancien-chef-de-l-etat-du-tchad.html, accessed 5/16/2021.

2. See the testimony of the former president of Senegal on the conditions of Hissein Habré's arrival in Senegal: Abdou Diouf, *Mémoires* (Paris: Editions du Seuil, 2014).

3. Chad. Decree Creating the Commission of Inquiry into the Crimes and the Misappropriations Committed by Ex-President Habré, his Accomplices and/or Accessories, Decree no. 014/P.CE/CJ/90 (December 29, 1990). Reprinted in Neil J. Kritz, ed., *Transitional Justice: How Emerging Democracies Reckon with Former Regimes.* Vol. 3 (Washington, DC: United States Institute of Peace Press, 1995), 48–50.

4. For a copy of the report in French, Tchad, Rapport de la commission nationale d'enquête du ministère tchadien de la justice, *Les crimes et les détournements*

de l'ex-président Habré et de ses complices (Paris: L'Harmattan, 1993). An English translation of the report can be found in Neil J. Kritz, ed., ibid., 51–93.

5. Commission nationale d'enquête du ministère tchadien de la justice, *Les crimes et les détournements de l'ex-président Habré et de ses complices*, video, 52 minutes, 1992.

6. Souleymane Guengueng, *Prisonnier de Hissene Habré. L'expérience d'un survivant des geôles tchadiennes et sa quête de justice* (Paris: L'Harmattan, 2012), 85–90.

7. See the complaint, *Plainte avec Constitution de Partie Civile, Suleymane Guengueng et al., A Monsieur le Doyen Des Juges d'instruction près le Tribunal régional hors classe de Dakar*, January 2000, available online https://www.hrw.org/legacy/french/themes/habre-plainte.html, accessed 5/16/2021.

8. Souleymane Guengueng, op. cit., note 6, 93–94.

9. Reed Brody, "The Prosecution of Hissène Habré: International Accountability, National Impunity," in *Transitional Justice in the Twenty-First Century: Beyond Truth versus Justice*, ed. Naomi Roht-Arriaza and Javier Mariezcurrena (Cambridge: Cambridge University Press, 2014), 286, 292.

10. Ibid., 286.

11. Read Brody and Michael Ratner, ed., *The Pinochet Papers: The Case of Augusto Pinochet in Spain and Britain* (The Hague: Kluwer Law International, 2000).

12. Reed Brody, *Contra Terror in Nicaragua: Report of a Fact-Finding Mission: Sept. 1984-Jan. 1985* (Boston, MA: South End Pr. 1985).

13. Larry Rohter, "Nicaragua Rebels Accused of Abuses," *New York Times*. March 7, 1985, Section A, 1.

14. Ronald Reagan, Remarks at a Fundraising Dinner for the Nicaragua Refugee Fund (Speech), April 15, 1985. https://www.reaganlibrary.gov/research/speeches/41585f, accessed 5/16/2021.

15. Reed Brody, "'Contra' Terrorism Is, Unfortunately, True," *New York Times*, April 26, 1985.

16. Ronald Reagan, *Remarks Following Meetings with President Hissein Habre of Chad*, June 19, 1987. https://www.reaganlibrary.gov/research/speeches/061987g, accessed 5/16/2021. For some details on United States' support to the Hissein Habré and his regime, see chapter 13.

17. See the complaint, *Plainte avec Constitution de Partie Civile, Suleymane Guengueng et al.*, op. cit. note 7.

18. Information provided by the Senegalese government, see, CAT, *Suleymane Guengueng, et al. v. Senegal*, Communication no. 181/2001, CAT/C/36/D/181/2001, May 17, 2006, para. 7.2.

19. For all the information on the decision of the investigating judge, see Cour d'appel de Dakar (Tribunal Régional Hors Classe de Dakar, Cabinet de M. Demba Kandji Juge d'instruction, no. du Parquet: 482, no. de l'instruction: 13/2000), *Procès-verbal d'interrogatoire de première comparution*, February 3, 2000.

20. Human Rights Watch, *Ex-Chad Dictator Indicted in Senegal*, News Release, February 3, 2000.

21. République du Sénégal, Cour d'appel de Dakar (Chambre d'accusation), Arrêt no. 135 du 04-07-2000/ Accusation.

22. The complaint is available online on the website of Human Rights Watch, http://www.hrw.org/french/themes/habre-plainte.html, accessed 5/16/2021.

23. Cour de cassation (Sénégal), *Souleymane Guengueng et autres c. Hissène Habré*, Arrêt no. 14 du 20-3-2001 Pénal.

24. On the analysis of the troubling decisions, see Press Release of the United Nations Rapporteurs on Torture and on the Independence of Judges and Lawyers, Dato' Param Cumaraswamy and Sir Nigel Rodley, August 2, 2000; Reed Brody, "Prosecution of Hissène Habré. An 'African Pinochet,'" in *Livre noir: Terrorisme et responsabilité pénale internationale: recueil des contributions préparatoires au Colloque du 5 février 2002,* organisé par SOS attentats, Assemblée Nationale (Paris, 2002), 317; Moussa Samb, "Etat des lieux de la justice. Réflexions sur une justice en crise," in *Senegal (2000-2012). Les institutions et politiques publiques à l'épreuve*, ed. Momar-Coumba Diop (Dakar-Paris: CRES-Karthala, 2013), 363; Human Rights Watch, *Chad: The Victims of Hissène Habré Still Waiting for Justice*, July 2005, Vol. 17, No. 10 (A); Human Rights Watch, *Le Sénégal a compétence sur les crimes commis par Hissène Habré*, May 10, 2000, online: https://www.hrw.org/legacy/french/docs/2000/05/10/chad7339.htm, accessed 5/16/2021; Human Rights Watch, *Les Agissements Déplorables du Sénégal*, July 4, 2000. https://www.hrw.org/legacy/french/press/2000/habre0705-fr.htm, accessed 5/16/2021.

25. In Senegal, the "Conseil supérieur de la magistrature" is an institution that plays a role in the appointment of Senegalese judges. See Article 90 of the Constitution of Senegal.

26. Souleymane Guengueng, op. cit., note 6, 131 (Translation from French).

27. Human Rights Watch, *Hissène Habré, les archives de l'horreur, les archives de la police politique*, 2003.

28. Ibid.

29. See, for example, the complaint of Souleymane Abdoulaye Tahir, December 3, 2001. https://www.hrw.org/legacy/french/themes/PlainteSouleymaneAbdoulaye.pdf , accessed 5/16/2021.

30. Belgium, *Loi relative à la répression des infractions graves aux Conventions de Genève du 12 août 1949 et aux Protocoles I et II du 8 juin 1977*, June 16, 1993.

31. Belgium, *Loi relative à la répression des violations graves du droit international humanitaire*, February 10, 1999. Belgium limited the scope of its law on universal jurisdiction in 2003: Belgium, *Loi du 5 août 2003 relative aux violations graves du droit international humanitaire*.

32. Chad, *Lettre du ministre de la justice du Tchad levant l'immunité dont M. H. Habré pourrait se prévaloir*, October 7, 2002.

33. See ICJ, Questions Relating to the Obligation to Prosecute or Extradite (*Belgium v. Senegal*), Judgment, ICJ Reports 2012, para. 21.

34. Ibid.

35. Cour d'appel de Dakar (Chambre d'accusation), arrêt no. 138, November 25, 2005.

36. Ibid. (Translation from French).

37. Senegal, Communiqué du Ministère des Affaires étrangères. November 27, 2005. https://www.hrw.org/legacy/french/docs/2005/11/27/chad12130.htm, accessed 5/16/2021.

38. CAT, *Suleymane Guengueng et autres C/ Sénégal*, Communication Présentée au Comité contre la torture (Article 22 de la Convention) pour violation des Articles 5 et 7 de la Convention, April 18, 2001. https://www.hrw.org/legacy/french/themes/habre-cat.html, accessed 5/16/2021.

39. Ibid.

40. Ibid.

41. Letter of the United Nations Office of High Commissioner for Human Rights to Reed Brody, Reference G/SO 229/31 SENE (1), April 27, 2001.

42. CAT, *Suleymane Guengueng and others v. Senegal*, op. cit., note 18.

43. AU, Decision on The Hissene Habre Case and the African Union. Doc. Assembly/Au/8 (Vi)) Add.9. January 23–24, 2006.

44. Report of the Committee of Eminent African Jurists on the Case of Hissene Habré, July 2, 2006, para. 3.

45. Ibid., para. 28.

46. Ibid., para. 31.

47. Ibid., para. 29.

48. AU, Decision on the Hissene Habre Case and the African Union. Doc. Assembly/Au/3 (Vii). July 2, 2006.

49. Sénégal, Présidence de la République-Le Ministre Porte-Parole, *Le Sénégal prépare activement le jugement de M. Hissène Habré*, Communiqué, Dakar, November 2, 2006.

50. Ibid.

51. Ibid.

52. Senegal, Loi no. 2007-02 du 12 février 2007 modifiant le Code pénal, JO 2007-03-10, no. 6332; Loi no. 2007-05 du 12 février 2007, modifiant le Code de procédure pénale relative à la mise en œuvre du Traité de Rome instituant la Cour pénale internationale.

53. Senegal, Loi no. 2007-02, ibid., Article 2. See also new articles of the Senegalese Criminal Code: 431-1, 431-2, 431-3, and 431-5.

54. Senegal, Loi no. 2007-05 du 12 février 2007, modifiant le Code de procédure pénale relative à la mise en œuvre du Traité de Rome instituant la Cour pénale internationale, Article 2. See also the new article 669 of the Senegalese Code of Criminal procedure.

55. Senegal, Loi no. 2007-05 du 12 février 2007, ibid., Article 1.

56. Ibid. For the crime of torture, see article 295-1 of the Senegalese Criminal Code.

57. Senegal, Loi constitutionnelle no. 2008-33 du 7 août 2008, Article 1. See also Article 9 of Senegal Constitution.

58. Comité de Pilotage du Comité International pour le Jugement Equitable de Hissène Habré, Lettre ouverte à la communauté internationale et africaine, Avril 15, 2008. https://www.hrw.org/fr/news/2008/04/15/lettre-ouverte-la-communaute-internationale-et-africaine, accessed 5/16/2021.

Cheikh Yérim Seck, "Accusé Madické Niang," *Jeune Afrique*, April 21, 2008. https://www.jeuneafrique.com/86140/politique/accus-madick-niang/, accessed 5/16/2021.

59. Human Rights Watch News, *Les victimes accusent Hissène Habré de crimes contre l'humanité. Plaintes déposées au Sénégal contre l'ex-dictateur du*

Tchad, September 16, 2008. https://www.hrw.org/legacy/french/docs/2008/09/15/senega19817.htm, accessed 5/16/2021.

60. For the arguments, see ECOWAS Court of justice. *Hissein Habré v. République du Sénégal*, doc. no. ECW/CCJ/APP/07/08 ARRET NO: ECW/CCJ/JUD/06/10, November 18, 2010.

61. Ibid., para. 61.

62. Ibid.

63. Ibid.

64. ACtHPR, *Michelot Yogogombaye c. République du Sénégal*, Req. 001/2008, Arrêt, December 15, 2009, para. 1.

65. Ibid., paras. 20–21.

66. Ibid., para. 37.

67. ICJ, Application Instituting Proceedings, Questions Relating to the Obligation to Prosecute or Extradite (*Belgium v. Senegal*), filed in the Registry of the Court on February 19, 2009.

68. Ibid., paras. 10–12.

69. Ibid.

70. ICJ, Request for the Indication of Provisional Measures submitted by the Government of the Kingdom of Belgium, February 19, 2009.

71. ICJ, Questions Relating to the Obligation to Prosecute or Extradite (*Belgium v. Senegal*). Request for the Indication of Provisional Measures, Order, May 28, 2009, paras. 70–73.

72. Table ronde des donateurs pour le financement du procès d'Hissène Habré, Document final, Dakar, November 24, 2010, paras. 15–16.

73. Ibid., para. 17.

74. AU, *Progress Report of the Commission on the Hissene Habre Case*, Doc. Assembly/AU/12 (XVIII) Rev.1, January 29–30, 2012, para. 3. AFP, "*Abdoulaye Wade va renvoyer l'ex-président Hissène Habré au Tchad*," Dépêche, July 8, 2011; "Le retour annoncé d'Hissène Habré au Tchad provoque la confusion," *Le Monde*, July 9, 2011.

75. See the Statement by the president of the UN Security Council, Doc. UN, S/PRST/2008/3, February 4, 2008.

76. See a document of the French national Assembly, *Proposition de résolution de M. André GERIN et plusieurs de ses collègues tendant à la création d'une commission d'enquête sur l'engagement de la France dans le conflit tchadien*, doc. no. 782, April 4, 2008.

77. Le Comité de Pilotage du Comité International pour le Jugement Equitable de Hissène Habré, *La condamnation d'Hissène Habré au Tchad n'a aucune incidence sur les obligations du Sénégal*, Communiqué de presse, August 18, 2008.

78. ONU info, *L'ONU appelle le Sénégal à revoir sa décision d'extrader Habré au Tchad*, July 10, 2011 ; FIDH, *Le Sénégal devrait extrader Hissène Habré en Belgique pour un procès équitable plutôt que de l'envoyer au Tchad où il risque sa vie*, Communiqué, July 10, 2011.

79. AU, *Progress Report of the Commission on the Hissene Habre Case*, op. cit. note 74, para. 4; UN News, *UN rights chief hails Senegal's decision not to repatriate former dictator to Chad*, July 12, 2011.

80. AU, Decision on the Hissene Habre Case, Doc. Assembly/Au/8(Xvii), 2011.

81. AU, Decision on the Hissene Habre Case, Doc. Assembly/Au/12(Xviii), 2011.

82. Interview of a Member of the working group.

83. Ibid.

84. ICJ, Questions Relating to the Obligation to Prosecute or Extradite, Judgment, op. cit., note 33, para. 122.

85. Ibid.

86. Agreement between the Government of the Republic of Senegal and the African Union on the Establishment of the EAC within the courts of Senegal, August 22, 2012.

87. Ibid., Article 3.

Chapter 2

The Construction of the Legal Framework of the Hissein Habré Trial

The Extraordinary African Chambers (EAC)

THE PROGRESSIVE EMERGENCE OF THE IDEA OF ESTABLISHING THE EAC

The construction of the legal framework for the trial of Hissein Habré was gradual. It was the result of a conjunction of political and judicial factors. The decision of Senegal not to extradite Hissein Habré to Belgium and the priority given by the African Union to an "African solution" led to the search for an appropriate African judicial court. Three main factors fueled this search.

First, in 2006, the report of the Committee of Eminent African Jurists mandated by the African Union to propose judicial options in the Habré case considered Senegal to be the most appropriate state to try the former Chadian head of state.[1] However, it envisaged other possible solutions, including the creation of an ad hoc regional tribunal, which could be "established in any African State."[2]

Second, in 2010, while condemning Senegal's failure to respect the authority of res judicata and the non-retroactivity of criminal law in the Habré case, the ECOWAS Court of Justice proposed an alternative to trial before Senegalese courts: trying Hissein Habré in the framework of an ad hoc international procedure.[3] The ruling of the ECOWAS Court of Justice contradicted the African Union's proposition to envisage a trial before the Senegalese courts without taking into account the possible violation of the rights of the accused. Whether or not the decisions handed down by Senegalese judges in the early 2000s, which claimed the incompetence of the Senegalese courts, were open to criticism, it was clear to the ECOWAS Court that a retrial could not take place within the restricted framework of the

Senegalese courts without raising questions as to whether certain principles of the law like the non-retroactivity of criminal law and the authority of res judicata would be violated.

With regard to the principle of the non-retroactivity of criminal law, ad hoc international criminal tribunals are established after the commission of international crimes.[4] Consequently, they generally rule on crimes committed before their creation. While the question of the non-retroactivity of criminal law was debated at the International Military Tribunals in Nuremberg in 1945 and Tokyo in 1946, it no longer seems to pose any real problems in the area of the ad hoc international tribunals since it is widely accepted that international crimes such as genocide, crimes against humanity and war crimes are punishable under international law. In Africa, for example, the International Criminal Tribunal for Rwanda (ICTR) and the Special Court for Sierra Leone (SCSL) examined international crimes committed before their establishment in 1994 and 2002, respectively.[5] Thus, recourse to an ad hoc tribunal with an international nature was likely to silence criticism of the violation of this principle. However, contrary to what the ECOWAS Court had noted in its decision, the fact that the crimes allegedly committed by Hissein Habré were already prohibited, at least under international law, constituted a relevant objection to the argument that the Senegalese authorities would violate the non-retroactivity of criminal law principle, in particular by relying on new Senegalese laws recognizing international crimes to try the former Chadian head of state.[6]

With regard to the principle of res judicata, the problem may seem more delicate in the context of the Habré case. The statutes of the ad hoc international criminal tribunals provide that they may try individuals who have already been tried at the national level,[7] in particular when the trial has been conducted at the national level only to exonerate these individuals from criminal responsibility or when the principles of a fair trial have not been respected. Here, there did not seem to be any reason in principle to oppose the trial of Hissein Habré before an ad hoc international tribunal. However, it should have been demonstrated that a trial against Hissein Habré had taken place in Senegal in the 2000s, that the Senegalese procedures of the 2000s were aimed solely at absolving him of responsibility, and that fair trial principles had not been respected. The ECOWAS Court of Justice did not address these issues when it proposed the possibility of establishing an ad hoc tribunal of an international nature. Despise the criticism that might be leveled at the ECOWAS Court of Justice,[8] its suggestion of setting up an international criminal procedure was the first decisive step toward the creation of an ad hoc court of international character to prosecute Hissein Habré. It was a median solution. On the one hand, it circumvented the possible violation, if any, of the principles of the authority of res judicata and the non-retroactivity of criminal law. On the other hand, it ensured the respect of victims' right to justice by opening the door to a new option.

Third, the international and regional context certainly played a significative role in the decision to try Hissein Habré in Africa and not in Europe, especially in Belgium that was requesting his extradition. Indeed, at the time the efforts to try Hissein Habré were gaining momentum, a debate on the fight against impunity in Africa was underway. One of the central elements of the debate was the controversies surrounding the indictment or prosecution of African leaders and officials under universal jurisdiction in some European countries, or by the ICC established in 1998 and based in The Hague, the Netherlands.[9]

With regard to universal jurisdiction, between 2000 and 2009, several African officials faced complaints or indictments and prosecutions in European countries for alleged international crimes perpetrated in Africa.[10] With regard to the ICC, it had become public knowledge that it had been accused of indicting and trying only Africans suspected of committing international crimes in Africa, while other regions of the world were also affected by the commission of crimes within its jurisdiction. High-ranking African political leaders, including heads of state, were indicted by the ICC during the process of establishing a tribunal to try Hissein Habré. For example, after the referral of the situations of Darfur (Sudan) and Libya to the ICC by the UN Security Council, arrest warrants were issued against African incumbent head of states: in 2009 and 2010 against Ahmad Al Bashir, then head of state of Sudan, and in 2011 against Muammar Gaddafi, then head of state of Libya.[11] In 2003, Côte d'Ivoire authorities accepted the jurisdiction of the ICC over international crimes committed on its territory and, in 2010 and 2011, confirmed that acceptance.[12] After investigations on alleged crimes committed in Côte d'Ivoire, the ICC issued an arrest warrant in 2011 against Laurent Gbagbo, the former head of state of Côte d'Ivoire.[13] During the same period, prosecutions were also launched by the ICC against several other African individuals from Sudan, Congo, Uganda, Côte d'Ivoire, and Kenya.[14]

This situation generated some of the most passionate debates in Africa, from the citizens who spoke about this remote ICC with imperialist overtones to the victims of international crimes who claimed that the Court was an adequate response to their suffering. In Africa, a continent that saw colonization by European countries in its recent history, indictments of Africans and their prosecution outside Africa looked like a breach of the sovereignty of African states or a new sign of neocolonialism. The mistrust of some African states became real. Alongside the African Union, they began to protest.

The Assembly of Heads of State and Government of the African Union issued three decisions expressing the concern that some European countries were targeting African leaders with investigations, indictments, and prosecutions based on universal jurisdiction, and complained about "the abuse of the principle of universal jurisdiction."[15] In several decisions, it complained about the ICC after the indictment of African head of states.[16] In 2009 and in the early 2010s, African Union also started to examine the possibility to prosecute international crimes such as genocide, crimes against humanity, and war crimes in Africa. Propositions arose on the creation of an International Criminal Law Section within the African Court of Justice and Human Rights.[17] A Protocol establishing an International Criminal Law Section within the African Court of Justice and Human Rights was later adopted in June 2014.[18] The Protocol was probably the African Union's response to the "abuse of the principle of universal jurisdiction" and ICC, which tried only Africans and issued arrest warrants against Africans, including sitting African presidents. Later, the African Union also threatened the ICC with a massive withdrawal of African states from the Rome Statute, the treaty that created the ICC.[19] Three African states, Gambia, South Africa, and Burundi, initiated proceedings to withdraw from the Statute of the ICC.[20] Only Burundi eventually withdrew from the Statute.[21]

Thus, part of this global context existed when there were attempts to try Hissein Habré and it was quite unlikely that Hissein Habré would be tried outside Africa. Of course, the ICC could not have jurisdiction over the crimes allegedly committed by Hissein Habré between 1982 and 1990. The ICC was created in 1998 and had "jurisdiction only with respect to crimes committed after the entry into force of [its] Statute."[22] This Statute entered into force on July 1, 2002, which meant that the ICC could only examine crimes committed after that date. But one could not expect that the African Union, which was opposing indictments and prosecutions of Africans outside Africa, would strongly support an extradition of the former head of state to Belgium, for example. The preference for an African criminal tribunal was consistent with the international and regional context and the will of Africans to provide an African solution.

Fueled by these three factors, the African Union Commission made propositions. In a report published in January 2011, the commission listed five options for the trial of Hissein Habré: "1) Establishment of Extraordinary Chambers in the Competent Court of Senegal; 2) Establishment of Extraordinary Chambers in the Competent Court of Chad; 3) Establishment of Extraordinary Chambers in the Competent Court of any other African Country; 4) Setting up an Ad hoc Tribunal and 5) Extradition to Belgium."[23] When examining the first option, Establishment of Extraordinary Chambers in the Competent Court of Senegal, the AU Commission strongly indicated that "the Senegalese judicial system" was the "best option for the trial of Hissene Habre."[24] Taking note of the AU

Commission report, the African Union Assembly of Heads of State and Government requested

> the Commission to undertake consultations with the Government of Senegal in order to finalise the modalities for the expeditious trial of Hissene Habre through a special tribunal with an international character consistent with the Economic Community of West African States (ECOWAS) Court of Justice Decision.[25]

THE CHOICE OF AN AD HOC CRIMINAL TRIBUNAL WITH AN INTERNATIONAL CHARACTER: THE MODEL OF THE EXTRAORDINARY CHAMBERS IN THE COURTS OF CAMBODIA

While the proposition to create an ad hoc criminal tribunal with an international character was considered, its specific form and provisions remained to be determined. Generally, in this type of situation, it is common for legal experts to look for a solution in precedents. At the international level, there was no shortage of examples of previously established courts. Several criminal courts of an international nature had been established in recent years. They ranged from the international criminal tribunals set up in the former Yugoslavia and in Rwanda to hybrid tribunals, mixing national and international elements, set up, for example, in Timor-Leste, Sierra Leone, Kosovo, Bosnia and Herzegovina, and Cambodia.[26] It was common knowledge that these courts had often tried individuals who held the highest offices of the state. For example, the International Criminal Tribunal for the former Yugoslavia (ICTY) tried the former Serbian president Slobodan Milošević. The ICTR tried the former Rwandan prime minister Jean Kambanda. The SCSL did the same with Charles Taylor, the former Liberian head of state. Thus, international criminal justice offered the African Union and Senegal a wide range of choices for the form and provisions of the tribunal.

The hypothesis for the creation of an ad hoc tribunal that was based on the model of the Extraordinary Chambers in the Courts of Cambodia (ECCC) emerged during negotiations between the African Union and Senegal. Ben Kioko, who was the legal counsel for the African Union and engaged in the negotiations with Senegal, revealed that they "recommended to Senegal the establishment of the 'African Extraordinary Chambers', modelled on the extraordinary Chambers in the Courts of Cambodia," and that "Senegal endorsed this proposal."[27] They also drafted several documents, notably the AU/Senegal Agreement and the tribunal statute that "were dispatched to Senegal for comments and observations."[28] The former legal counsel also mentioned that in this process, they received inputs from individuals who worked for Human Rights Watch, ICTR, and UN High Commissioner for Human Rights Office, and that they met with representatives of the European Commission and many countries including Senegal, France, Germany, Switzerland, United Kingdom, the Netherlands, Belgium, and United States of America.[29]

So, in order to prosecute and try Hissein Habré, there were plans to create chambers in the courts of Senegal similar to those in Cambodia. In early 2000, the United Nations and Cambodia reached an agreement to establish the ECCC to prosecute individuals responsible for crimes committed in Cambodia between 1975 and 1979.[30] This court operated in Cambodia and was staffed by Cambodian and international personnel.[31] On the basis of this Cambodian model, the envisaged African tribunal would therefore not be a court-created ex nihilo, but a court that would fit into the framework of the existing Senegalese judicial system. Despite this, in 2011, the Senegalese authorities did not seem to have the will to try Hissein Habré, even though the idea was now firmly anchored in the discussions. Against this backdrop of the international pressure that was being exerted on Senegal, the insistence on the implementation of the recommendations of the Committee against Torture, the decision of the ICJ, and the election of President Macky Sall negotiations were accelerated. On August 22, 2012, an agreement was concluded between the African Union and Senegal on the establishment of a tribunal with an international nature. The agreement named the tribunal the EAC within the Senegalese courts. This agreement and the EAC Statute, which was annexed to the agreement, set out the contours of the tribunal.

MAIN FEATURES OF THE TRIBUNAL

Composition

The EAC were composed mainly of judges, prosecutors, registrars, and an administrator. According to Article 11 of the EAC Statute, the EAC comprised four chambers, each composed of judges and alternate judges: the Extraordinary African Investigative Chamber within the Regional High Tribunal of Dakar (four judges and two alternate judges), the Extraordinary African Indictment Chamber within the Court of Appeal of Dakar (three judges and one alternate judge), the Extraordinary African Assize Chamber within the Court of Appeal of Dakar (three judges and two alternate judges), and the Extraordinary African Assize Appeals Chamber within the Court of Appeal of Dakar (three judges and two alternate judges).

Article 12 of the EAC Statute provided for a general prosecutor and three deputy prosecutors, Article 13 for registrars, and Article 15 for an administrator.

The Mandate

According to Article 1 of the agreement establishing the EAC within Senegalese courts, the chambers were responsible for "prosecuting the person or persons most responsible for the crimes and serious violations of international law, international custom and international conventions ratified by Chad, committed on Chadian territory during the period from 7 June 1982 to 1 December 1990." This role assigned to the tribunal seemed to break with the history that presided over its creation. That history focused on efforts to bring to justice Hissein Habré, who was not named in the agreement.

The designation of a person in an international legal instrument, such as the person to be prosecuted, is not unknown in international criminal law. After the First World War, Article 227 of the 1919 Treaty of Versailles provided for a tribunal to be set up to try William II, the former German emperor, who was named as being responsible for violations of international rules during the war. The tribunal was not created and the will to judge the emperor faded. Apart from this historical example, however, no international or hybrid criminal court had been granted jurisdiction *ratione personae* over an explicitly designated individual.

The choice of the agreement between the African Union and Senegal not to name Hissein Habré was part of the recent history of international criminal courts. After their creation, these courts decided which individuals were to be prosecuted.

However, it was hard to imagine a tribunal, which was created to bring an individual to justice, making the decision not to prosecute that individual. The history of the EAC and their constitution showed that they were tailor-made for a trial of Hissein Habré. On the one hand, the jurisdiction *rationae temporis* of the tribunal, which covered the period from June 7, 1982, to December 1, 1990, corresponded to the period during which Hissein Habré ruled Chad. On the other hand, while it was not explicitly mandated to prosecute Hissein Habré, it was clear that the phrase "to prosecute the person or persons primarily responsible" in Article 1 of the agreement implicitly referred to Hissein Habré, while implying that the court may independently decide not to confine itself to the case of Hissein Habré, or decide to prosecute other individuals accused of perpetrating crimes under his regime.

Crimes within the Jurisdiction of the EAC

The EAC had jurisdiction over four crimes: genocide, crimes against humanity, war crimes, and torture.[32]

The crime of genocide was defined as "acts committed with intent to destroy, in whole or in part, a national, ethnical, racial or religious group, as such."[33] Five acts were listed: intentional homicide of members of the group; causing serious bodily or mental harm to members of the group; deliberately inflicting on the group conditions of life calculated to bring about its physical destruction in whole or in part; imposing measures intended to prevent births within the group; and forcibly transferring children of the group to another group.

Crimes against humanity were defined as acts committed as part of a widespread or systematic attack directed against any civilian population. These acts included rape, sexual slavery, enforced prostitution, enforced sterilization, or any other form of sexual violence of comparable gravity; voluntary homicide; extermination; deportation; the crime of apartheid; enslavement or widespread and systematic practice of summary executions; kidnapping of persons followed by their disappearance; torture or inhuman acts causing intentionally great suffering, serious injury to body or to mental or physical health inspired by political, racial, national, ethnic, cultural, religious, or gender grounds.[34]

War crimes were divided into two categories.[35] First, a list of acts committed against members of the armed forces, prisoners of war, civilians, or property protected under the provisions of the Geneva Conventions of August 12, 1949: voluntary homicide; torture or inhuman treatment, including biological experiments or willfully causing great suffering to body or mental health; destruction and appropriation of property, not justified by military necessity and carried out unlawfully and wantonly; compelling a prisoner of war or other protected person to serve in the armed forces; willfully depriving a prisoner of war or other protected person of the rights of fair and regular trial; and deportation or unlawful transfer or unlawful confinement and taking of hostages. Second, a list of serious violations of Article 3 common to the Geneva Conventions and of the 1977 Protocol Additional II added to these Conventions: violence to life, health, and physical or mental well-being of persons, in particular murder as well as cruel treatment such as torture, mutilation, or any form of corporal punishment; collective punishments; taking of hostages; acts of terrorism; outrages upon personal dignity, in particular humiliating and degrading treatment, rape, enforced prostitution, and any form of indecent assault; pillage; the passing of sentences and the carrying out of executions without previous judgment pronounced by a regularly constituted court, affording all the judicial guarantees which are recognized as indispensable by civilized peoples; threats to commit any of the foregoing acts.

Torture was defined as follows:

> Any act by which severe pain or suffering, whether physical or mental, is intentionally inflicted on a person for such purposes as obtaining from him or a third person information or a confession, punishing him for an act he or a third person has committed or is suspected of having committed, or intimidating or coercing him or a third person, or for any reason based on discrimination of any kind, when such pain or suffering is inflicted by or at the instigation of or with the consent or acquiescence of a public official or other person acting in an official capacity. It does not include pain or suffering arising only from, inherent in or incidental to lawful sanctions. No exceptional circumstances whatsoever, whether a state of war or a threat of war, internal political instability or any other public emergency, may be invoked as a justification of torture.[36]

The Main Steps of the EAC Criminal Procedure

The EAC criminal procedure was summed up in four steps that were structured around the four Chambers.[37]

The Extraordinary African Investigative Chamber task was to investigate the case after a referral by the prosecution.[38] After investigation, it had to decide whether to refer the accused to the Extraordinary African Assize Chamber for a trial.[39]

The Extraordinary African Indictment Chamber considered motions against the decisions of the Investigative Chamber.[40] Its decisions could not be appealed.[41]

The Extraordinary African Assize Chamber was the Trial Chamber. Its role was to try individuals referred by the Investigative Chamber, to acquit or convict these individuals, and to sentence them to penalties in case of a conviction.[42]

The Extraordinary African Assize Appeals Chamber function was to examine applications against the judgments of the Extraordinary African Assize Chamber in the event of a procedural or substantive error of law, or a fact that has led to a denial of justice.[43] Its decision was not subject to appeal.[44]

The EAC criminal procedure was part of the inquisitorial system. It is a system based on civil law and generally found in continental Europe.[45] Judges play an important role at all levels of the criminal procedure.[46] For example, investigating judges gather evidence and build the case. Trial parties, that is, prosecutors, lawyers for civil parties, and the defense lawyers, discuss the elements of the investigation file during the trial. The judges may ask questions and participate in the search for and manifestation of the truth. This system is very different from the common law adversary system, in which, while the prosecutor and defense lawyers discuss the case during the trial when all the facts are presented, judges are relatively passive and "independent decision-maker[s]."[47]

This criminal procedure structured around the four chambers also corresponded to the criminal procedure in Senegal. The EAC thus had a strong link with Senegal while maintaining its international aspects, all of which reflected its hybrid nature.

THE HYBRID NATURE OF THE TRIBUNAL

The development of international criminal law has led to the emergence of two main categories of tribunals: international criminal tribunals and hybrid criminal tribunals. International criminal tribunals, such as the ICC, the ICTY, and the ICTR, are international because all elements concerning, for example, their establishment, composition, organization, and functioning are international. Hybrid tribunals are different because domestic elements, usually related to a particular state, are added to the international elements related to, for example, their establishment and functioning. Thus, they combine international and national characteristics. Such courts have been established, for example, in Sierra Leone, Timor-Leste, Cambodia, Kosovo, Bosnia, and the Central African Republic.[48] The EAC fell into the category of hybrid tribunals because they combined international and domestic elements.

International Elements

An agreement concluded between Senegal and the African Union, an international organization, created the EAC. Thus, the tribunal was the result of an international agreement, which is nothing less than a treaty.

The EAC Statute provided for substantive jurisdiction under international law. Its Article 3 referred to "crimes and serious violations of international law, international custom and international conventions ratified by Chad." The definitions of the crimes to be considered by the EAC were either those already found in international law or clearly based on international law.[49] The definition of genocide was based on the definition provided by the 1948 Convention on the Prevention and Punishment of the Crime of Genocide, the definition of crimes against humanity and war crimes on the statutes of previous international criminal tribunals and the definition of the crime of torture on the 1984 Convention against Torture.[50]

The composition of the EAC judges was partly international. Article 11 of the Statute provided that the presidents of the Extraordinary African Assize and Appeals Chambers were to be nationals of an African state other than Senegal. In addition, the African Union played a role in the appointment of EAC judges. Under Articles 11 and 12 of the EAC Statute, the chairperson of the African Commission appointed all the judges and prosecutors of the EAC on the proposal of the Senegalese minister of justice.

With regard to immunities and privileges, Article 29 of the EAC Statute called upon international law to protect the staff of the EAC on the basis of the 1961 Vienna Convention on Diplomatic Relations.

In the context of appeal procedures, which could be implemented after a judgment, Article 25, paragraph 3, of the EAC Statute provided that the Extraordinary African Assize Appeals Chamber could rely on the jurisprudence of international criminal courts or tribunals.

The Statute resolutely followed in the footsteps of the statutes of previous international or hybrid criminal tribunals by adopting similar rules and principles.[51] These included the non-applicability of statutory limitations within the jurisdiction of the EAC (Article 9), the *non bis in idem* rule (Article 19), the rights of the accused (Article 21) strengthened by the creation of a defense office,[52] the prohibition of amnesty (Article 20), and the non-exemption from criminal responsibility based on official capacity, or a superior or subordinate position (Article 10).

With regard to reparations, the EAC Statute was inspired by the ICC Statute.[53] Like the ICC Statute, it distinguished three forms of reparation: restitution, compensation, and rehabilitation (Article 27). It also provided for the establishment of a "Trust Fund for Victims" to which states, international institutions, nongovernmental organizations, or "other sources" should contribute on a voluntary base (Article 28).

In the same vein, some elements related to the organization of the EAC were in line with those of the ECCC. As in the Cambodian case, EAC were not administered by the registry as in several international and hybrid criminal tribunals.[54] The ECCC were administered by a director and a deputy director of the Office of Administration.[55] Article 15 of the EAC Statute entrusted their administration to an administrator. In both systems, registrars were provided for and assisted, inter alia, the judges. In addition, victims could be civil parties and have representatives before the EAC[56] and ECCC.[57]

Domestic Elements

As a central state actor in the trial, Senegal remained at the heart of the Statute of the EAC. As we have seen, the organization of the tribunal was a reflection of Senegalese criminal justice. The four chambers of the EAC were created within Senegalese judicial courts (Article 2 of the EAC Statute) and the judicial organization of the tribunal around four separate chambers (investigation, indictment, trial, and appeal) corresponded to the criminal procedure in Senegal.

Senegal had a role to play in the appointment of staff members to the EAC. Under the terms of Articles 13 and 15 of the EAC Statute, the minister of justice of Senegal alone was responsible for appointing the registrars and the administrator of the EAC. Certainly, the chairperson of the African Commission was set to appoint the judges and prosecutors of the EAC. However, this appointment was to be made on the proposal of the minister of justice of Senegal.

Senegal was also at the heart of the law applicable by the EAC. Situations and matters that were not contemplated in the EAC Statute were governed by Senegalese law according to Article 16 of the EAC Statute. However, it would be erroneous to conclude that Senegalese law could only be invoked in the event that the Statute was silent. The EAC Statute explicitly provided for the applicability of Senegalese law in several matters. Thus, Senegal's Code of Criminal Procedure applied to hearings,[58] the conduct of public proceedings,[59] the determination of the powers of the registry,[60] and to provisions related to the participation of victims not provided for in the Statute.[61] Thus, while governing a residual category where the Statute was silent, Senegalese law was a central set of rules within the EAC Statute.

This impression was even clearer on closer examination of the international rules provided for in the Statute. Even if they did not have any decisive influence or constitute an important change, some elements of the Senegalese law were incorporated in these international rules in the context of the transposition of international law. For example, based on the definition of genocide in the 1948 Convention on the Prevention and Punishment of the Crime of Genocide, Article 5 of the EAC Statute provided a list of genocidal acts that included "intentional homicide" and not "the killing of members of the group" as found in that Convention. By referring to "intentional homicide" and not "the killing of members of the group," Article 5 of the EAC Statute followed the Senegalese Act of February 12, 2007, which, in transposing international law, also provided for such substitution.[62]

This blend of international and national elements in the EAC Statute alongside the importance of Senegalese law and other features raised some questions about the specificities of the hybrid nature of the tribunal.

EAC: A SUI GENERIS HYBRID TRIBUNAL?

Because of some of their special features, including their mode of establishment, the absence of a specific set of rules of procedure and evidence, and their jurisdiction, the EAC raised the question of whether they were sui generis in nature and quite different from other international and hybrid criminal tribunals.

Created by an Agreement between a Regional Organization and a State

Created in 2012 by an agreement between a regional international organization (the AU) and a state (Senegal), the EAC had a regional nature that was unprecedented in the area of a hybrid criminal tribunal. In Cambodia and Sierra Leone, for example, hybrid criminal courts had been established under an agreement between the United Nations and these states.[63] It was not until three years later that a hybrid criminal court was established after negotiations between a state and a regional organization. Indeed, in 2015, a hybrid tribunal was set up in Kosovo following a 2007 report by the Parliamentary Assembly of the Council of Europe, and after collaboration and agreement between the European Union and Kosovo.[64]

No Specific Rules of Procedure and Evidence Adopted

On the procedural level, the EAC Statute did not provide for the adoption of rules of procedure and evidence, unlike the system adopted for several international and hybrid criminal courts. Admittedly, EAC were not the only tribunal with this peculiarity. In Cambodia and Timor, the hybrid tribunals did not adopt rules of procedure and evidence. In Timor, the United Nations Transitional Administrator (UNTAET) had issued transitional rules on criminal procedure, the content of which regularly referred to international law.[65] In Cambodia, Article 12 of the 2003 agreement between the United Nations and Cambodia and Articles 20, 23, and 33 of the 2004 Law on the Establishment of the ECCC envisaged the procedural applicability of Cambodian law. These legal instruments also indicated that solutions should be sought in international rules in the event of difficulties. The ECCC adopted internal rules to consolidate applicable Cambodian procedure for their proceedings and incorporated additional rules that they found necessary.[66]

Moving away from these solutions, Articles 16 and 17(1) of the EAC Statute provided for the applicability of Senegalese law in the event that the Statute was silent. However, Article 1, paragraph 4, of the agreement to which the EAC Statute was annexed provided that the tribunal shall apply the "Statute, international criminal law, Senegalese Criminal Code and Code of Criminal Procedure and other relevant Senegalese laws." It suggested, based on the order of the elements cited, that the EAC apply "international criminal law" before Senegalese law. It thus seemed to contradict the Statute, which provided that the Chambers were to apply the Statute and, in the event of the Statute being silent, Senegalese law. All in all, and despite these uncertainties, the Senegalese law appeared under the EAC Statute as the rule of procedure and evidence of the EAC.

The Individual Responsibility "for Serious Violations of Human Rights, International Law and International Custom"

The EAC Statute gave a special place to individual responsibility by providing that the court "shall pass sentences and impose penalties and sanctions on persons convicted of serious violations of human rights, international law and international custom."[67] There was something unprecedented and curious about this formulation.

It was unprecedented because until the creation of the EAC, while the statutes of international or hybrid criminal courts have sometimes referred to individuals responsible for violations of international humanitarian law[68] or individuals responsible for crimes,[69] they had not explicitly set out the responsibility of individuals for serious human rights violations. While the Law Establishing the ECCC referred to those most responsible for violations of international conventions recognized by Cambodia, it did not explicitly refer to individuals responsible for human rights violations. The EAC Statute thus moved away from international criminal law and closer to international human rights law. Indeed, international human rights law jurisprudence deals with the obligation of states to bring to justice those responsible for serious human rights violations.[70]

The wording of Article 23 also appeared curious because it referred to persons responsible for violations of international law and international custom. By citing both international law and one of its sources, international custom, Article 23 raised questions about the reasons for insisting on that particular source. One might wonder, without having a clear answer, in what way international custom appeared particular in the framework of the EAC Statute. It would have been more consistent to link the "jurisdiction" of the EAC under Article 3 of the Statute to Article 23, and to provide that the EAC could pass sentences and impose "penalties and sanctions on persons convicted" of the violations or crimes provided for in its Statute. This was the choice made, in particular, by Article 22, paragraph 1, of the ICTR Statute, and Article 23, paragraph 1, of the ICTY Statute. According to these statutes, the two courts could impose penalties and sanctions on the perpetrators of serious violations of international humanitarian law, international humanitarian law being the cornerstone of their substantive jurisdiction.[71]

The Scope of Their Substantive Jurisdiction and the Particularity of Universal Jurisdiction

Until the creation of the EAC, the statutes of hybrid criminal courts had provided for substantive jurisdiction that covered crimes under national law. This was the case in Sierra Leone, Cambodia, Kosovo, Timor-Leste, and Bosnia.[72] The EAC Statute did not provide for any crimes that were strictly governed by national law. The scope of the EAC's substantive jurisdiction was restricted to international crimes. This was certainly due to the difference between the previous cases and the EAC. The crimes brought before the previous hybrid courts had been generally committed on the territory of the states concerned, making the mobilization of national law relevant. In the case of EAC being based in Dakar, Senegal, the crimes were mainly committed abroad, in Chad.

Thus, the EAC were a hybrid criminal tribunal with universal jurisdiction. Prior to the EAC, most hybrid criminal courts were created to try crimes committed on the territory of the states in which they were sitting. The Special Tribunal for Lebanon (STL) was an exception as its headquarters was in The Hague.[73] However, the opening of an STL office in Beirut, Lebanon, gave a local dimension to the tribunal.[74] In the case of Sierra Leone, there had also been a relocation of the trial of the former Liberian head of state Charles Taylor to The Hague.[75] However, the seat of the SCSL was in Freetown, Sierra Leone.[76] It was not until 2016 that a hybrid court emerged following the same location logic as the EAC. Indeed, the Specialist Chambers and Prosecutors for Kosovo have been based in The Hague, the Netherlands.[77] However, the Netherlands was not as involved in the creation of the Kosovar hybrid tribunal as Senegal was in the creation of the EAC.

So, the EAC were a sui generis tribunal among hybrid criminal tribunals. They owed this characteristic to the development of the Habré case. The creation of the EAC was the result of the failure to implement two procedures relating to universal jurisdictions in Belgium and Senegal. The implication of Senegal in the establishment of the tribunal and its procedures could also explain that particularity of the EAC. These procedures that were applied to the Habré case started with the investigation phase that preceded the trial and the appeal phases.

NOTES

1. Report of the Committee of Eminent African Jurists on the Case of Hissein Habré, July 2, 2006, para. 29.
2. Ibid., paras. 31 and 33.

3. ECOWAS Court of Justice, *Hissein Habré v. République du Sénégal*, no. ECW/CCJ/APP/07/08, arrêt no. ECW/CCJ/JUD/06/10, November 18, 2010.

4. See, for example, the International Military Tribunal of Nuremberg created after the Second World War (Agreement of London, August 8, 1945), the International Criminal Tribunal for the former Yugoslavia created after the perpetration of international crimes during the war in the former Yugoslavia (UN Security Council Resolution 808, Doc. UN, S/RES/808, 22 February 1993).

5. For ICTR, Resolution 955 of the UN Security Council, Doc. UN, S/RES/955, November 8, 1994. For the SCSL, Agreement between the United Nations and the Government of Sierra Leone on the establishment of a SCSL, January 16, 2002.

6. For a debate regarding the application of the principle of the non-retroactivity of criminal law in the Habré case, see Alain Didier Olinga, "Les droits de l'homme peuvent-ils soustraire un ex-dictateur à la justice? L'affaire Hissène Habré devant la Cour de justice de la C.E.D.E.A.O.," *Revue trimestrielle des droits de l'homme* 87, (2011): 735–746; Valentina Spiga, "Non-Retroactivity of Criminal Law: A New Chapter in the Hissène Habré Saga," *Journal of International Criminal Justice* 9, no. 1 (March 2011): 5–23.

7. See, for example, Article 10 para. 2 of the ICTY Statute, Article 9 para. 2 of the ICTR Statute and Article 9 para. 2 of the SCSL Statute.

8. More generally, for the criticisms of the ECOWAS Court of Justice ruling, see Alione Sall, *L'affaire Habré. Aspects judiciaires nationaux et internationaux* (Paris: L'Harmattan, 2013), 57–74.

9. Rome Statute of the International Criminal Court, opened for signature July 17, 1998, 2187 UNTS 3 (entered into force July 1, 2002).

10. For example, in the context of universal jurisdiction for international crimes, an arrest warrant was issued on April 11, 2000, by Belgium against the then Minister of Foreign Affairs of the Democratic Republic of Congo (DRC). DRC filed a complaint against Belgium before the International Court of Justice (ICJ). In 2002, the ICJ ruled that the issue of that arrest warrant "failed to respect the immunity from criminal jurisdiction and the inviolability which the incumbent Minister for Foreign Affairs of the Democratic Republic of the Congo enjoyed under international law," see Arrest Warrant of April 11, 2000 (*Democratic Republic of the Congo v. Belgium*), Judgment, ICJ Reports 2002, 34. For a detailed list of the cases under universal jurisdiction, see Council of the European Union, *The AU-EU Expert Report on the Principle of Universal Jurisdiction*, Doc. 8672/1/09 REV 1, April 16, 2009, 27–29.

11. ICC, *The Prosecutor v. Omar Hassan Ahmad Al Bashir*, Warrant of Arrest for Omar Hassan Ahmad Al Bashir, no. ICC-02/05-01/09-1, March 4, 2009; ICC, *The Prosecutor v. Omar Hassan Ahmad Al Bashir*, Second Warrant of Arrest for Omar Hassan Ahmad Al Bashir, no. ICC-02/05-01/09-95, July 12, 2010; ICC, Situation in Libya, *The Prosecutor v. Saif Al-Islam Gaddafi*, no. ICC-01/11-01/11, Case Information Sheet, November 2009.

12. ICC, *The Prosecutor v. Laurent Gbagbo and Charles Blé Goudé*, no. ICC-02/11-01/15, Case Information Sheet, July 2021.

13. ICC, *The Prosecutor v. Laurent Gbagbo*, Warrant of Arrest for Laurent Koudou Gbagbo, no. ICC-02/11-01/11-1, November 23, 2011.

14. All the information about the cases are available on the website of the ICC: https://www.icc-cpi.int/pages/situation.aspx, accessed 5/16/2021.

15. AU, Decision on the Report of the Commission on the Abuse of the Principle of Universal Jurisdiction, Doc. Assembly/AU/14 (XI), 2008, paras. 5 and 7; AU, Decision on the Implementation of the Assembly Decision on the Abuse of the Principle of Universal Jurisdiction, Doc. Assembly/AU/3(XII), February 1–3, 2009, para. 4; AU, Decision on the Abuse of the Principle of Universal Jurisdiction. Doc. Assembly/AU/11(XIII), July 3, 2009, para. 4.

16. AU, Decision on the Application by the International Criminal Court (ICC) Prosecutor for the Indictment of the President of the Republic of the Sudan, Doc. Assembly/AU/Dec.221(XII), February 3, 2009; AU, Decision on the Meeting of African States Parties to the Rome Statute of the International Criminal Court (ICC), Doc. Assembly/AU/13(XIII), July 3, 2009; AU, Decision on the Progress Report of the Commission on the Implementation of Decision Assembly/Au/Dec.270(XIV) on the Second Ministerial Meeting on the Rome Statute of the International Criminal Court (ICC), Doc. Assembly/AU/10(XV), July 27, 2010; AU, Decision on the Implementation of the Decisions on the International Criminal Court, Doc. EX.CL/639(XVIII), January 31, 2011; AU, Decision on the Implementation of the Assembly Decisions on the International Criminal Court, Doc. EX.CL/670(XIX), July 1, 2011; Decision on the Progress Report of the Commission on the Implementation of the Assembly Decisions on the International Criminal Court (ICC), Doc. EX.CL/710(XX), January 30, 2012.

17. AU, Decision on the Implementation of the Assembly Decision on the Abuse of the Principle of Universal Jurisdiction, Doc. Assembly/AU/3(XII), February 3, 2009, para. 9; AU, Decision on the Meeting of African States Parties to the Rome Statute of the International Criminal Court (ICC), Doc. Assembly/AU/13(XIII), July 3, 2009, para. 5; AU, Decision on the Abuse of the Principle of Universal Jurisdiction, Doc. EX.CL/606(XVII), July 27, 2010, para. 5; AU, Decision on the Implementation of the Assembly Decisions on the International Criminal Court, Doc. EX.CL/670(XIX), July 1, 2011, para. 8; AU, Doc. Min/Legal/ACJHR-PAP/3(II) Rev. 1.5.

18. Protocol on Amendments to the Protocol on the Statute of the African Court of Justice and Human Rights, June 27, 2014 (Annex).

19. See the following documents of the AU: EX.CL/952(XXVIII), January 30–31, 2016; EX.CL/987(XXIX), July 17–18, 2016; EX.CL/1006(XXX), January 30–31, 2017. In June 2021, 33 African States are parties to the Rome Statute of the International Criminal Court.

20. AU, Doc. AU, EX.CL/1006(XXX), January 30–31, 2017, para. 6.

21. Burundi, *Withdrawal*, C.N.805.2016.treaties-xviii.10, October 28, 2016; South Africa, *Withdrawal of Notification of Withdrawal*, C.N.121.2017.treaties-xviii.10, March 7, 2017; Gambia, *Withdrawal of Notification of Withdrawal*, C.N.62.2017. treaties-xviii.10, February 16, 2017.

22. Article 11, para. 1 of the ICC Statute.

23. AU, Progress Report of the Commission on the Hissein Habré Case (In the Implementation of Decision Assembly/Au/Dec.297(XV)), Doc. Assembly/ AU/9(XVI) Rev.1, January 30–31, 2011, para. 23.

24. Ibid., para. 24.
25. AU, Decision on the Hissein Habré Case, Doc. Assembly/Au/9(XVI), 2011, para. 9.
26. For an overview, Robert Cryer et al., *An Introduction to International Criminal Law and Procedure*, 4th edition (Cambridge: Cambridge University Press, 2019).
27. Ben Kioko, "Creating the EAC in Senegal. Perspectives from the African Union," in *The President on Trial: Prosecuting Hissene Habré*, ed. Sharon Weill, Kim Thuy Seelinger, and Kerstin Bree Carlson (New York: Oxford University Press, 2019), 72.
28. Ibid.
29. Ibid.
30. Agreement between the United Nations and Cambodia for the Prosecution of Crimes Committed during the Period of Democratic Kampuchea, 2003.
31. Ibid., for example, Article 3.
32. Article 4 of the EAC Statute.
33. Article 5, ibid.
34. Article 6, ibid.
35. Article 7, ibid.
36. Article 8, ibid.
37. Article 2, ibid.
38. See Article 17, para 4, ibid., and EAC (Chambre d'instruction), Ordonnance de non-lieu partiel, de mise en accusation et de renvoi devant la Chambre africaine extraordinaire d'assises, February 13, 2015, 7.
39. Articles 169 and 175 of the Criminal Procedure Code of Senegal.
40. Article 31, para. 1 (b), of the EAC Statute.
41. Ibid.
42. Article 23, ibid.
43. Article 25 para. 1, of the EAC Statute.
44. Article 25, para. 4, ibid. For more on the EAC organization and criminal procedure, see Sharon Weill, Kim Thuy Seelinger, and Kerstin Bree Carlson, "Hissene Habre on Trial: Mapping the Long Road to Justice," in *The President on Trial: Prosecuting Hissene Habré*, ed. Sharon Weill, Kim Thuy Seelinger, and Kerstin Bree Carlson (New York: Oxford University Press, 2019), 5–6.
45. Bryan A. Garner, ed., *Black's Law Dictionary* (West Publishing Co., 2009), 864.
46. Ibid.
47. Ibid., 62.
48. On hybrid criminal courts, see, for example, Aaron Fichtelberg, *Hybrid Tribunals: A Comparative Examination* (New York: Springer, 2015).
49. Articles 4 to 8 of the EAC Statute.
50. Ibid. For genocide, Article 2 of the 1948 Convention on the Prevention and Punishment of the Crime of Genocide; for crimes against humanity, Article 3 of the ICTR Statute, Article 5 of the ICTY Statute and Article 7 of the ICC Statute; for war crimes, Article 8 of the ICC Statute; for torture, Article 1, para. 1, and Article 2, para.

2, of the 1984 Convention against Torture and Other Cruel, Inhuman or Degrading Treatment or Punishment.

51. See, for example, the Statutes of the ICTY, ICTR, ICC, and SCSL.

52. Amendment to the Agreement Establishing the EAC, July 24, 2014. This office was not finally set up and operational.

53. Articles 75 and 79 of the ICC Statute.

54. See, for example, Article 43 of the ICC Statute and Article 16 of the Statute of the SCSL.

55. Article 8 of the Agreement between the United Nations and Cambodia for the Prosecution of Crimes Committed during the Period of Democratic Kampuchea, 2003.

56. Article 14 of the EAC Statute.

57. Rules 12 ter and 23 ter of the Rules of Procedure of the ECCC, January 16, 2015.

58. Article 22 of the EAC Statute.

59. Article 12, para. 3, and Article 17, para. 1, ibid.

60. Article 13, para. 1, ibid.

61. Article 14, para. 5, ibid.

62. Loi n° 2007-02 du 12 février 2007, op. cit. For more on the influence of Senegalese law on the EAC, see Marina Eudes and Emmanuel Guematcha, "Quels apports des Chambres africaines extraordinaires?," *Revue belge de droit international*, no. 1 (2017): 93–214.

63. Agreement between the United Nations and Cambodia for the Prosecution of Crimes Committed during the Period of Democratic Kampuchea, 2003; Agreement Between the United Nations and the Government of Sierra Leone on the Establishment of a SCSL, 2002.

64. Law No. 04/L-274 on Ratification of the International Agreement between the Republic of Kosovo and the European Union on the European Union Rule of Law Mission in Kosovo, April 23, 2014; Law No.05/L-053 on Specialist Chambers and Specialist Prosecutor's Office, August 3, 2015.

65. UNTAET, Regulation 2000/30.

66. ECCC, Internal Rules (Rev.9), as Revised on January 16, 2015.

67. Article 23 paragraph 1, of the EAC Statute.

68. For example, see the Statutes of the ICTR (Articles 1 and 22), ICTY (Articles 1 and 23), and SCSL (Article 1).

69. For example, ICC Statute (Article 1), Timor Regulation 2000/15 (section 2).

70. See, for example, IACDH, *"Las Dos Erres" Massacre v. Guatemala*, Judgment, November 24, 2009, Series C no. 211, para 232; ECHR, *Marguš v. Croatie*, n° 4455/10, May 27, 2014, para. 127; African Commission on Human and Peoples' Rights, Communication no. 74/92, *Commission nationale des droits de l'homme et des libertés v. Chad*, 18th Ordinary Session, October 1995, para. 21.

71. Article 1 of the ICTR Statute and Article 1 of the ICTY Statute.

72. See the statutes of these hybrid tribunals.

73. Agreement between the Kingdom of the Netherlands and the United Nations concerning the Headquarters of the Special Tribunal for Lebanon, December 21, 2007.

74. Memorandum of Understanding between Lebanon and the Special Tribunal for Lebanon concerning the Office of the Special Tribunal in Lebanon, June 17, 2009.

75. See Doc. UN, S/2006/207, April 3, 2006.

76. Article 10 of the SCSL Statute.

77. Agreement between the Kingdom of the Netherlands and the Republic of Kosovo concerning the Hosting of the Kosovo Relocated Specialist Judicial Institution in the Netherlands, February 15, 2016.

Chapter 3

The Investigation Phase

After the adoption of the Statute of the Extraordinary African Chambers (EAC), everything began to accelerate. On December 28, 2012, the president of Senegal promulgated the law adopted by the Senegalese Parliament authorizing the ratification of the international agreement that created the EAC.[1] The prosecutors (the general prosecutor, Mbacké Fall, and his deputies, Youssoupha Diallo, Anta Ndiaye Diop, and Moustapha Ka) and the administrator (Ciré Aly Bâ) of the EAC were appointed.[2] The judges of the Extraordinary African Investigative Chamber (Jean Kande, Souleymane Teliko, Absatou Ly Diallo, Abdoul Aziz Diallo) and the alternate judges (Barou Diop and Oumar Fall) were appointed, as were the judges of the Extraordinary African Indictment Chamber (Assane Ndiaye, André Bob Séne, Lamine Sow) and its alternate judge (Hyppolite Anquediche Ndèye).[3] The judges of the Assize and Appeals Chambers were appointed later, just before the start of the trial phase and the appeal phase for which they were responsible.[4] Registrars, communication and administrative staff, assistants, drivers, and so on were also recruited. Senegalese police officers were responsible for ensuring the security of the tribunal.

The inauguration of the EAC took place on February 8, 2013.[5] Shortly after the inauguration, the pretrial investigation phase was launched. This phase, which preceded the trial and appeals phases, corresponded to the work of the Investigative Chamber after referral by the prosecutors and to the possible proceedings before the Indictment Chamber in case of motions against the decisions of the Investigative Chamber.

THE INITIATION OF PUBLIC ACTION AND THE WORK OF INVESTIGATING JUDGES

After the inauguration of the EAC, the prosecutors began their work. They started to gather information on the crimes committed in Chad under the Hissein Habré regime and sought information.[6] They traveled to Belgium where investigation work on the crimes had been carried out. They also visited Chad which, to facilitate the work of the EAC, concluded a judicial cooperation agreement with Senegal on May 3, 2013.[7] Received with open arms by the Chadian authorities, the prosecutors met many victims of the Habré regime and the organizations that defended them. Based on the information they gathered, the prosecutors demanded the arrest of Hissein Habré on their return to Dakar. On June 30, 2013, Hissein Habré was taken into custody.

On July 2, 2013, by an introductory indictment, the general prosecutor of the EAC referred the case to the Extraordinary African Investigative Chamber. Having noted that serious crimes were perpetrated in Chad between 1982 and 1990, the prosecutors requested that Hissein Habré and five of his former collaborators be indicted for crimes against humanity, war crimes, and torture. The five collaborators were Saleh Younouss and Guihini Korei, two former directors of the DDS (the Hissein Habré regime political police); Mahamat Djibrine known as El Djonto; and Abakar Torbo Rahma and Zakaria Berdei, individuals who held various positions within the DDS and other security bodies of the Hissein Habré regime. The prosecutors also called for the pretrial detention of Hissein Habré and the issuance of international arrest warrants against the five collaborators. The prosecutors based their request in particular on numerous documents accumulated during the many years of trying to bring Hissein Habré to justice, and particularly on the work of the Belgian judiciary, which had made available the file it had compiled during the investigation phase of the Habré case in Belgium.

On the same day of July 2, 2013, after an interrogation by the investigating judges, Hissein Habré was indicted by the Extraordinary African Investigative Chamber for crimes against humanity, war crimes, and torture committed during his presidency. He was remanded into custody.

In the days and months that followed, the investigating judges issued international arrest warrants against the five former collaborators. Accompanied by prosecutors, the investigating judges traveled to Chad. Several international letters rogatory were executed in Chad, where more than 2,500 victims and witnesses were heard with the assistance of the Chadian judicial authorities. An international letter rogatory was executed in France to hear a former DDS agent residing there.

In Chad, investigating judges and prosecutors visited the secret jails of the former regime that still existed and the mass graves and other places where massacres were allegedly perpetrated. Information was collected, locations photographed, videos made, archives examined, and certified copies made.

At the end of 2014, the Extraordinary African Investigative Chamber had a massive dossier at its disposal. To this wealth of information were added the documents of several experts appointed by the tribunal to work on the political and military history of Chad, on the mortality rate in Chadian prisons, on writings and forensic analyses, and so on. Faced with this arsenal of documents and a procedure that was clearly leading toward a trial against him, Hissein Habré rejected the validity of the EACs.

HISSEIN HABRÉ'S COUNTERATTACK: TRYING TO INVALIDATE THE CREATION OF THE EAC

From the start of the proceedings against him in 2000, Hissein Habré had benefited from the services of lawyers he had appointed himself. Until 2012, his lawyers had succeeded in thwarting attempts to bring him to justice. With the creation of the EAC, their inauguration in February 2013 and the start of their procedures, the vice seemed to be inexorably tightening around Hissein Habré. But the former head of state did not intend to be impressed by the EACs. He decided to challenge their legality. During his interrogation by the investigating judges of the EAC on July 2, 2013, he asserted that his arrest was an "illegal abduction," a "kidnapping," and described the EAC as an "administrative service."[8] Then, he refused to answer any questions put to him by prosecutors and investigating judges. He informed the investigating judges that proceedings were under way before the ECOWAS Court of Justice, which would rule on the "legality of the African Chambers."[9]

Indeed, a few months earlier, on March 27, 2013, Hissein Habré had brought an application before the ECOWAS Court of Justice to challenge the creation of the EAC.[10] According to him, the creation of the new tribunal in Senegal constituted a violation of the ECOWAS Court of Justice's decision of November 18, 2010, which concluded that there was a likelihood that his rights would be violated by Senegal's attempt to retry him.

However, in the new decision issued on November 5, 2013, the ECOWAS Court of Justice ruled against Hissein Habré's claim. The court implicitly held that by setting up the EAC under an agreement with the African Union, Senegal was complying with the ruling that it issued in 2010, and that suggested that Hissein Habré could be tried within the framework of an international tribunal.[11] The ECOWAS Court of Justice held that it was incompetent to control the legality of international agreements such as the agreement that established the EAC.[12]

Although unfavorable, the ECOWAS Court of Justice's decision did not entirely destroy the Hissein Habré's intent to demonstrate the illegality of the EAC. His lawyers also acted in Senegal and pointed out that elements relating to the agreement establishing the EAC violated the Senegalese Constitution. They took the matter to the Supreme Court of Senegal, which referred it to the Senegalese Constitutional Council, an institution vested with the power of reviewing the constitutionality of legislation.[13] They presented legalistic and technical arguments.

They argued that a decree authorizing the appointment of Senegalese judges by the chairperson of the African Commission was issued on the basis of the agreement establishing the EAC, even though the law and decree ratifying the agreement had not been published.[14] According to Hissein Habré's lawyers, as the agreement had not entered into force, this appointment procedure constituted a violation of the Constitution of Senegal, which laid down rules on the ratification of treaties. They also considered that the signature of the agreement of August 22, 2012, by the Minister of Justice of Senegal invalidated the treaty, as the minister was not vested with full powers to bind the state internationally, as required by Article 7 of the 1969 Vienna Convention on the Law of Treaties. The lawyers added that the appointment of Senegalese judges by the chairperson of the African Commission was contrary to the Senegalese Constitution, which reserved this prerogative for the president of the Republic of Senegal.

The Constitutional Council of Senegal rejected the claims of Hissein Habré's lawyers on March 2, 2015.[15] The Council considered that the treaty establishing the EAC was an agreement in simplified form and that its validity did not depend on a ratification law. For the Council, the Minister of Justice was qualified to commit Senegal. The exceptional and international character of the EAC authorized the appointment of Senegalese judges by the chairperson of the African Commission. The Council also rejected two further arguments by the lawyers, which referred to an error in the dating of the ratification law and a lack of consultation with the Constitutional Council on the conformity of the agreement creating the EAC with the Senegalese Constitution. The Constitutional Council pointed out that the dating error was not the cause for invalidating the law and that the Senegalese Constitution did not provide for a mandatory consultative phase before the adoption of an international agreement.

The decisions of the ECOWAS Court of Justice on November 5, 2013, and of the Senegalese Constitutional Council of March 2, 2015, were a real blow to the former president of Chad. They sounded the death knell for his hopes of having EAC declared illegal and of avoiding a lawsuit. There were no more legal obstacles in the way of a trial he would have to undergo. In pretrial detention, he was condemned to defending himself, either within the legal framework of the EAC or in a nonjudicial forum, in the media for example, through his lawyers who could speak on his behalf. But, before the 2015 Senegalese Constitutional Council's decision, Hissein Habré had already chosen to keep quiet.

Indeed, on February 5, 2014, he had informed the EAC that he no longer wished to participate in future hearings.[16] Thus, Hissein Habré remained silent during the hearings. How to explain the silence of the former Chadian head of state during much of the investigation phase? Did he think he was pre-convicted? Was he aware that there was overwhelming evidence against him and that he had no chance in the event of a trial? Was his silence simply a way of expressing all his disdain for this criminal procedure which he considered illegal? One could only speculate.

In any case, the silence of the main defendant and the absence of his lawyers, who no longer participated in the proceedings despite invitations from the judges, did not disrupt the course of the investigation phase that continued at the pace of international letters rogatory, hearings, investigations, expert appraisals, and the exploitation of documents during 2014 and the early months of 2015.[17] The investigation and proceedings were resolutely turned toward Chad, whose cooperation, more than that of other states, was crucial for the success of the EAC criminal procedures.

CHAD'S POSITION: FROM COOPERATION TO MISTRUST

In the context of trials with an international dimension, the importance of state cooperation for the efficiency of justice is well known. In particular, international criminal tribunals need the cooperation of states to arrest the persons being prosecuted and to authorize the collection of evidence on their territory. The proceedings leading up to the trial of the former Chadian head of state did not deviate from this requirement.[18] As we have seen, the investigating judges and prosecutors of the EAC went to Belgium at the beginning of their work and an international letter rogatory was executed in France to hear a former DDS agent. However, it was to Chad that the EAC turned as their main source of information. That was not surprising. Chad was the place where the crimes were allegedly committed. It was on the Chadian territory that several material elements important to the proceedings were located: mass graves, jails, archives, victims, witnesses, and many alleged perpetrators. On the basis of the judicial agreement concluded between Senegal and Chad on May 3, 2013,[19] the EAC requested the cooperation of Chad for the collection of material and testimonial evidence on the one hand, and for the arrest and transfer of the five individuals being prosecuted on the other.

With regard to the collection of evidence, Chad was very cooperative for several months. It warmly welcomed prosecutors and investigating judges at the start of investigations. International letters rogatory were executed in Chad without difficulty for several months. In the context of judicial cooperation, the Chadian judicial authorities actively participated in the work of the EAC by collecting testimonies from thousands of victims and witnesses and recording them in legal minutes. This active judicial cooperation came to a halt in July 2014 when Chad refused to execute an international letter rogatory from the EAC. The investigating judges demanded the hearing of Goukouni Weddeye, a former head of state of Chad, a former brother in arms of Hissein Habré who had become his enemy. According to the Chadian authorities, Goukouni Weddeye had expressed his wish not to be heard.

With regards to the arrest and transfer of persons prosecuted by the EAC, Chad's judicial cooperation was very problematic. The Chadian authorities did not execute the arrest warrants issued by the EAC in 2013 against the five Habré collaborators. In October 2014, they indicated that they would not follow up on the request of the EAC for the indictment of the former director of the DDS Saleh Younouss and a former DDS agent, Mahamat Djibrine, known as "El Djonto." They noted that both persons were being prosecuted in Chad. On December 2, 2014, the Senegalese judicial authorities informed the investigating judges of the EAC that the arrest warrants against the five collaborators could not be executed, in other words, that Chad had refused to cooperate.

Chad's attitude raised questions: Why was it cooperating with the EAC at the beginning of its procedures and why was it being less inclined to do so in mid-2014? Two assumptions could be made in this regard: the unsuccessful attempt of Chad to fully participate in the trial and the fear of the potential consequences of the trial by the Chadian authorities.

Chad's Unsuccessful Attempt to Fully Participate in the Trial

Beyond judicial cooperation, Chad intended to participate in the ongoing proceedings before the EAC. This willingness to participate in the proceedings aimed at bringing Hissein Habré to justice was not new. During the Belgian proceedings against Hissein Habré, the Chadian authorities had pointed out that the immunity of the latter, a former head of state, had been lifted by a Chadian National Conference in 1993.[20] According to the Chadian authorities, the former head of state could not claim immunity in criminal proceedings pending before the Belgian courts. Chad had also indirectly participated in the process of establishing the EACs by promising to provide funding to the tribunal during the 2010 donor round table.[21]

In February 2014, Chad no longer wished to limit itself to such a distant role. In an attempt to take advantage of the EAC Statute, which provided for the possibility for victims to become civil parties, it requested to be recognized as a civil party to the trial and sought compensation for the economic damage suffered as a result of the alleged looting and misappropriation of public funds by Hissein Habré. Chad's request raised legal challenges. In principle, the possibility for legal persons, including states, to become civil parties in criminal proceedings is not prohibited in the inquisitorial legal system of some states like Senegal.[22] As other civil parties in the criminal proceedings, states have access to the documents related to the case when they are civil parties. However, the request for a state to bring a civil claim before a hybrid criminal court was unprecedented in the international criminal field where proceedings are oriented toward international crimes committed by individuals.

The Extraordinary African Investigative Chamber rejected Chad's request on May 21, 2014. It considered that the state was not among the victims of the crime of genocide, crimes against humanity, and the crime of torture provided for in Articles 5, 6, and 8 of the EAC Statute. On the basis of the case law of the ICC, it decided that in the case of looting constituting war crimes under Article 7 of the EAC Statute, a state could only be considered a victim when the act was committed in the territory occupied by an enemy power. In the Habré case, it pointed out as a reminder; it was an individual who was suspected of having committed looting against the state of which he was a national. Dissatisfied, the Chadian state's lawyers challenged the decision before the Extraordinary African Indictment Chamber. The Indictment Chamber confirmed the decision of the Investigative Chamber in a decision issued on August 27, 2014. Chad's attempt to participate in the proceedings other than through judicial cooperation failed. Thus, Chad's lack of diligence in the area of judicial cooperation may appear to be a form of reprisal against the EAC.

Chadian Justice Preferred Because of Fear of the Potential Consequences of the Hissein Habré Trial?

As relations between the EAC and Chadian authorities seemed to take a problematic turn in 2014, the Chadian judicial authorities decided to organize the trial of several former collaborators of Hissein Habré in Chad. Two individuals under arrest warrants issued by the EAC, Saleh Younouss and Mahamat Djibrine, were among those being prosecuted, as were several former collaborators of Hissein Habré who, as the EAC investigation was underway, were likely to provide information on the repressive machinery of the former president's regime. The trial of the collaborators began in November 2014 before the criminal court of the Court of Appeal of N'Djamena and, on March 25, 2015, the court rendered its decision.[23] Assassinations, torture, kidnapping, arbitrary detention, assault, intentional and fatal bodily harm and other barbaric acts were reported in the decision. The Court condemned the accused and the Chadian state was declared civilly responsible to pay 75 billion CFA francs (more than 114 million euros) to the civil parties, the victims.[24] It also condemned several defendants to heavy sentences for crimes committed under Hissein Habré's regime. Saleh Younouss and Mahamat Djibrine were sentenced to hard labor for life.[25] These defendants were now out of the control of the EAC. The Chadian criminal procedure against the collaborators, even if it was a form a justice for the victims, could be analyzed as a legal pretext for the Chadian authorities to stop cooperating with the EAC and not to execute arrest warrants.

For years, the victims had unsuccessfully tried to bring their former torturers to justice. After the publication of the report of the Chadian National Commission of Inquiry in 1992, the new Chadian authorities could have tried the collaborators. Instead, they chose to reintegrate several of them into the administrative or security state services.[26] For example, the NGO Human Rights Watch asserted that Mahamat Djibrine, cited in the Chadian National Commission of Inquiry report as one of the main torturers of Hissein Habré's regime,[27] held important positions in the Chadian police and had even been integrated into a contingent of Chadian peacekeepers sent to Côte d'Ivoire as part of UNOCI (the United Nations Operation in Côte d'Ivoire).[28] Mahamat Djibrine was dismissed from the contingent following a complaint filed by Human Rights Watch to the United Nations.[29] According to Human Rights Watch, Saleh Younouss, also prosecuted by the EAC, held a position at the Chadian Ministry of Posts and Telecommunications.[30] By indicting former DDS agents holding public service functions in Chad, the EAC might have sent the signal that any Chadian could be targeted, and given rise to fears of a domino effect that could affect other people who collaborated with the former regime, including Idriss Déby Itno, the then current head of state of Chad who worked for the Hissein Habré regime for several years.

Indeed, until his rebellion in 1989 against Hissein Habré, who allegedly attempted to assassinate him, Idriss Déby Itno was his military advisor and, before, had actively contributed to the seizure of power by Hissein Habré in 1982, had worked to consolidate the Hissein Habré regime and fought its enemies.[31] Because of this relative proximity between the regime of Hissein Habré and Idriss Déby Itno, it was possible to suspect the apprehensions of the Chadian regime of Idriss Déby Itno which, if it decided to arrest and transfer the former collaborators to the EAC would open a Pandora's box with devastating effects.

Consequently, by arresting, judging and sentencing the former collaborators of the Hissein Habré regime to heavy sentences, and above all imprisoning them, Chad gave the impression that it was insidiously cutting the grass under the feet of the EAC, which could no longer try these collaborators if they so desired, or hear them as witnesses if they so wished. Whatever the reason, Chad's lack of cooperation during 2014 had effects on the proceedings initiated by the EAC.

COMPLETION OF THE INVESTIGATION: HISSEIN HABRÉ REFERRED TO TRIAL

After the Investigative Chamber completed its work, the general prosecutor of the EAC made his final submission to the Investigative Chamber on February 6, 2015, and asked for a trial of Hissein Habré. In their order of February 13, 2015, the investigating judges decided to refer only Hissein Habré to the Extraordinary African Assize Chamber for a trial. They considered that there was sufficient evidence that Hissein Habré committed or participated in the commission of crimes against humanity, war crimes, and torture during his presidency.[32]

The five collaborators of Hissein Habré, targeted by the general prosecutor as perpetrators, were not referred to the Assize Chamber. The investigating judges were unable to gather sufficient evidence about Zakaria Berdei, one of the collaborators.[33] Although they had gathered information on the other four collaborators, they noted the lack of cooperation of Chad and non-execution of the arrest warrants issued.[34] They confirmed the impossibility of trying Saleh Younouss, Guihini Korei, Abakar Torbo Rahama, and Mahamat Djibrine.[35]

PREPARATION OF THE TRIAL IN COURT

So, the instruction phase was coming to an end. Hissein Habré was to be tried by the Extraordinary African Assize Chamber, the Trial Chamber. The chairperson of the African Commission appointed the judges of the Trial Chamber in April 2015: one Burkinabe judge, Gustave Kam who was appointed president of the Chamber, and three Senegalese judges—Amadou Diouf, Moustapha Ba (assessors judges), and Pape Ousmane Diallo (alternate judge).[36]

After their appointments, the judges examined the file and the information gathered by the investigating judges. On June 3, 2015, the president of the Extraordinary African Assize Chamber interrogated Hissein Habré, who remained silent.[37]

The judges of the Trial Chamber held a status conference, with the aim of organizing the trial, on June 29, 2015.[38] The prosecutors, registrars, and lawyers of the victims (civil parties) were present. Hissein Habré's lawyers, although invited, were absent. The defense of the former head of state later explained the reasons for the absence. To the president of the Assize Chamber, who asked them for an explanation, the defense team replied that Hissein Habré was refusing to participate in the proceedings that were in progress and in the trial which he considered "illegal, irregular and illegitimate."[39] The absence of Hissein Habré's lawyers during the status conference then began to raise questions: Would Hissein Habré be tried if he had no lawyers? While the trial was set to begin on July 20, 2015, no one really knew what would happen that day.

NOTES

1. Senegal, Loi no. 2012-25 du 28 décembre 2012 autorisant le Président de la République à ratifier l'Accord entre le Gouvernement de la République du Sénégal et l'Union africaine sur la création de Chambres africaines extraordinaires au sein des juridictions sénégalaises.

2. Information available on the website of the Extraordinary African Chambers: http://www.chambresafricaines.org/index.php/presentation-des-chambres/administration/administrateur.html and http://www.chambresafricaines.org/index.php/presentation-des-chambres/contexte-de-creation.html, accessed 5/16/2021.

3. See the website of the Extraordinary African Chambers http://www.chambresafricaines.org/index.php/presentation-des-chambres/contexte-de-creation.html, accessed 5/16/2021.

4. This was consistent with Article 31, paragraph 1(c), of the EAC Statute.

5. See http://www.chambresafricaines.org/index.php/le-coin-des-medias/communiqu%C3%A9-de-presse/567-communiqu%C3%A9-du-collectif-des-avocats-des-victimes-du-r%C3%A9gime-de-hiss%C3%A8ne-habr%C3%A9.html, accessed 5/16/2021.

6. All the investigation phase presented in the lines that follow is detailed in Réquisitoire introductif, as cited in EAC, Ordonnance de renvoi, 2015, 7–9, and EAC (Extraordinary African Assize Chamber), *Ministère public v. Hissein Habré*, Judgment, May 30, 2016, 18–26 (hereafter, *Ministère public v. Hissein Habré*, Judgment, May 30, 2016).

7. Accord de coopération judiciaire entre la République du Sénégal et la République du Tchad pour la poursuite des crimes internationaux commis au Tchad durant la période du 7 juin 1982 au 1er décembre 1990, May 3, 2013.

8. *Ministère public v. Hissein Habré*, Judgment, May 30, 2016, 18, para. 62 .

9. Ibid.

10. ECOWAS Court of Justice, *Hissein Habré v. Republic of Senegal*, no. ECW/CCJ/RUL/05/13, November 5, 2013, para. 2.

11. Ibid., para. 42.

12. Ibid., paras. 44–45.

13. See Article 74 of the Constitution of Senegal. All the elements and arguments relating to the application before the Senegalese Constitutional Council are set out in Senegal, Conseil constitutionnel, Affaire no. 1C2015, Décision du 2 mars 2015.

14. All the arguments are exposed in Senegal, Conseil constitutionnel, Affaire no. 1C2015, ibid.

15. Ibid.

16. *Ministère public v. Hissein Habré*, Judgment, May 30, 2016, 21, para. 75.

17. See EAC, Ordonnance de renvoi, 2015, 7–10, and *Ministère public v. Hissein Habré*, ibid., 18–26.

18. On the cooperation of Chad and for all the lines that will follow, see EAC, Ordonnance de renvoi, 2015, 7–9 and 184; *Ministère public v. Hissein Habré*, ibid., 19–24 and 26.

19. Accord de coopération judiciaire entre la République du Sénégal et la République du Tchad, op. cit., note 7.

20. Chad, *Lettre du ministre de la justice du Tchad levant l'immunité dont M. H. Habré pourrait se prévaloir*, October 7, 2002.

21. *Table ronde des donateurs pour le financement du procès d'Hissène Habré*, November 24, 2010, para. 15.

22. Articles 2 and 3 of the Senegal Criminal Procedure Code.

23. Chad, Cour d'appel de N'Djamena, *Ministère Public et Ismael Hachim et autres c. Saleh Younous Ali, Waroun Fadoul ali et autres*, Répertoire n°01/15, March 25, 2015.

24. Ibid.

25. Ibid.

26. Souleymane Guengueng, 2012, Souleymane Guengueng, *Prisonnier de Hissene Habré. L'expérience d'un survivant des geôles tchadiennes et sa quête de justice* (Paris: L'Harmattan, 2012), 93–94.

27. Rapport de la commission nationale d'enquête du ministère tchadien de la justice, 39.

28. Rapport Human Rights Watch, *Tchad: Les victimes de Hissène Habré toujours en attente de justice*, vol. 17, no. 10 (A), July 2005, 28.

29. Ibid.

30. Ibid., 39.

31. See, for example, Jeremy Rich, "Idriss Déby Itno," in *Dictionary of African Biography*, ed. Emmanuel Kwaku Akyeampong and Henry Louis Gates (New York: Oxford University Press, 2012), 172–173.

32. EAC, Ordonnance de renvoi, 2015, 185–187.

33. Ibid., 184.

34. Ibid.

35. Ibid.

36. AU, Directorate of Information and Communication, Press Release no. 089/2015, April 6, 2015.

37. *Ministère public v. Hissein Habré*, Judgment, May 30, 2016, 27.

38. Ibid.

39. Ibid., para. 103.

Chapter 4

The Trial in the Courtroom

A FALSE START

July 20, 2015, the official opening ceremony of the trial was scheduled to take place in Courtroom No. 4 of the Palais de Justice in Dakar. The public and the media were there.[1] The president of the Extraordinary African Assize Chamber made a preliminary statement and passed the floor successively to the general prosecutor, the lawyers for the civil parties, and the representative of the president of the Senegalese Bar. The general prosecutor made a strong speech and justified the referral of Hissein Habré to the Assize Chamber for a trial. The lawyers for the civil parties introduced themselves and recalled their role in defending victims of heinous crimes. The representative of the president of the Senegalese Bar emphasized the importance of the presumption of innocence and the impartiality of judges.

The accused, Hissein Habré, and his lawyers were absent. A few hours before the official opening ceremony of the trial, Hissein Habré was forced into the courtroom. He started gesticulating, shouting, and screaming, expressing his contempt for the EAC. His supporters joined him and created skirmishes and outbursts, forcing the police to remove him from the courtroom.

Noting the absence of the accused, the president of the Assize Chamber committed a bailiff to summon Hissein Habré to appear in the courtroom. Hissein Habré replied by sending a message denouncing the EAC:

> These Chambers, which I call myself, the Extraordinary Administrative Committee, are illegitimate and illegal. Those who sit on it are not judges but mere civil servants fulfilling a politically ordered mission. I was illegally imprisoned following an act of kidnapping and have been illegally detained ever since.

> Therefore, I have nothing, I do not have to answer to any action of this administrative committee whose existence and activities are illegitimate and illegal.[2]

Whispers rose in the courtroom after the reading of Hissein Habré's message which challenged the Trial Chamber. Its president ordered that the next day, July 21, 2015, Hissein Habré was to be brought by force.

The next day, Hissein Habré was brought in without major incident.[3] Surrounded by two armed guards, he sat draped in a large white boubou, turbaned and wore clear glasses. Sitting with his back to the public and facing the stage reserved for the judges and the prosecutors, he looked nervous, stared left and right, raised his head, lowered it, and touched his fingers. He was not accompanied by his lawyers, who so far had officially defended him.

The judges of the Extraordinary African Assize Chamber entered the courtroom and sat. The president of the Assize Chamber addressed Hissein Habré, asking him to stand before the Chamber. A few long seconds went by. Hissein Habré did not react. Resuming the floor, the president of the Trial Chamber inquired whether the accused's lawyers were present. Nobody replied. The president of the Assize Chamber took note of the silence of the accused and the absence of his lawyers. From that moment on, questions hovered over the continuation of the trial.

If the right to silence or to be silent during a trial was guaranteed in criminal law, whether at a national or international level, was the refusal to be assisted by a lawyer an extension of this right? Could Hissein Habré be tried without lawyers? Could public defenders be appointed? Was it possible, according to law, to defend someone who refused to be defended and was mute? The observation of several international trials showed that when accused persons refused to participate in the proceedings, public defenders or at least a standby counsel were appointed to assist and represent them. This was notably the case during the trial of Jean-Bosco Barayagwiza before the ICTR in 2000 and the Akhbar Be/Rut S. A. L. Ibrahim Mohamed Ali Al Amin trial before the STL in 2014.[4] In these cases, far from the usual situations in which lawyers are appointed ex officio because of the indigence of the accused, the appointment of counsel ex officio was mainly motivated by the interests and administration of justice. For its part, Article 21(4)(d) of the EAC Statute provided that public defenders may be appointed to defend accused persons "whenever the interests of justice so required." Senegal's Code of Criminal Procedure, applicable to EAC proceedings, provided for the mandatory presence of a lawyer in criminal proceedings and the possibility for judges to appoint one ex officio.[5]

After a quick recess, the Extraordinary African Assize Chamber made the decision, which was based on the Senegal's Code of Criminal Procedure, to commit three ex officio lawyers to Hissein Habré. Mounir Ballal, Mbaye

Sene, and Abdoul Gning, all lawyers in Senegal, were appointed. Then, the trial was adjourned for 45 days while the new defense lawyers reviewed the file in order to defend the former head of state.

The judges of the Assize Chamber left the courtroom. Hissein Habré rose from his seat and made the "V for Victory" toward his supporters present in the courtroom. His supporters clapped loudly. Forty-five days later, on September 7, 2015, Hissein Habré returned, carried in by prison guards into an overheated courtroom and a chaotic atmosphere.

THE TRIAL BEGINS

The trial of Hissein Habré really only began on September 7, 2015, in Courtroom No. 4 of the Palais de Justice in Dakar.[6] Indeed, the tumultuous din and uproar that marked the accused's entry into the courtroom gradually faded and was replaced by a peaceful serenity. The president of the Extraordinary African Assize Chamber asked the registrars to read the "ordonnance de renvoi," the document that accused Hissein Habré of perpetrating crimes against humanity, war crimes and torture, and that referred him for trial. As the minutes went by, Hissein Habré got quiet. The ritual of the trial and the hearings was put in place. The main participants in this ritual attended by the public each had a role to play in the manifestation of the truth about the innocence or guilt of Hissein Habré. On the one hand, judges, prosecutors, and lawyers asked questions. On the other, witnesses, experts, and victims made preliminary presentations before answering these questions.

Judges, Prosecutors, and Lawyers

There were three judges, plus one alternate. The president of the Assize Chamber was the senior judge. He was the master of ceremonies for the trial. He conducted the debates and gave or withdrew the floor accordingly to all those participating in the trial. He called for calm in the event of disturbances and redirected those involved in the trial when it was deemed necessary. And he announced the decisions taken by all the judges.

There were four prosecutors, one general prosecutor and three deputy prosecutors. They represented the public prosecutor's office. The general prosecutor was the head of that office. In principle, during the trial, it was up to him to speak when the public prosecutor was invited to do so. He could decide to turn the floor over to one of the three deputy prosecutors if he wished to do so.

The lawyers for the civil parties appeared to be a specific feature of the EAC. The civil parties were the victims who participated in the criminal proceedings, just as the prosecution and the defense. Their presence was one of the vivid illustrations of the influence of the continental inquisitorial system on EAC proceedings. In the Anglo-Saxon adversary system, it is not possible for victims to be civil parties in criminal proceedings. In several states applying the continental inquisitorial procedure, such as France and Senegal, victims can become civil parties and participate fully in criminal proceedings. These victims are represented by lawyers called "civil parties lawyers" who defend their interests. As the EAC had opted for an inquisitorial procedure, the victims were represented by more than ten Chadian, African, and European lawyers who were organized into two distinct groups: the counsel of the civil parties under the name of Clément Abaïfouta and others, and the counsel of the civil parties under the names of Réseau des associations des droits de l'homme du Tchad (RADHT—Network of Human Rights Associations of Chad) and AVCPR.[7]

The three defense lawyers, appointed ex officio, ensured the defense of the accused while contributing to the manifestation of the truth.

Witnesses, Experts, and Victims

These were the most numerous participants in the trial. The Extraordinary African Assize Chamber heard from 96 people.[8] In this context, the public prosecutor's office was in charge of the timetable and decided on their order of appearance, in principle in consultation with the other parties to the proceedings and the administrator of the EAC.

Thus, the following were invited to testify: a historian, members or former members of NGOs, a former Belgian investigating judge who worked on the Habré case in Belgium, the former president of the Chadian Commission of Inquiry set up after the collapse of the Hissein Habré regime, numerous experts, Chadian politicians, a former agent of the repressive Hissein Habré regime, several witnesses, and many victims already heard during the investigation phase. A few people testified by videoconference from Chad. All of these actors were called upon to enlighten the Extraordinary African Assize Chamber and to contribute to the manifestation of the truth by presenting elements, facts, accounts, and testimonies within a well-defined legal framework.

Public Hearings and the Judicial Ritual of the EAC

In accordance with Article 22 of the EAC Statute, the EAC was to hold public hearings. Article 36 provided that the hearings "shall be filmed and recorded for the purpose of dissemination unless this contravenes measures necessary for the protection of witnesses and other participants."[9] The EAC also funded a consortium of NGOs to raise public awareness about the former president's trial.[10] The consortium, inter alia, created a website on which numerous legal documents related to the trial have been published.[11] It also created a YouTube playlist on which almost all of the hearings before the Assize Chamber can be found.[12] The trial hearings were broadcast in a slightly delayed version by Radio Télévision Sénégalaise (RTS). They were also broadcast in Chad, Senegal, and on the EAC website.[13]

During the trial, the hearings of experts, witnesses, and victims followed a simple judicial routine. When they were called to testify, witnesses, experts, and victims, sometimes assisted by Arabic or English translators when they did not speak French, presented their account—the conclusions of their expertise for the experts, and the events that they experienced or witnessed for the witnesses and victims. When they were finished, the president of the Assize Chamber and the other judges had the option of asking them questions. The prosecutors, the lawyers for the civil parties, and the defense lawyers asked questions. Usually judges asked questions on points they wanted to clarify. Prosecutors and lawyers of civil parties directed their questions toward points that were intended to demonstrate the guilt of the accused. Defense lawyers directed their questions toward elements that were intended to exonerate the accused. They also attempted to cast doubt on the credibility of those who testified against the accused. As for Hissein Habré, the accused, although he assiduously attended the hearings of the trial, remained silent.

The Silent Accused

With his head and face partially buried in a turban despite a ruling of the Extraordinary African Indictment Chamber that had banned the wearing of turbans, a decision that the Extraordinary African Assize Chamber refused to execute in order to "maintain the serenity of the debates and in the interest of justice,"[14] Hissein Habré was silent after the loudly shouted words at the beginning of the hearing on September 7, 2015. It was noted, as the hearings unfolded, that he crossed his legs, taped his feet lightly, rested his elbows on the armrests of his comfortable seat, interlaced his fingers, closed his eyes behind his sunglasses, bent his head slightly and rested it on the folded fingers of his right hand.[15] Nervous ticks? Reflection? Asleep? Tired? Willing to show that he was in no way concerned about what was going on? For those in the court, it was difficult to reach a definitive conclusion on their meaning. As for his silence, did it reveal anything?

On the opening day of the trial, the general prosecutor of the EAC stated in a serious and severe manner that the silence of the accused was not to be considered as a defense strategy, but could be considered an admission of the alleged crimes.[16]

Charged with investigating Hissein Habré's personality by the EAC, the experts produced a report without having been able to meet with him or his close family. They pointed out to the Assize Chamber, based on statements they had collected, that Hissein Habré was said to be, among other things, calm, courteous, kind, implacable with his enemies, proud, Muslim, and a stakes man.[17] Was it possible, for example, to find an explanation of silence in the pride, calm, or piety described by these experts? One could consider that Hissein Habré refused to lower himself to the level of this "illegal" court which tried him, a former head of state. Or one could say that, faced with a situation that he deplored, he decided, calmly and piously, to give free rein to his fate as an innocent martyr sacrificed on the altar of human injustice. In any case, here, the silence of the accused could give rise to various interpretations.

Whatever the reason, Hissein Habré's silence contrasted sharply with the behavior often displayed by former heads of state accused of international crimes and brought to justice. They did not hesitate to use trials as a forum to denounce the criminal proceedings against them, while calling the whole world to witness the injustice they were enduring.

Like Hissein Habré, the former Yugoslav president Slobodan Milošević had at the beginning of his trial proclaimed the illegality of the ICTY which was to try him, calling it a tribunal set up to justify the war crimes committed by North Atlantic Treaty Organization (NATO) in the former Yugoslavia.[18] However, he then actively participated in the hearings. Unassisted by counsel during the hearings and defending himself during part of his trial, Slobodan Milošević conducted cross-examinations of those who testified against him, sometimes pushing them to the limit and destabilizing them.[19]

Charles Taylor, the former president of Liberia, assiduously took notes during his trial at the SCSL, making it clear that he intended to deconstruct all the prosecution arguments. He answered the questions put to him and denied the commission of the crimes of which he was accused.[20]

Saddam Hussein, brought before the Iraqi Special Tribunal, described the tribunal as illegitimate. During his trial, he never ceased to address the judges individually, to proclaim his innocence, to denounce his trial, the relentlessness and insults of the Americans who, according to him, wanted to execute him.[21]

Polite in his first address to the ICC, Laurent Gbagbo, the former president of Côte d'Ivoire, calmly denounced the conditions of his overthrow, arrest, and transfer to The Hague and castigated in particular the role played by the French army.[22] During his trial, he defended himself with determination until he and his lawyers succeeded in obtaining an acquittal.[23]

Hissein Habré's attitude was therefore the antithesis of the usual combativeness of former heads of state. But his attitude did not stop his trial.

The appearance of witnesses, experts, and victims on the trial scene opened the door to the search for the truth about the crimes of which he was accused and the examination of his criminal responsibility. In this context, an examination of the historical context appeared to be the essential prerequisite for understanding what happened in Chad under the presidency of Hissein Habré.

NOTES

1. All the information regarding the opening ceremony can be found in the online, EAC, *Cérémonie d'ouverture officielle du procès de Hisséne Habré*, July 21, 2015: https://www.youtube.com/watch?v=D_Ys8grgcpI, accessed 5/16/2021; see also, Le Monde, "Procès Hissène Habré : atmosphère tendue au tribunal de Dakar," video, July 20, 2015: https://www.dailymotion.com/video/x2yoa9t, accessed 5/16/2021. Most of the recordings and videos of the trial hearings were published online by the *Forum interactif sur les CAE.* See the YouTube playlist: https://www.youtube.com/channel/UCgING8GqD65mKzs8NALpd2g/playlists, accessed 5/16/2021 (hereafter, Online Playlist of the *Forum interactif sur les CAE*).

2. Transcripts, EAC, July 20, 2015, quoted in *Ministère public v. Hissein Habré*, Judgment, May 30, 2016, 9, note 59. This excerpt, like the other excerpts from the EAC documents, is in French and has been translated into English.

3. EAC, Transcripts, July 21, 2015; EAC, July 21, 2015: https://www.dakaractu.com/VIDEO-Le-proces-de-l-ancien-president-Tchadien-Hissene-Habre-du-Mardi-21-Juillet-2015_a93801.html, accessed 30/09/2018; CAE, Cérémonie d'ouverture du Procès Hissein Habré, 20 et 21 juillet 2015, Online Playlist of the *Forum interactif sur les CAE.*

4. ICTR, *Le Procureur c. Jean-Bosco Barayagwiza*, Décision sur la requête des conseils de la défense en retrait de leur commission d'office, no. ICTR-97-19-T, November 2, 2000; STL, *Akhbar Be/Rut S.A.L. Ibrahim Mohamed Ali Al Amin*, no. Stl-14-06/Pt/Cj, Motifs de la décision Relative à la commission d'office d'un Conseil, June 5, 2014.

5. Article 273 of the Senegalese Procedural Code.

6. See CAE, 07-09-2015, in Online Playlist of the *Forum interactif sur les CAE*; Transcripts, CAE/07-09-2015/Habré/Procès/T3.

7. For the long list of these lawyers, see the first pages of Ordonnance de renvoi, 2015, and of *Ministère public v. Hissein Habré*, Judgment, May 30, 2016.

8. *Ministère public v. Hissein Habré*, Judgment, May 30, 2016, 29, para. 116.

9. Translation from French.

10. Premium Africa Consulting, RCN Justice & Democracy, Cabinet Magi Communications, *Fiche Programme-CAE Sensibilisation de la population aux activités menées par les Chambres Africaines Extraordinaire*, https://rcn-ong.be/wp-content/uploads/2020/01/Fiche-projet-CAE.pdf, accessed 5/16/2021.

11. http://www.forumchambresafricaines.org/, accessed 30/09/2018.

12. Playlist of the *Forum interactif sur les CAE*, https://www.youtube.com/channel/UCgING8GqD65mKzs8NALpd2g/playlists, accessed 5/16/2021.

13. www.chambresafricaines.org, accessed 5/16/2021.

14. *Ministère public v. Hissein Habré, Judgment*, May 30, 2016, paras. 77 and 109.

15. See, for example, Online Playlist of the *Forum interactif sur les CAE*: Vidéo 08/09/2015 - Procès Hissein Habré / Part 1, 55:59 and 1:03:40; Vidéo_Après Midi 07/09/2015 - Procès Hissein Habré / Part 2, 3:45, 56:39; Vidéo du 08/09/2015 - Procès Hissein Habré / Part 2, 18:07; EAC, Hearing of Arnaud Dingammadji, 09/09/2015, Part 1, 39:49.

16. EAC, Cérémonie d'ouverture officielle du procès de Hissène Habré, July 20, 2015, Online Playlist of the *Forum interactif sur les CAE*; EAC, Transcripts, July 20, 2015.

17. EAC, Hearing of Yakhara Diop Gassama, September 10, 2015, Online Playlist of the *Forum interactif sur les CAE*. EAC, Transcripts, September 10, 2015.

18. ICTY, *Prosecutor v. Slobqdan Milosevic*, Transcripts, July 3, 2001.

19. For more, see the account of the former ICTY chief prosecutor Carla Del Ponte, "Difficulties for the Participants Indictment Correct, Trial Impossible," in *The Milosevic Trial: An Autopsy*, ed. Timothy William Waters (New York: Oxford University Press, 2013) 147.

20. See, for example, SCSL, *The Prosecutor of the Special Court v. Charles Ghankay Taylor*, Case no. SCSL-2003-01-T, Transcripts, July 14, 2009.

21. For an account of the trial, see for example the book written by the coordinator of the defense team of Saddam Hussein, Abdul-Haq Al-Ani, *The Trial of Saddam Hussein* (Atlanta: Clarity Press, 2008), 214–215.

22. ICC, *The Prosecutor v. Laurent Koudou Gbagbo*, no. ICC-02/11-01/11, Transcripts, December 5, 2011.

23. ICC (Appeals Chamber). *The Prosecutor v. Laurent Gbagbo and Charles Blé Goudé*. Judgment in the appeal of the Prosecutor against Trial Chamber I's decision on the no case to answer motions, no. ICC-02/11-01/15-1400, March 31, 2021; ICC, *Trial Chamber I decides to release Laurent Gbagbo and Charles Blé Goudé following acquittal*, no. ICC-CPI-20190116-PR1428, Press Release, January 16, 2019; ICC, *The Prosecutor v. Laurent Gbagbo and Charles Blé Goudé*, Reasons for oral decision of January 15, 2019, on the Requête de la Défense de Laurent Gbagbo afin qu'un jugement d'acquittement portant sur toutes les charges soit prononcé en faveur de Laurent Gbagbo et que sa mise en liberté immédiate soit ordonnée, no. ICC-02/11-01/15-1263, July 16, 2019.

Chapter 5

The Context of the Commission of the Crimes

The History of Chad in the Trial

International crimes such as crimes against humanity, genocide, and war crimes are usually committed in specific contexts. Thus, international criminal trials are often an opportunity to revisit a part of the history of the state in which these crimes took place. Consideration of the history of the state makes it possible to clarify the chronological sequence of events and to grasp the political, social, and even cultural and economic dynamics that presided over the crimes and atrocities. Even if some scholars such as Hannah Arendt, in her book *Eichmann in Jerusalem*, rightly considered that the purpose of a criminal trial was not to make history but to judge guilt or innocence,[1] the analysis of history has become a standard feature of international criminal trials. It has emerged in the course of the development of international criminal law as a necessary element in understanding the context of the criminal mechanics of atrocities. For example, after the Second World War, the Nuremberg Trials were an opportunity to dissect the history of Nazism and the Nazi National Party.[2] During the 1990s, the ICTY focused on the history of the former Yugoslavia in the *Tadiç* case and the ICTR on the history of Rwanda in the *Akayesu* case.[3] Since the 2000s, the ICC acted similarly in the *Lubanga* case for the history of parts of the Democratic Republic of the Congo territory,[4] the SCSL in the *Charles Taylor* case for the history of Sierra Leone,[5] and the ECCC in the case of *Kaing Guek Eav* alias *Duch* for the history of Cambodia.[6] In order to enlighten judges, historians are often invited to produce a report on the historical context and to testify as expert witnesses. The presentation of the history of the state is often focused on the period during which the crimes were committed and, if it goes back further, it is usually to establish causal links between historical events and the abuses committed during the period under consideration by the court.

The trial of Hissein Habré did not depart from this practice. During the trial, the hearings did not emphasize the fact that Chad had been a colony of France which had artificially built this state on a territory of more than 1 million square kilometers that was occupied by varied and culturally diverse populations and ethnic groups.[7] The details about the disparities in levels of development—particularly between the south of Chad, developed by the former colonial power, and the less developed north—were not deeply discussed. The trial of Hissein Habré did not focus on the many animist populations that made up Chad; or on the 1960 movement that saw several former French colonies, including Chad, gain independence; or on the unrest that has beset this now independent state, which experienced neither lasting peace nor stability and endured numerous coups d'état and several leaders before Hissein Habré came to power in 1982. During the trial, it was the history of Chad in relation to the regime of Hissein Habré during the period 1982 to 1990 that was presented in detail.

The Chadian historian Arnaud Dingammadji complied with this task. This expert was the author of two voluminous monographs on Chad.[8] The EAC commissioned him to write a report on the historical context of the crimes perpetrated under the Hissein Habré regime. He was called to testify about the report that he wrote and submitted to the tribunal.

Arnaud Dingammadji presented himself before the EAC judges with a serene air.[9] Behaving like he was justifying his presence at the trial, he began his presentation with developments on the importance of historians in trials for international crimes, recalling for example the role they played for the ICTY, the ICTR, and the "Khmer Rouge" trial in Cambodia. He warned the judges that he was born in 1976, that he was only six years old when Hissein Habré took power in 1982, and only 14 when he was ousted in 1990. He presented his curriculum vitae in great detail, talked about the books and articles he had published and the universities he had attended. He explained that he was trying to demonstrate that his scientific qualities were the only reasons for his appointment as an expert historian by the EAC. This surreal scene of an expert presenting himself in great detail and justifying his presence before a court of law was astonishing. Even more astonishing was the lack of reaction from the judges of the Extraordinary African Assize Chamber, who did not interrupt the historian during his monologue. The explanation for this situation could be sought outside the courtroom.

A few weeks earlier, announced as an expert witness to the EAC, historian Arnaud Dingammadji was violently attacked. His objectivity and competence were questioned. He was designated as an opponent of Hissein Habré's regime.[10] According to the general prosecutor, Hissein Habré declared that Arnaud Dingammadji was not neutral that he had always militated against his regime and lacked impartiality.[11] This is certainly why he mentioned his age and presented his CV, as if to silence these critics. His precautions were not enough. After his hearing before the Assize Chamber, he was taken to task again on the Internet by the defenders of Hissein Habré.[12] He was blamed for his young age because he did not experience the facts he presented. The veracity of some of the information provided during the hearing was challenged and bias was alleged. It was noted that he was living in Chad's Christian south and was accused of being the visible face of a cabal against Hissein Habré.

But Arnaud Dingammadji did not yet know that he would be torn to pieces despite his presentation, which sought to set the historical context of the crimes committed in Chad under the regime of Hissein Habré. He introduced Hissein Habré and related the events leading up to his seizure of power. He then summarized the voluminous report he had presented to the tribunal, dealing in particular with the different phases of the Chadian armed conflicts after Hissein Habré took power and with the repression of certain communities by his regime.

THE CHADIAN ARMED CONFLICTS UNDER HISSEIN HABRÉ

The North

Hissein Habré faced two main armed conflicts in northern Chad after he took power. Arnaud Dingammadji presented the two main armed conflicts in northern Chad. On the one hand, there was the armed conflict that opposed Hissein Habré's troops to the Government of National Unity of Chad (GUNT—Gouvernement d'Union nationale du Tchad) of Goukouni Weddeye, his former ally. On the other hand, there was the armed conflict that saw Chad confront Libya then led by Muammar Gaddafi. He explained the troubled role of Libya, which supported opponents of Hissein Habré's regime and then engaged in direct armed conflict against Chad. Hissein Habré's troops scored dazzling victories against GUNT in 1982–1983 and then against Libya in the late 1980s. Later, victims and former prisoners of war (POWs) told their stories to the Assize Chamber and shed light on the course of the Chadian wars described by the historian.

Concerning the war against the GUNT, a former prisoner of war named Bichara Djibrine Ahmat gave an enlightening account of the victory of Hissein Habré's troops at Faya-Largeau, a city in northern Chad, and its aftermath.[13] At the time of his testimony before the Assize Chamber, Bichara Djibrine Ahmat was an elderly man who asked to sit down because of the pain he felt in his feet. The president of the Assize Chamber gave him permission to do so. Bichara Djibrine Ahmat said he fought for the GUNT against the armed forces led by Hissein Habré in 1980. Victorious, the GUNT had taken power and installed Goukouni Weddeye at the head of the Chadian state. But in 1982, Hissein Habré returned with his troops, drove out the GUNT, and took the reins of the Chadian state. Bichara Djibrine Ahmat fled to Libya with other GUNT soldiers. He returned with them to Chad in an attempt to regain power. But in a violent battle at Faya-Largeau, GUNT was defeated by Hissein Habré's troops. He was taken prisoner along with other GUNT soldiers at the airport where they were stationed. Hissein Habré's soldiers asked the GUNT soldiers to take off their shoes and belts, and left them under surveillance as they waited outside in the sun. Bichara Djibrine Ahmat said that he saw Hissein Habré at Faya-Largeau. Hissein Habré had rejoiced in his victory in front of the captured soldiers.

Bichara Djibrine Ahmat and other POWs were taken to a jail where they were kept before being transferred to N'Djamena. During the transfer to the Chadian capital, they were beaten by the Zairian soldiers to which Hissein Habré's troops had handed them over for a short time.[14] During the long transfer to N'Djamena, they were given neither food nor drink. When they arrived in N'Djamena, they were presented to the population, who were invited to come and see captured "Libyan mercenaries." People were shouting hostile comments. The POWs were then crammed into cells in a detention center, again without food or water. The press was then invited to film the POWs who, for the occasion, had been taken out of their cells.

The subsequent fate of the POWs was fatal. The regime of Hissein Habré executed several of them. Bichara Djibrine Ahmat reported that one day, about 150 POWs, including himself, were taken from the prison cells and chained in groups of two or three. They had been selected by a person named Issa, head of the prison, presumably an agent of the DDS, the Chadian political police. Bichara Djibrine Ahmat was unaware of the criteria for selecting individuals. The POWs were loaded into a truck, and soldiers also got in. Other vehicles were escorting that truck. The trucks started up and they began to move. Later, the vehicles stopped and the POWs were told to get off the truck. The regime's soldiers surrounded the prisoners, pointed their weapons at them, and fired long shots.

Bichara Djibrine Ahmat lay down quickly during the execution, had a finger of his hand broken, and was slightly grazed by bullets on his forearm and thighs. Other POWs fell on him and their bodies formed a protective shield. The soldiers stopped firing at one point, got back in the truck, and drove off. The other POWs had died, but Bichara Djibrine Ahmat had survived. Slowly he emerged from the inert, bullet-riddled bodies. He managed to remove his chains—using techniques he had learned in his commando training, he would later say—and at first crawled and then began to walk away. He walked for a long time and, after a long journey that took him to Cameroon where he received health care, he went to Libya where he was again treated and recovered his health. The defense team of Hissein Habré asked questions about the circumstances of his escape after he survived the execution, noting that Bichara Djibrine Ahmat had claimed to have recited a verse from the Quran to stop one of his wounds from hemorrhaging. With a touch of poorly concealed irony, a defense lawyer wanted to know if this technique had also been taught to him as part of his commando training. The former POW replied that this was a technique that every Muslim knew, causing the defense lawyer to give the witness a look of incredulousness. However, he remained constant on the fact that 150 POWs had been executed by Hissein Habré's soldiers. When asked by a judge about the fate of the other arrested POWs, Bichara Djibrine Ahmat replied that he did not know what had become of them. He noted that they had not been seen since their arrest, implicitly suggesting that they must have died.

This victory of Hissein Habré's troops in Faya-Largeau over the Libyan-backed GUNT, witnessed by Bichara Djibrine Ahmat, marked the beginning of Hissein Habré's control and command of all Chadian territory. The Libyans had been occupying part of northern Chad, but Hissein Habré waged war on them and succeeded in driving them out of the territory. The Chadian historian explained that it was with the support of foreign states, notably France, the United States, and Zaire, that Hissein Habré's regime had succeeded in ridding itself of its enemies and gradually regained total control of northern Chad. This aid from two Western states in the 1980s hinted at the influence of the Cold War context on the armed conflict in Chad.

Called to testify, Facho Balaam, a former opponent of Hissein Habré and a member of the GUNT, evoked that context.[15] Acknowledging that the GUNT received military support from Libya, Facho Balaam stated that the context of the Cold War had favored the political division of Chad. A distinction was made between the communists, to whom he was supposed to belong, and the capitalists led by Hissein Habré who were receiving help from the West.

The South

In addition to the armed conflicts against GUNT and Muammar Gaddafi's Libya between 1982 and 1987, Hissein Habré's regime faced armed rebellions in southern Chad, according to the Chadian historian Arnaud Dingammadji. The historian presented the tumultuous relations that existed between the armed forces of President Hissein Habré and several rebel armed groups from the south, organized under the name of Codos, that opposed him from 1983 onward. He recalled that these rebels opposed to the government of Hissein Habré had been the object of fierce repression. As tacticians, Hissein Habré and his regime had in the end brilliantly and cynically used negotiations to successfully rally rebels who were already extremely weakened by the fierce repression being conducted against them. Giving weight to the report of Arnaud Dingammadji and his testimony, several victims later told the Assize Chamber that people, rightly or wrongly suspected of being members, supporters, or sympathizers of the Codos rebellion, had been subjected to repression and massacres by Habré's forces.

A Chadian state official named Mallah Ngabouli claimed that in 1984 while he was working as a "poor civil servant," he was arrested by agents of Habré's regime who accused him of financially aiding the rebels.[16] He denied these facts. The agents beat him viciously and broke his teeth and jaw. Imprisoned in a jail in Sarh, a town in southern Chad, he was then transferred to a jail in N'Djamena. Several of his colleagues had disappeared during the crackdown. He only regained his freedom in 1987 as part of the reconciliation process initiated with the rebels by Habré's regime. After his release, he was received by Hissein Habré himself—he still "did not know why," he noted—who asked him to return home without holding any rancor.

Djokota Prosper Kladoumngué, a Chadian teacher, recounted that in 1984 the security forces of Habré's regime arrived in Koumra in southern Chad and executed several inhabitants suspected of being Codos.[17] His uncle was killed and he attended his funeral. The regime's soldiers killed people and left their bodies in plain sight. The inhabitants were afraid of reprisals and refrained from burying the dead.

Mbaïssouroum Manda René stated that in 1985 soldiers came to his village, rounded up the villagers, and questioned them about their activities.[18] The people living there were farmers but the military suspected them of being Codos rebels. The military selected 17 people, including Mbaïssouroum Manda René, and fired on them. He was wounded and came out of it miraculously alive. Thirteen of the 17 people had died.

Djimingaye Halta recounted how in the southern Chadian town of Ngalo, Chadian soldiers arrived and arrested the men living in the village.[19] He had taken refuge in a well that was not deep. Several men from the village were executed. The soldiers were looking for Codos rebels, but the inhabitants of the village were not Codos rebels. Djimingaye Halta pointed out that two soldiers accused of being responsible for the massacres were publicly executed on the orders of Hissein Habré. According to an official of the regime, the former president insisted he was innocent and did not send them to commit the massacres.

Thus, throughout his time in power, Hissein Habré and his regime were confronted with clashes or armed conflicts in both northern and southern Chad. These events were the occasion for the perpetration of crimes. However, from a historical perspective, acts of repression were not limited to clashes and armed conflicts.

INTERNAL REPRESSION FROM A HISTORICAL PERSPECTIVE

Indeed, according to the Chadian historian Arnaud Dingammadji, the repression exercised by Habré's regime was also directed against members of populations or ethnic groups suspected of being opposed to the regime.

Habré's regime attacked several Chadian Arabs. In the context of the war against Libya, Arabs were often suspected of collusion with that state. Later, the story of Hawa Brahim was significant in revealing the trouble experienced by some Chadians in that context.[20] Hawa Brahim told the Assize Chamber that she was arrested in 1985 by DDS agents who were looking for her Libyan mother, Hadje Mabrouka. The DDS agents took her away and detained her as "bail" because they did not find her mother. She was taken hostage to pressure her mother into surrendering to the DDS. Her mother finally came forward and was arrested too. The DDS agents did not release Hawa Brahim despite the surrender of her mother, who was tortured during detention. Hawa Brahim indicated that she did not know why they had been arrested and detained. The general prosecutor informed her that, according to the DDS archives, they were suspected of collusion with Libya, the state against which Chad was fighting.

According to the historian, Habré's regime had also attacked members of certain ethnic groups which had allied with President Hissein Habré's ethnic group, the Goranes, and had brought him to power and supported his regime.

The first ethnic group concerned was the Hajaraï, the population of south-central Chad, inhabitants of the mountains known as the "highland people."[21] In 1984, the death of an elite member of this ethnic group, Idriss Miskine, foreign affairs minister of the Habré regime, was said to have been the starting point of a process that would lead to repression. This high dignitary of the Republic of Chad was said to have died of neuro-malaria. However, there was a widespread rumor that he had been murdered (poisoned) on the orders of Hissein Habré. Some scholars have written that a malaise was said to have set in between Hissein Habré and Idriss Miskine because the latter had support in France and was likely to overshadow the president of Chad.[22] Hissein Habré, suspicious and anxious to eliminate any threat against his power, was suspected to have ordered his elimination.

The Chadian doctor who wrote Idriss Miskine's death certificate testified at the African Extraordinary Assize Chamber and shed edifying light on the causes of his death.[23] Dr. Nahor Ngawara confessed that he incorrectly concluded that the former foreign minister died of malaria. It was obvious to him that Idriss Miskine had been poisoned. But, at the time, he could not reveal the cause of death without risking his life. According to the doctor, some Chadian political authorities wanted the former minister dead. While Idriss

Miskine was in agony, the request for hospitalization and medical evacuation that he had made as a doctor were ignored. Asked by a defense lawyer about the Hippocratic Oath which he had clearly violated as a doctor by lying about the causes of death, Dr. Nahor Ngawara replied that he had to protect his life. However, the doctor was unable during his testimony to provide any evidence explicitly linking Hissein Habré to the murky circumstances of Idriss Miskine's death, leaving open questions about the individual responsibility of the former Chadian head of state for the death of the Hajaraï leader.

In any case, whatever the cause of this death, a persistent rumor had circulated about the responsibility of Hissein Habré and the disenchantment between the regime and many Hajaraï was born. Several members of the Hajaraï ethnic group had also engaged in armed opposition by creating a movement, the Movement for the National Salvation of Chad (MOSANAT). Habré's regime responded brutally by repressing members of the Hajaraï community, first targeting some of its elites by imprisoning them in secret detention centers and murdering them, then targeting other members of this ethnic group suspected of collusion against the Chadian authorities by arresting, detaining, humiliating, or torturing them, dispossessing them of their property or executing them. Later, giving consistency to the historical reference points presented by the historian Arnaud Dingamadji, Hajaraï victims came in front of the judges of the Assize Chamber, recounting their experiences and linking them to their belonging to the Hajaraï ethnic group and to the suspicion of their opposition to the Habré regime.

For example, Mariam Hassan Bagueri reported how one night in 1987, Chadian soldiers arrested her husband, Hissein Seid Nanga known as "Michelin," a prosperous Hajaraï businessman who traded between Cameroon and Chad.[24] She was pregnant at the time of the arrest. The reasons for the arrest remained unclear to her. She still thought he had been arrested because he was part of the Hajaraï elite, many of whom had rebelled against the Habré regime. She had not seen her husband since that night in 1987. After the arrest, the soldiers of the regime returned to her home, settling in the courtyard of her house, arresting and interrogating all those who visited them. The military seized her husband's property. But she managed to hide some of it. She and her family were evicted from the family home, which was then occupied by people she did not know. Her husband was not a politician, she said after a question from a prosecutor who revealed links between him and the former Chadian head of state. Her husband was a friend of Hissein Habré and used to deliver vehicles to his regime. In fact, the vehicles used by the soldiers present at her house were part of it. She also revealed that there was a persistent rumor about her husband's disappearance. Hissein Habré was said to have murdered her husband himself. The former head of state had allegedly slit her husband's throat. The general prosecutor asked her if a friend would be likely to slit a friend's throat. "Only God knows," she replied thoughtfully.

Zenaba Bassou Ngolo, widow of Saleh Ngaba, a former Chadian radio journalist and correspondent for Radio France Internationale (RFI), Agence France Presse, and the US news agency, also talked about her husband's disappearance during the Habré regime.[25] Her husband was arrested by agents of the regime. She learned about the arrest on Chadian radio, then on RFI. She was a student, pregnant at the time, and she had not heard from her husband since. She had had to drop out of school and convert to a small retail business to survive. She wanted Hissein Habré to tell her where her husband was and what had become of him.

When asked by a judge why she thought Hissein Habré had ordered her husband's arrest, she replied that she was certain that he was the one who ordered it. After questions from the prosecutors, she explained that her husband often criticized the Chadian authorities for persecuting the Hajaraï, the ethnic group to which he belonged. Her husband participated in meetings aiming to organize opposition against the regime. Sensing an imminent arrest, her husband had fled to Mongo, hundreds of kilometers from N'Djamena, to hide from the regime which was looking for him. She was told that her husband was denounced by one of his cousins, arrested, brought back to N'Djamena, taken to the Chadian presidential palace, then to the offices of a repressive body called BSIR (Brigade spéciale d'intervention rapide—Special Brigade for Rapid Intervention), before being imprisoned in the Camp des martyrs, a detention center of the regime.

After her husband's arrest, terrorized by the anti-Hajaraï atmosphere and often followed in the streets, she had not dared to ask the Chadian authorities where her husband was. A prosecutor informed her that traces of her husband's incarceration had been found in the DDS archives. According to these, he died of "chronic amoebic dysentery." Alifa Gaston, one of the nurses in charge of looking after people held in the secret detention centers of the Habré regime, referred to the case and confirmed that Saleh Ngaba had been arrested and detained.[26] He added that the Hajaraï journalist was sleeping on the floor of a bare cement cell that was two meters long and two meters wide, was weakened, and did not eat.

Fatimé Toumle, a Chadian civil servant who presented herself as an indirect victim of the repression against members of the Hajaraï ethnic group, indicated that she was married to Haroun Godi, a Hajaraï leader.[27] Her husband, a Chadian diplomat who held posts in Brussels and Bucharest before being appointed a member of the Chadian government, had played a role in bringing the Habré regime closer to one of its fierce opponents, Maldoum Abbas. He was dismissed at the end of the successful mission. In this context, her husband had learned that Hissein Habré was preparing to arrest him. He told her the seriousness of the situation and that he did not intend to be humiliated in front of his family. Thus, after 15 years of living together, he decided to leave and gave her 300,000 CFA francs. It was in 1987. She later learned on the radio that the "traitor Haroun Godi," her husband, had been executed. The agents of Habré's regime emptied the family home and expelled her and her children from it. After a question from a prosecutor, she added that some Goranes, the ethnic group to which Hissein Habré belonged, occupied her family home. The defense team of Hissein Habré questioned the possession of a weapon by Haroun Godi, who had been a police commissioner before becoming a diplomat and then a member of Hissein Habré's government. The lawyers of Hissein Habré sought to show that her husband was certainly part of the armed rebellion. However, Fatime Toumle affirmed and maintained that her husband was not part of the Hajaraï armed rebellion against Hissein Habré.

According to the historian Arnaud Dingammadji, harassed members of the Hajaraï community later joined the Zaghawa, an ethnic group from eastern Chad that is also found in western Sudan.[28] Members of the Zaghawa group were targeted by the Habré regime beginning in 1989. As in the case of the Hajaraï, it was Hissein Habré's mistrust of the Zaghawa elite that was said to have triggered the hostilities. Hissein Habré was said to have gradually become suspicious of the important place of this elite within his regime. Hassan Djamous, in particular, a Zaghawa and former chief of staff of the Chadian army and hero of the war against Libya, was reportedly praised by the media, especially the foreign media. Hissein Habré was said to have seen this as a threat to his regime because, at the same time, the rising influence of personalities of the Zaghawa ethnic group, particularly that of his successor Idriss Déby Itno, was growing. According to another version of the facts, the Zaghawa elite wanted to eliminate Hissein Habré in a coup d'état in order to seize power. Despite this variety of explanations, it was certain that in April 1989, several Zaghawa elites, including Idriss Déby Itno and Hassan Djamous, had distanced themselves from the regime and fled N'Djamena. Many Zaghawa people then became a target of the Habré regime. Some Zaghawa elites, including Hassan Djamous, had been murdered, others thrown into prison and tortured.

As an illustration of this repression reported by the Chadian historian Zakaria Fadoul Kitir, a Zaghawa professor of literature at the University of N'Djamena, later testified that he was arrested because he belonged to this ethnic group.[29] Habré's regime accused him of being part of a new government envisaged in the event of a successful coup d'état that was in preparation. The scholar insisted that he knew nothing about this putschist project. Several members of his family, who were Zaghawa like him, had been arrested or had disappeared. The story of one of his relatives, Sidikh

Fadoul Kitir, was of particular interest. Sidikh Fadoul Kitir was a member of the GUNT and a former opponent in exile. Hissein Habré had asked him to return to Chad. Through Hassan Djamous, one of the most influential men in the regime, he had promised him an important position if he returned. Sidikh Fadoul Kitir did return to Chad and was staying with Hassan Djamous. But the agents of the regime arrested him. Hassan Djamous had told Zakaria Fadoul Kitir that he had pleaded Sidikh Fadoul Kitir's case with Hissein Habré and insisted that he keep his word. Hissein Habré had replied that he should let the police do their job. Sidikh Fadoul Kitir was not released. Hassan Djamous was offended. For Zakaria Fadoul Kitir, this was one of the reasons why Hassan Djamous, the former hero of the Chadian army, had joined the rebellion against Hissein Habré, a rebellion that was fatal to him. According to the academic, after his rebellion, Hassan Djamous was reportedly wounded and arrested during the fighting against forces loyal to Hissein Habré, taken to hospital, then to the Chadian presidential palace and interrogated by Hissein Habré himself. He allegedly died after the torture he had undergone. A photo of him, lying on the ground and bare chested, had been found in the DDS archives by the Chadian National Commission of Inquiry. As for Sidikh Fadoul Kitir, he reportedly was removed from the cell in which he was imprisoned and never seen again.

This latest act of repression, unlike the previous ones, did not consolidate Habré's regime. Idriss Déby Itno managed to escape despite the regime's desire to get rid of him. Oumar Déby Itno, Idriss Déby's half-brother and a civil servant in Chad, later testified before the Assize Chamber and related how in April 1989, when he was only 11 years old, 400–500 Chadian soldiers surrounded their family home in N'Djamena before bursting in.[30] The military executed two people who were visiting them. Together with his brothers, he climbed the wall separating the family home from that of their immediate neighbors, Americans living in a house owned by Chadians. Helped and hidden by the caretaker of the neighbors' house, he took refuge there with his brothers for two days before leaving it, briefly becoming a street child and going in search of his mother, whom he later found in another locality in Chad. He and his mother headed for the bush and the mountains where they found other Zaghawas who, like them, were fleeing the repression of the Habré regime.

But Hissein Habré was not going to hold on to power for long. According to the Chadian historian Arnaud Dingammadji, the repression of the Zaghawa would be the last. Led by a Zaghawa, Idriss Déby Itno, armed troops stormed N'Djamena and defeated Hissein Habré toward the end of 1990.

The historian's account of Chad's history and Habré's regime depicted a Hissein Habré with many faces. The former head of state seemed to be a cold and ruthless man who did not hesitate to implement fierce repression against his enemies or people who were supposed to be his enemies. He was also a fine tactician, a hero of his country who had put the powerful Libyan army out of action in Chad, a strategist who cleverly played with the Cold War and the East-West confrontation, reconciling with his enemies while remaining distrustful. Facho Balaam, former opponent of Hissein Habré, later told the judges of the EAC how, after successful negotiations, he returned to Chad and held an important political position within a regime that was always on the lookout.[31]

The alleged crimes of Hissein Habré had therefore been committed in a particular historical context. It was on these aspects of Hissein Habré's politics that his court-appointed lawyers dwelt on during the historian's interrogation in order to cast doubt on the criminal responsibility of Hissein Habré. Prosecutors and lawyers for the civil parties focused on the crimes against POWs, on the repression of the Chadian population by the regime and on the individual responsibility of Hissein Habré.

However, the historian's testimony did not make it possible to get a clear picture of the internal functioning of the repressive machinery set up by the regime, without which the crimes allegedly committed by Hissein Habré could not have been perpetrated.

NOTES

1. Hannah Arendt, *Eichmann in Jerusalem : A Report on the Banality of Evil* (New York: Viking Press, 1964).

2. International Military Tribunal (Nuremberg), Judgment, October 1, 1946, 15–25 (Section entitled "The Nazi regime in Germany").

3. ICTY (Trial Chamber), *The Prosecutor v. Dusko Tadiç*, Case no. IT-94-1-T, Judgment, May 7, 1997, paras. 53–129; ICTR, *The Prosecutor v. Jean-Paul Akayesu*, no. ICTR-96-4-T, September 2, 1998, paras. 78–111.

4. ICC (Trial Chamber I), *The Prosecutor v. Thomas Lubanga Dyilo*, no. ICC-01/04-01/06, Judgment pursuant to Article 74 of the Statute, March 14, 2012, paras. 67–90.

5. SCSL (Trial Chamber), *The Prosecutor v. Charles Ghankay Taylor*, no. SCSL-03-01-T, Judgment, May 18, 2012, paras. 18–70.

6. ECCC, *Kaing Guek Eav alias Duch*, Case File/Dossier no. 001/18-07-2007/ECCC/TC, Judgment, July 26, 2010, paras. 59–81.

7. On Chad History, see, for example, Mario J. Azevedo and Samuel Decalo, *Historical Dictionary of Chad* (Lanham: Rowman and Littlefield, 2018).

8. Arnaud Dingammadji, *Ngalta Tombalbaye: parcours et rôle dans la vie politique du Tchad, 1959-1975* (Paris: L'Harmattan, 2007); *Les gouvernements du Tchad: de Gabriel Lisette à Idriss Déby Itno, 1957-2010* (Paris: L'Harmattan, 2011).

9. EAC, Hearing of Arnaud Dingammadji, September 9, 2015, Online Playlist of the *Forum interactif sur les CAE*. EAC, Transcripts, September 9, 2015.

10. See the document published by the supporters of Hissein Habré: La cellule de communication avec la collaboration des Avocats, *Le Sénégal « juge » le Président Hissein Habré* (June 2015), 58–59.

11. EAC, Hearing of Arnaud Dingammadji, September 9, 2015, Online Playlist of the *Forum interactif sur les CAE*. EAC, Transcripts, September 9, 2015.

12. See, for example, François SERRES (Avocat HABRE), «Procès Habré : Chroniques d'injustice, Jour 1», September 10, 2015, online: https://www.dakaractu.com/Proces-Habre-Chroniques-d-injustice-Jour-1_a97175.html; accessed 5/16/2021; La cellule de communication du Président HH, «L'audience du mardi 9 septembre: Arnaud Dingammadji, prétendu Expert tchadien des Chambres africaines, ignore tout de son pays», publication facebook «non au procès de Hissein Habré par le Sénégal», September 15, 2015, online: https://www.facebook.com/notes/266304674726492/?__xts__[0]=68.ARDdK_M0U8YrI-rLvJm337tijCT6TrteUbdAkDjlLP2q0cPutSLXMQjph6Tx5pIn6cOvU2m6ZKkFDPOMY4VBWUVqvkryjIwAwWy7XFqM8TdSml0a-d3qNdeiSjT7pUQM2cDjNwTEM00YHmou4po0UdO7pRp_kajZsWohgENDvvLoKGHI1WG2DDijngWA2k5ypU-81p7jK-RuQXoHZajLWKX8SPYoeuT5e2wiRZ7hrXkaxIx23dAUGSGBYtOucpsmKxXM-9BVYU7mlTDylbFwCWaiIxSO79OBUwYm0NQCbpUQ8QBj_6QY0hGxeu0p_IAHFhGhA7uzN9tccxccdk53U1hg, accessed 5/16/2021.

13. EAC, Hearing of Bichara Djibrine Ahmat, December 8, 2015, Online Playlist of the *Forum interactif sur les CAE*. EAC, Transcripts, December 8, 2015.

14. Zaïre was the name of the Democratic Republic of the Congo.

15. EAC, Hearing of Facho Balaam, September 10, 2015, Online Playlist of the *Forum interactif sur les CAE*. EAC, Transcripts, September 10, 2015.

16. EAC, Hearing of Mallah Ngabouli, October 27, 2015, Online Playlist of the *Forum interactif sur les CAE*. EAC, Transcripts, October 27, 2015.

17. EAC, Hearing of Djokota Prosper Kladoumngué, October 27, 2015, ibid.

18. EAC, Hearing of Mbaïssouroum Manda René, November 12, 2015, Online Playlist of the *Forum interactif sur les CAE*. EAC, Transcripts, November 12, 2015.

19. EAC, Hearing of Djimingaye Halta, November 16, 2015, Online Playlist of the *Forum interactif sur les CAE*. EAC, Transcripts, November 16, 2015.

20. EAC, Hearing of Hawa Brahim, October 21, 2015, Online Playlist of the *Forum interactif sur les CAE*. EAC, Transcripts, October 21, 2015.

21. Harold D. Nelson et al., *Area Handbook for Chad* (Washington, DC: Foreign Areas Studies Division, American University 1972), 55.

22. See, for example, Marielle Debos, *Le métier des armes au Tchad: le gouvernement de l'entre-guerres* (Paris: Karthala, 2013), 87; Ahmad Allam-Mi, *Autour du Tchad en Guerre. Tractation politiques et diplomatiques 1975-1990* (Paris: L'Harmattan, 2014), 188–189.

23. EAC, Hearing of Nahor Ngawara, November 17, 2015, Online Playlist of the *Forum interactif sur les CAE*. EAC, Transcripts, November 17, 2015.

24. EAC, Hearing of Mariam Hassan Bagueri, September 29, 2015, Online Playlist of the *Forum interactif sur les CAE*. EAC, Transcripts, September 29, 2015.

25. EAC, Hearings of Zenaba Bassou Ngolo and Service Brahim, October 6, 2015, Online Playlist of the *Forum interactif sur les CAE.* EAC, Transcripts, October 6, 2015.

26. EAC, Hearing of Alifa Gaston, October 14, 2015, Online Playlist of the *Forum interactif sur les CAE.* EAC, Transcripts, October 14, 2015.

27. EAC, Hearing of Fatime Toumlé, October 5, 2015, Online Playlist of the *Forum interactif sur les CAE.* EAC, Transcripts, October 5, 2015.

28. K.P. Moseley, "Zaghawa," in *Ethnic Groups of Africa and the Middle East: An Encyclopedia: An Encyclopedia*, ed. John A. Shoup (Santa Barbara: ABC-CLIO, 2011), 333.

29. EAC, Hearings of Zakaria Fadoul Kitir, September 30, 2015, and October 1, 2015, Online Playlist of the *Forum interactif sur les CAE.* EAC, Transcripts, September 30, 2015 and October 1, 2015.

30. EAC, Hearing of Oumar Déby Itno, October 19, 2015, Online Playlist of the *Forum interactif sur les CAE.* EAC Transcripts, October 19, 2015.

31. EAC, Hearing of Facho Balaam, September 10, 2015, Online Playlist of the *Forum interactif sur les CAE.* EAC Transcripts, September 10, 2015.

Chapter 6

The Machinery of Crimes and the Central Role of the Directorate of Documentation and Security

It is well known that the establishment of a repressive machinery in a dictatorial regime requires the creation of monitoring systems and special bodies which, generally, cultivate the secrecy of their activities while at the same time having obscure missions and arousing fear and terror among the population.[1] These bodies are sometimes referred to as political police or secret police. The Schutzstaffel (SS) of the Nazi regime or the Staatssicherheit (STASI) of the former German Democratic Republic, to cite only these examples, are illustrations of this totalitarian system responsible for the protection and cost-cutting maintenance of a dictatorial regime. The system usually aimed to put all real or supposed threats out of action. Within this framework, state resources are mobilized by leaders and recourse to exactions and crimes against individuals appears to be a normal mode of operation. Hissein Habré's regime operated in this vein.

OVERVIEW OF THE MECHANISMS OF REPRESSION

There was indeed a police force and a judicial organization in Chad during the presidency of Hissein Habré. However, several agencies had been set up as part of a parallel police and penitentiary system.[2] At the head of this system was a body created by Hissein Habré in 1983 and called Directorate of Documentation and Security (DDS).[3] Before and during the trial, this body was regularly cited in the testimonies of victims and witnesses. It appeared to be a genuine secret police and intelligence service unofficially responsible for protecting Habré's regime and tracking down its opponents and people who were rightly or wrongly suspected of threatening it.[4]

Officially placed under the Chadian Ministry of the Interior,[5] the DDS was suspected of being in reality the repressive arm of the former Chadian president. The report of the Commission of Inquiry set up after the fall of Habré's regime had concluded that the DDS was under the control of the former president.[6] During his testimony before the Extraordinary African Assize Chamber, the former president of the Commission of Inquiry, Mahamat Hassan Abakar, insisted on the pivotal role played by Hissein Habré in controlling and using the DDS as an instrument of terror.[7] It was also in the abandoned premises of the DDS that archives uncovering the atrocities of the Habré regime were discovered by Reed Brody of Human Rights Watch, which were later analyzed and exploited to build the case against Hissein Habré.[8]

DDS was not the only frightening symbol of repression in Chad during Habré's regime. Several bodies or services, such as the intelligence services, the security services of the Chadian presidency, and even the political party of Hissein Habré (UNIR—Union nationale pour l'indépendance et la révolution) contributed to the terror.[9] Among the various testimonies that helped the judges of the Assize Chamber and the public expose the intricate network of Chad's repressive bodies was that of an inside man, a former DDS agent, whose appearance was a key moment in the trial.

THE TESTIMONY OF BANDJIM BANDOUM, FORMER DDS AGENT

Bandjim Bandoum was the former DDS agent who gave an enlightening account of the regime's repressive machinery.[10] He was a man with an imposing build, who, when he appeared before the judges, was wearing a pair of small glasses, which he removed. At the time of his testimony, he lived in France where he was a building caretaker. His hearing at the Extraordinary African Assize Chamber was eagerly awaited. The press had been echoing this for several weeks, presenting as a sensational event the forthcoming hearing of a former DDS agent at the Extraordinary African Assize Chamber.[11] As he began to introduce himself, the audience in the courtroom learned that he was a former gendarme and DDS agent, and the public prepared to plunge into the heart of Hissein Habré's parallel repressive system in Chad. But the hearing of Bandjim Bandoum undoubtedly raised questions: What role did he play as a DDS agent? Did he commit crimes when he was an agent of the DDS? Was he not at risk of incurring the wrath of the victims and the press? Why was he not among the persons accused of perpetrating crimes during the Hissein Habré regime? Did he make an agreement with the prosecutors to testify in exchange for immunity? The audience in the courtroom got answers.

Bandjim Bandoum explained to the Assize Chamber why he had decided to testify. His son had learned that he worked for the DDS and asked him if he had killed people. Surprised by his son's question, he had answered that if the opportunity ever arose, he would tell the truth to a tribunal about these events which very often still troubled his conscience. And the day of his testimony before the Assize Chamber was the day of the fulfilment of the promise to his son; a testimony by virtue of a promise that had become a moral obligation. He would have wanted his son to be in Dakar with him and hear him testify before the tribunal. But it had not been possible.

Through the testimony of the former DDS agent, the audience in Courtroom No. 4 of the Palais de Justice of Dakar discovered that within the DDS and the repressive system of Habré's regime, Bandjim Bandoum held several positions. Bandjim Bandoum worked in the BSIR. According to him, this body was the "armed arm" of the DDS, made arrests, and often abused those arrested and detained. He held a secretarial position there, typing arrest orders and drawing up lists of prisoners which he forwarded to the brigade commander. He held the position of "deputy head of documentation," a service office within the DDS. He archived the documents of the DDS, which were established and collected outside of the usual legal system, and included, for example, orders for arrest, execution, or release. He also carried out missions in southern Chad for the Habré regime, in the context of the armed rebellion put down by the N'Djamena government, and was later appointed head of the Department of Operations (Chef service d'exploitation) at the DDS.

In his testimony and when he answered questions from the prosecutors and civil parties' lawyers, Bandjim Bandoum established a link between the DDS and the accused. Hissein Habré was, according to him, the real head of the DDS, whose director he appointed. Within this repressive body, everything was recorded in minutes: shadowing reports, names of arrested persons, hearing sheets that sometimes showed the results of the "exploitation" of arrested persons who were detained in the cells, prisons or secret jails that the regime had progressively built, and so on. The director of the DDS used to go daily to the Chadian presidential palace with these minutes. Bandjim Bandoum was convinced that the hearing sheets were intended for Hissein Habré himself. The president of the Republic of Chad, Hissein Habré, consulted, read the minutes, and annotated them. He marked them in French: "seen," "to be released" or "E," which meant "execution." Asked by a civil party's lawyer to explain the meaning of "E" and "execution," Bandjim Bandoum said that a DDS agent named Issay Arawaï, a notorious DDS torturer according to the report of the Chadian National Commission of Inquiry,[12] was in charge of the executions. At night, detainees were taken out of their cells to the outskirts of N'Djamena and executed. Bandjim Bandoum insisted that the decision to release or execute people was never made by the director of the DDS, who did not in fact have that authority. Only President Hissein Habré had that power. He had complete control over the DDS's actions. Bandjim Bandoum noted that Hissein Habré often came to the DDS premises. He saw him there. However, he could not say for certain whether Hissein Habré visited the DDS detention facilities when he came.

Bandjim Bandoum recounted his daily professional life and the repression that had become a commonplace: arbitrary arrests and detentions, atrocious acts of torture, appalling detention conditions, and deaths. People were arrested, detained, tortured, and died. The system of repression was perfectly organized. Its deployment made it possible to crush any hint of opposition and preserve the life of the regime.

In a silent courtroom, Bandjim Bandoum recounted that he had even heard that there were prison cells within the presidential palace where Hissein Habré lived. They were under the control of the SIP (Service d'investigation présidentiel—Presidential Investigation Service), another repressive body of the regime. According to Bandjim Bandoum, Hissein Habré stayed and slept in the same place as those who were arrested and detained by his regime. Like those in other secret prisons, they were probably tortured.

Bandjim Bandoum described a funeral ritual reserved for those who died in the prison cells of the Habré regime. Detainees often shared cells with the bodies of the dead. Souleymane Abdoulaye Taher, a former detainee, later told the Assize Chamber that because of the heat in the cells, detainees often huddled against the fresh bodies of dead prisoners.[13] They were absorbing a little coolness from the bodies of those who had given up their souls and who would soon be taken away by the gravediggers. At nightfall, continued Bandjim Bandoum, DDS agents, assisted by selected detainees, loaded the bodies of the dead detainees into a car, took them to a vacant lot on the edge of N'Djamena where, after summarily digging the ground, they buried them.

Faced with his testimony, a civil party lawyer questioned Bandjim Bandoum about his participation in arrests and torture. Bandjim Bandoum responded, forcefully denying any physical involvement in the perpetration of atrocities. No, no, he said, he had never arrested, tortured, or killed anyone. Yet a few years earlier, in a documentary film, a victim named Ginette Ngarbaye, arrested by Habré's regime, claimed that he had tortured her.[14] Was she lying? Bandjim Bandoum said that he was in the office of Issay Arawaï, a DDS torturer at the time, when Ginette Ngarbaye was being tortured. But, he insisted, he had never personally tortured anyone. In this regard, the defense lawyers requested a confrontation between Bandjim Bandoum and Ginette Ngarbaye, which meant that both individuals had to appear in court at the same time to argue the facts. The president of the Assize Chamber replied that the tribunal would judge this necessity. The confrontation never happened. A few weeks later, Ginette Ngarbaye testified before the Assize Chamber and confirmed the testimony of the former DDS agent.[15] Bandjim Bandoum was present when Issay Arawaï tortured her, but he had not tortured her.

Beyond his role in the DDS, Bandjim Bandoum was also a victim. He explained that the Habré regime sometimes turned against its servants. He himself had been arrested and tortured. His arrest and subsequent detention had taken place in circumstances that he still could not understand. Recovering from an illness after a short stay in his village, he had returned to N'Djamena where he wanted to resume his work with the DDS. The deputy director of the DDS had offered to take over the position he held before his departure. But someone else was occupying it and refusing to give it back to him. When he was ready to leave and give up, the deputy director asked him to wait on the spot until he spoke to the director of the DDS. A few minutes later, DDS agents came back and told him that he was under arrest. Immediately. The reasons for the arrest remained unclear. It was explained to him that he had worked with someone who had since become an opponent of the Habré regime. He was accused of having a cousin in France who had decided to join a rebel group, that of Idriss Déby Itno, who was then militarily opposed to Habré's regime. He did not know at the time of his testimony before the EAC who had ordered his arrest: the then-president Hissein Habré or the director of the sinister DDS. He had ended up in the jails of the regime he served. He was ill in prison when he finally benefited from the leniency and pity of his jailers, former colleagues, who took him to hospital before returning him to his family and to his village. He had entered prison after an illness from which he had been cured, and he had come out of it with an illness!

One was still surprised to have sympathy for Bandjim Bandoum when one learned, following questions from a lawyer for the civil parties, that he had been receiving anonymous calls since he began to collaborate in the proceedings against Hissein Habré. He was being threatened. To ensure his wife's safety, he had had to divorce her because he was living in France and she was living in Chad. Unknown persons had attacked his wife. She had been shot and had a broken leg.

After Bandjim Bandoum's testimony and his responses to the prosecutors and having answered the questions of the lawyers for the civil parties, the defense lawyers endeavored to question his account and his presentation of the bodies of repression. Questioning the credibility of Bandjim Bandoum, they established differences between his oral assertions before the Assize Chamber and those he had made during the investigation. For example, he had said to the Assize Chamber that the former president of the Republic of Chad had appointed him to the DDS. Instead, in the minutes of his hearing during the investigation phase, he had stated that a former DDS director, Ahmat Allachi, had appointed him head of the operations department.

Bandjim Bandoum replied that he had certainly expressed himself poorly during the investigation hearing. He reconsidered the facts surrounding this appointment, explaining that the then director of the DDS had offered him to return to work at the DDS. He had told him that he would speak to the former president Hissein Habré about it so that he could be appointed. Bandjim Bandoum had declined the proposal. The director of the DDS threatened him at the time. If he refused to return to work, he would be arrested and incarcerated again. He gave in, and two days later, a decree signed by Hissein Habré appointed him head of the operations department at the DDS. While the director of the DDS had certainly chosen him, he had done so with the agreement of the president, who had signed the appointment decree.

The defense lawyers also raised questions about the link between the DDS and the Chadian Ministry of the Interior. That link was established by Article 2 of the decree that created the DDS in 1983. The defense lawyers sought to exonerate Hissein Habré from responsibility for crimes committed by DDS agents. Bandjim Bandoum noted that reality contradicted the law. According to him, the DDS had never been under the authority of the Ministry of the Interior, but rather under that of the presidency of the Chadian Republic.

The defense lawyers casted doubt on the alleged meetings between the director of the DDS and the former president of the Republic of Chad. Could Bandjim Bandoum say with certainty that the director of the DDS met with the former president when he went to the presidential palace? No, certainly not, since Bandjim Bandoum was not there with the director of the DDS. However, in a clear response, Bandjim Bandoum insisted on the meetings organized by the DDS director on his return from the presidential palace, which he attended as a DDS officer. The director tirelessly repeated Hissein Habré's instructions, which made it clear that he had indeed met with the president.

In spite of the explanations of Bandjim Bandoum, the defense lawyers insisted on the autonomy of Hissein Habré's political police officers. At the same time, they tried to legitimize the brutal reaction of the Habré regime to the threat of a Libyan occupation of Chadian territory. With a touch of cold humor and irony, Bandjim Bandoum replied that in the event of war or armed conflict, the Geneva Convention—he did not say which one—must be respected, that people, when they are accomplices of the enemy and arrested, must be treated humanely and brought to justice. The defense lawyers attacked him head-on, citing his "immunity" and noting that he was free to appear before the Assize Chamber even though he had confessed to having participated in the repression during the Habré regime. Bandjim Bandoum replied that he was not shirking justice. He revealed to the Chamber that Chad had issued an international arrest warrant against him. If one day in Chad, he continued, there were to be a Republic that respects the law, he would go there to be tried at the request of that state. He was Chadian and had no other nationality, he said. He also indicated that he did not in any way negotiate his hearing before the Assize Chamber. His decision to accept a hearing before the Assize Chamber was "voluntary." He came to Dakar to testify and intended to get nothing in return.

The testimony of the former DDS agent was a strong indictment against Hissein Habré. Beyond the personal experiences of Bandjim Bandoum, his testimony presented the system of repression of the DDS, the crimes committed within and by the DDS, and the close link between the former president and the DDS.

Somewhat far from the institutional aspects of the DDS and the Chadian regime that had taken place between 1982 and 1990, other victims and witnesses gave more personal presentations to the Assize Chamber, which helped the court understand the crimes against humanity, the war crimes, and the crimes of torture of which Hissein Habré was being accused.

NOTES

1. Ernest Kohn Bramstedt, *Dictatorship and Political Police: The Technique of Control by Fear* (New York: Oxford University Press, 1945); Sheena Chestnut Greitens, *Dictators and Their Secret Police: Coercive Institutions and State Violence* (Cambridge: Cambridge University Press, 2016).
2. Tchad, Rapport de la commission nationale d'enquête du ministère tchadien de la justice, *Les crimes et les détournements de l'ex-président Habré et de ses complices* (Paris: L'Harmattan, 1993), 21 ff.
3. Président de la République du Tchad, Décret du 26 janvier 1983.
4. Rapport de la commission nationale d'enquête du ministère tchadien de la justice, op. cit., note 2, 31 ff.
5. See Article 2 of the Décret du 26 janvier 1983.
6. Rapport de la commission nationale d'enquête du ministère tchadien de la justice, op. cit., note 2, 30–32.
7. EAC, Hearing of Mahamat Hassan Abakar, September 15 and 16, 2015, Online Playlist of the *Forum interactif sur les CAE*. EAC Transcripts, September 15 and 16, 2015.
8. Human Rights Watch. *Hissène Habré, les archives de l'horreur, les archives de la police politique*. 2003.
9. Tchad, Rapport de la commission nationale d'enquête du ministère tchadien de la justice, op. cit., note 2, 32–34.
10. EAC, Hearing of Bandjim Bandoum, September 22 and 23, 2015, Online Playlist of the *Forum interactif sur les CAE*. EAC Transcripts, September 22 and 23, 2015.
11. See, for example, Rémi Carayol, "Tchad: Bandoum Bandjim, le repenti du système Habré," *Jeune Afrique*, July 27, 2015, online https://www.jeuneafrique.com/

mag/250203/societe/tchad-bandoum-bandjim-le-repenti-du-systeme-habre/, accessed 5/16/2021.

12. Rapport de la commission nationale d'enquête du ministère tchadien de la justice, op. cit., note 2, 43.

13. EAC, Hearing of Souleymane Abdoulaye Taher, November 10, 2015, Online Playlist of the *Forum interactif sur les CAE*. EAC, Transcripts, November 10, 2015.

14. Florent Chevolleau, *Hissène Habré: la traque d'un dictateur*, 2009, 57 mn.

15. EAC, Hearing of Ginette Ngarbaye, November 19, 2015. EAC, Transcripts, November 19, 2015, as quoted in EAC, *Ministère public v. Hissein Habré*, Judgment, May 30, 2016, para. 277.

Chapter 7

Victims Sharing Their Experiences of International Crimes

Repetitive Pattern of the Process of Crimes Reported by Survivors

International crimes are not just criminal qualifications used by lawyers and law experts. Actually, they are personal experiences of victims, a compilation of terrible suffering of which each individual victim has his or her own experience, perception, and story. The victims of the Habré regime presented their experiences of international crimes that demonstrated an eerie repetition. The testimonies delivered to the Extraordinary African Assize Chamber by most of the direct and surviving victims generally had in common that they began with an arrest in sometimes incredible and absurd circumstances, followed by a detention marked by interrogations, atrocious acts of torture and appalling detention conditions, and finally, for some of them, a release during the regime or after the fall of the regime. Whether they were Arabs, Hajaraï, Zaghawa, even Senegalese, or simply opponents of Habré's regime or perceived as such, these three stages were recounted repeatedly in the survivors' descriptions of their painful experiences. Some of them also experienced sexual violence.

ARRESTED, DETAINED, AND RELEASED BY HISSEIN HABRÉ'S REGIME

Clément Abaifouta

Clément Abaifouta was one of those who was arrested and held in the jails of the Habré regime before being released.[1] He was also one of the victims who got the media attention, one of the leading figures in the struggle leading up to the trial of Hissein Habré. A resident of N'Djamena, he was the president of an organization representing the victims of crimes committed during the Habré regime. He had been seen many times in the media vilifying the torturing regime, detailing the crimes committed, stressing the responsibility of the former head of state, and claiming his status as a victim, which he reiterated before the Assize Chamber during his testimony.

The usual course of his life suddenly changed in July 1985. One night, he heard knocking at his door. He opened it and stood in front of strangers. One of them asked him if he was Clément. He nodded. The strangers informed him that they had a few small questions to ask him and that they had to take him with them. They promised he would be back home soon. Clément Abaifouta followed them. They put him in a pickup truck with military personnel on board. On the way, the pickup truck made a stop. The military took another person on board. Clément Abaifouta was taken to the Directorate of Documentation and Security (DDS) office and interrogated about the reasons why he wanted to join the rebellion against Hissein Habré. He did not understand. He did not know what the DDS agents were talking about.

In fact, Facho Balaam, a former opponent of Hissein Habré who had also testified before the Extraordinary African Assize Chamber, had revealed that he was the uncle of Clément Abaifouta.[2] His support for Goukouni Weddeye in his armed struggle against Hissein Habré had earned him the latter's wrath. Having tagged him as a political opponent and armed fighter, the regime had attacked several of his relatives, including Clément Abaifouta. The arrest of Clément Abaifouta by the DDS was therefore linked to his uncle's opposition to Hissein Habré.

After the interrogation, the DDS agents kept Clément Abaifouta in a small room in which a pot of paint was being used as a latrine. In this cramped room, several people, presumably also arrested, were sitting on the bare floor. New people arrived as the days went by. After two weeks, there were more than 50 people in the room. Not having enough space to lie down on the floor, the inmates had to take turns sleeping or find other stratagems. They were served rice, black rice, obviously the residue from the bottom of a pot of burnt rice.

Clément Abaifouta was then taken to a prison called "Les locaux." He held several "jobs" while in detention there. The jailers put him in charge of cooking and washing and ironing the clothes of the soldiers and their families. He was also "appointed" a gravedigger. At night, he accompanied the DDS agents to the suburb of N'Djamena, a place called Hamral Goz, where the earth was summarily dug for the burial of the dead detainees. Usually, they had to be quick to avoid being seen by the locals. Transporting and burying the detainees was not an easy task from a psychological point of view. The skin of the dead people stuck to the hands of the gravediggers, and a white liquid flowed from their mouths. Clément Abaifouta later noted that he had told the Chadian National Commission of Inquiry where the people had been buried and added images of unearthed bones to his testimony.

The conditions of detention were appalling. In the cells, inmates sometimes rubbed their bodies against the walls if they were itchy. Disease, edema, dysentery, and death reigned. So did the jailers. They would pick up inmates and later return them to their cells after having interrogated and tortured them. They beat the detainees. Clément Abaifouta himself had been beaten and tortured. Women prisoners were raped. They talked about it. When the detainees were talking to each other, the jailers suspected them of attempting to escape. The prison cells were infiltrated by agents of the regime. The regime wanted to know what the inmates were saying to each other. The regime had assigned nurses and a doctor to the place of detention and an infirmary had been established. The inmates could expect care. But some of the nurses were mean. They insulted inmates. Inmates had died after receiving injections from the medical staff. In desperation, inmates prayed. One day, while they were praying, the director of the DDS arrived and asked them to be quiet and bow their heads.

Clément Abaifouta suddenly became moved by the recollection of his past experience. "What a waste," he said, before continuing his testimony.

Hissein Habré had shattered his future. At the time of his arrest, he had just passed his high school diploma, had been awarded a scholarship to East Germany, was to continue his medical studies in Europe, and had a bright future ahead of him. Sadly, he had lost everything. He would like Hissein Habré to explain to him how obtaining a scholarship was an attack on state security. He would like to know why he had suffered so much, why Hissein Habré had subjected Chad to a reign of terror for eight years. For him, Hissein Habré was behaving like a god. Hissein Habré himself whipped some prisoners, Ngali Ngotté, a Chadian politician, told him.

Habré's regime finally freed Clément Abaifouta following an agreement with his uncle and former opponent of Hissein Habré, Facho Balaam. Weary of war and after negotiations, Facho Balaam decided to join the "reconciliation" sought by Hissein Habré, returned to Chad, and held positions within the regime. This return facilitated the release of his relatives, including his nephew Clément Abaifouta.

In order to contradict the testimony of Clément Abaifouta, the defense lawyers used the context of the armed conflict in Chad to imply that Hissein Habré was only fighting against his country's enemies, including Libyan-backed rebels. The arrest of Clément Abaifouta was only part of Hissein Habré's efforts to protect his country. The defense lawyers asked questions about the scholarship from East Germany. Clément Abaifouta had obtained that scholarship after a proposal made by Facho Balaam to him. The defense lawyers presumably tried to sow doubt about the real intentions of the opponent. But nothing seemed to call into question the story of Clément Abaifouta, who was arrested, detained in appalling conditions, and later released.

Zakaria Fadoul Kitir

The story of the Zaghawa scholar Zakaria Fadoul Kitir was similar. A victim of the Habré regime, he recounted his story in a book published in 1998.[3] As we have seen, he was an academic and head of the Department of Literature and Linguistics at the University of N'Djamena in 1989.[4] He told the Assize Chamber how he was "arrested" at his workplace by DDS agents before being taken to a place of detention and released after having lived through a real ordeal.[5]

On April 26, 1989, at approximately 12:30 p.m., while he was receiving a student who insisted to have his dissertation corrected, a man, he did not know, entered his office. The man introduced himself as a security guard and announced: "I've come for you." Concerned, the scholar asked him if he had an arrest warrant. The man sneered and assured him that there was nothing to be alarmed about. He added that a police commissioner wished to speak with him for about 30 minutes. Reassured and without warning anyone, Zakaria Fadoul Kitir followed his visitor. He was taken to the DDS offices and questioned about his ethnicity. He answered that he was Zaghawa. His interrogator insisted, wanting to know to which subclan or subgroup of the Zaghawa he belonged. "Zaghawa-Kobe," he replied. He did not understand what was happening to him when, on the instructions of a DDS officer, he was taken by another officer to a prison called "La piscine"—"the swimming pool."

That prison with a strange name came up several times in the testimonies of victims and appeared as one of the symbols of repression in Chad. The investigating judges of the EAC, who visited the premises of La piscine during letters rogatory in Chad, gave a brief overview of that prison.[6] It was located within the new headquarters of the political police, the DDS. It was indeed an old swimming pool dating from the colonial period and used by the families of French soldiers. In 1987, Habré's regime transformed it into a secret prison. The walls around the pool were raised and a reinforced concrete slab was put into place as the roof. A front door had been installed. A staircase provided access to the swimming pool, which had been divided into 10 small cells with tiny windows. It was toward this old swimming pool, now a prison, that Zakaria Fadoul Kitir was dragged. Here began his detention.

The DDS officer opened the door of La piscine prison and made him run down the stairs into the corridor dividing the cells on either side of the pool and, at the end of which was a toilet with a foul odor. The scholar was struck down by the intense heat and smell emanating from the cell in which he was to be locked. He made a backward movement. The jailer maintained his trajectory and pushed him into the small room, closing the door behind him.

The cell was a filthy place: dirt on the walls, unbearable heat, foul smell, and a layer of urine on the cemented floor. In the cell was an individual who knew Zakaria Fadoul Kitir's family. They talked about their two families. The warmth of the cordial exchanges described by Zakaria Fadoul Kitir made the public of Courtroom No. 4 of the Palais de Justice forget for a moment the desperate nature of the place where the discussion took place. This feeling faded immediately when the Chadian scholar recounted what happened next.

Later on, other inmates joined them in the cell. A jailer suddenly opened the cell door and placed a plate of rice balls and pieces of meat on the floor. An inmate ate a bite. He spits it out right away. The food was sprinkled with sand and the jailers wanted them dead, he exclaimed. Once consumed, the sand would settle at the bottom of their stomachs and cause death. One of the inmates proposed a ploy: to decant the sand and separate it from the food by making a porridge out of it. They could use the sardine cans available in the cell as containers to hold the porridge, then the sand would gradually settle to the bottom of the cans. This would allow an acidic liquid free of sand to collect that they could drink without it being harmful to their health. The inmates followed the process and consumed the resulting liquid.

The scholar Zakaria Fadoul Kitir was taken from his cell for an interrogation with an uncertain outcome. He was brought before Mahamat Djibrine known as "El Djonto," a DDS agent described as a ruthless torturer by the Chadian National Commission of Inquiry report.[7] Welcoming Zakaria Fadoul Kitir as an important visitor whom he was delighted to see, El Djonto asked the academic what brought him there. For a moment, disconcerted by this grotesque situation, the scholar replied that he had been arrested and taken before him. "So you don't know anything?" continued El Djonto. Zakaria Fadoul Kitir added that he knew there were arrests and disturbances, but that he had nothing to reproach himself for. "Mr. Professor, the responsibility is collective," replied El Djonto accusingly. He then asked him about his relationship with Hassan Djamous, who was his brother-in-law, and Idriss Déby Itno one of his family members. It was here, as we have seen, that the scholar learned that he was suspected of being part of a Zaghawa elite plan to overthrow Hissein Habré and that he denied any involvement. A DDS agent standing behind Zakaria Fadoul Kitir wanted to torture him. El Djonto prevented him from doing so while intimidating the scholar with his gun.

An agent took the scholar back to his cell. Zakaria Fadoul Kitir thought his fate was sealed. He was going to be killed. There did not seem to be any other way out of the situation. Death would free him from the nightmare he had been plunged into. The scholar certainly met the frightened eyes of several starving inmates sitting on the cell floor, wounds, scrapes, and traces of dried blood on their skin. He read the incomprehension in the eyes of those who, appearing less damaged, had certainly been arrested recently. He saw Sudanese arrested and beaten with metal truncheons and detainees urinating and defecating on the cell floor because the empty cans of sardines were too small to use as latrines. Fresh air was scarce in the cell of the La piscine prison. One after the other, the inmates used to lie down and stick their noses close to the gap between the floor and the cell door to sniff the little fresh air that sometimes crept in.

On the tenth day of his detention, the scholar was taken out of his cell by a DDS agent who told him that he was being released, on one condition—a DDS ritual that was repeated in several victims' testimonies—in detention, he had seen nothing, he had heard nothing. Zakaria Fadoul Kitir nodded. While driving him out of the prison, the DDS officer asked Zakaria Fadoul Kitir how many of his brothers had been arrested. "Eight," he replied. And how many had he seen at the DDS, questioned the jailer. "Two," the scholar added. Suddenly, the DDS agent got angry, called him an idiot, reminded him that he had just told him that he should never reveal what he had seen at the DDS.

As this unfortunate sequence was being described, a few smiles and laughter, both mocking and compassionate, spontaneously erupted amid the courtroom public.

The officer took the scholar back to his cell, put him in, closed the door, and left. The scholar stayed there for five more days. On the 15th day of his detention, he was released by a man who came to remove him from his cell, a man he later learned was the director of the DDS, Guihini Korei. He was offered tea. He took a bath and was taken home to his family.

Two white Americans from the International Society of Linguistics, to which the scholar Zakaria Fadoul Kitir belonged, visited him later and burst into tears when they saw him.

The scholar paused for a moment in his testimony to point out that he had never seen white people cry before. "What have they done to you?" the two Americans asked, dismayed at the sight of his skin that was "gone." After 15 days of detention, he was simply unrecognizable.

Tears sometimes streamed down Zakaria Fadoul Kitir's cheeks during his testimony. The memories of his painful past still moved him.

Zakaria Fadoul Kitir told the judges of the Assize Chamber that after his release, he was informed of the circumstances that had contributed to his being removed detention. Worried about his disappearance, his wife had approached his cousin who was the Hissein Habré campaign manager. After an intervention by his cousin with the director of the DDS, then with Hissein Habré because the release had still not taken place, the scholar was released. This cousin later told Zakaria Fadoul Kitir that Hissein Habré himself had ordered his release. Strong international pressure, particularly from human rights organizations and the contacts he had established abroad in academic circles, had been decisive in his release.

Zakaria Fadoul Kitir had survived, unlike several members of his family arrested like him. He had set up an organization, inter alia, to establish the responsibility of those who had committed these crimes. He was astonished by the experience he had gone through. Yet he knew Hissein Habré, he revealed to the judges of the Assize Chamber. He had met him in Europe several years before he took power. Hissein Habré was then recruiting people to join the rebellion. Hissein Habré had come to see him in his room in Brussels but had left without telling him anything. Zakaria Fadoul Kitir had concluded that Hissein Habré must have felt that he did not look like someone who could join the rebellion. The scholar added that he admired Hissein Habré, who had qualities as a fighter for justice and freedom, who represented the symbol of the liberating man. However, he regretted the negative and progressive metamorphosis of his regime. While Hissein Habré was certainly aware of the actions of the agents of his regime, it could not be considered that Hissein Habré was always aware of everything his agents did. But, according to him, the former head of state had made the mistake of giving carte blanche to the DDS, covering its agents and their harmful and brutal actions no matter what.

After the testimony of Zakaria Fadoul Kitir, the prosecution and lawyers for the civil parties asked him questions focusing on Hissein Habré's responsibility. The defense lawyers, seizing the opportunity offered by the victim's statement of admiration for Hissein Habré, tried to push Zakaria Fadoul Kitir to present the accused in a favorable light, insisting that Hissein Habré was only fighting for justice and freedom in Chad when he attacked enemies and rebels. The defense lawyers also tried to discredit Zakaria Fadoul Kitir by being surprised that he, who had indicated during the investigation that he had been tortured while in detention, had then said before the Assize Chamber that he had never been tortured. Zakaria Fadoul Kitir admitted that there was certainly an error in the investigation report. The defense lawyers suggested that the account of his release, that he said was ordered by the former head of state, was hearsay and unsupported by evidence. However, this repetitive pattern of arrest, detention, and release by the regime was not really contested. Indeed, it was a recurring pattern that did not spare foreigners.

Abdourahmane Gueye

Abdourahmane Gueye, a Senegalese victim of Habré's regime who testified before the Assize Chamber,[8] had experienced the same scenario. Based in Bangui in the Central African Republic and authorized by the administration of that country to engage in commercial activities, he delivered gold jewelry and precious stones to the regiments of French soldiers who used to stop and stay there. He received orders that he had to deliver within two months.

It was in the context of this activity that in 1987 he received an order from a visiting regiment. As usual, he had to deliver the goods within two months. But, a month after the order was placed, he received a call from the regimental commander informing him that the regiment was going to Chad. He had started working on the delivery but was not ready yet. The regimental commander recommended that he contact his replacement when the work was completed. This replacement would tell him how to proceed with the delivery.

When he finished his work, he did as recommended by the regimental commander. The replacement told him to go to Chad to deliver the items ordered by the former regiment. To do so, a visa for Chad was required. Despite some setbacks at the Chadian Embassy, he obtained a visa, as did Demba Gaye, a Senegalese national who was going to travel with him.

They flew to Chad at midnight on a French military plane. They arrived in N'Djamena around 2:00 a.m. and landed at a French military base located near the civilian airport of N'Djamena. Because it was night, a lieutenant advised them to sleep in the base and wait until morning to carry out formalities for entry into Chadian territory. These formalities could only be carried out within the civil airport of N'Djamena. The two Senegalese agreed. The next day, after having breakfast with French soldiers, they received two temporary passes, which were to allow them to carry out the formalities for entering Chadian territory and to return the next day to take new passes authorizing them to go to the place where the goods would be delivered to the French regiment. But their lives were turned upside down when they left the French military base on foot to reach the Chadian civilian airport.

While they were walking, they saw a Peugeot 504 vehicle heading toward them. The car stopped next to them. A man with a walkie-talkie in his hand got out. He asked them to come into the car. In the car were two other people, military personnel. The two Senegalese had nothing to hide. They got into the car and it drove to N'Djamena. Once downtown, the car stopped at a building. They got out of the car and entered the building. They did not know where they were.

Abdourahmane Gueye was separated from Demba Gaye. He was taken to an office where he was interrogated by a Chadian agent. The officer asked him for identification. He presented his passport. The officer noticed that he traveled a lot because his passport was "full." He asked him why he had arrived in N'Djamena in the company of French soldiers. Abdourahmane Gueye replied that he was a trader and had to deliver goods to a regiment of French soldiers. To prove his good faith, he showed him the goods that were in envelopes. The envelopes were opened and the contents put on the table. The agent informed him that he and Demba Gaye were suspects, spies sent by the Libyan head of state Muammar Gaddafi. Abdourahmane Gueye burst out laughing and said that it was the French who had led them to Chad, and that the French were protectors of Chad. The agent replied that, in reality, the French were playing a double game and had helped a rebel named Kamougué, an opponent of Hissein Habré's regime. Abdourahmane Gueye suggested that the officer call the French military and hear their side of the story. The officer did not answer. He took a sheet of paper, noted the name of Abdourahmane Gueye and his passport number. He then asked him to sign at the bottom of the page. Abdourahmane Gueye refused, fearing that after signing, the agent would add compromising notes on the sheet of paper. The officer got angry and ordered him to strip. He did it and kept only his pants on. His passport was confiscated along with the goods.

A few hours later, he was put in a vehicle and driven to a place he did not know. He understood that he had just been put in prison when he was locked in a cell. A lot of people were there. A detainee, who later introduced himself as a captain in the Chadian army and belonging to the Hajaraï ethnic group, asked him in French why he had been arrested. He told his story and wanted to know if he could benefit from the services of a lawyer. The captain laughed. "A lawyer?" he exclaimed, mockingly. He added that there were no magistrates or lawyers. The prison was one of the places of detention of the DDS and was called Camp des martyrs, he informed him. For the inmate, the only thing left to do was to pray for his release.

Abdourahmane Gueye was taken out of his cell for interrogation without any physical act of torture, but he knew nothing. He was returned to his cell. The conditions of detention were appalling. It was hot, very hot. There were no lights. The food was stinky. The inmates would die in the cells. He sometimes heard screams of people presumably being tortured. One day, he heard someone screaming. The detainees claimed it was a Hajaraï named Saleh Ngaba. The Hajaraï captain told him that the Hajaraï were arrested. One night, the captain was removed from the cell by DDS agents and taken to an unknown destination.

Abdourahmane Gueye had fallen ill in prison. One day, some agents took him out of his cell. They took him to the place where he had been interrogated after his arrest. They sat him down. He did not understand what was going on. A doctor came to see him and gave him IV fluids. He was given food, but he couldn't eat. In that place, he heard people screaming. Tortured people? He stayed there for about 20 days. Then the director of the DDS came to pick him up and he was taken to the office of the Chadian Ministry of the Interior. The Minister of the Interior, the Senegalese Ambassador to Chad, and the first secretary at the embassy, whom he knew, were there. The Minister of the Interior asked him to sit down. He informed him of the death of his compatriot Demba Gaye. He apologized to him, noting that Senegal and Chad were sister countries. Speaking to the Senegalese ambassador, the minister of the interior clarified that he had nothing to do with the DDS and the arrests because the DDS was under the authority of the president of the Republic of Chad. The ambassador announced to Abdourahmane Gueye that he would be compensated, but that this compensation would be made on a state-to-state basis. Abdourahmane Gueye was therefore released in 1988 after spending 11 months in detention.

He was later told about the conditions of his release. Informed of the arrest and pressured by the Senegalese people, the Senegalese authorities had sought information. The then-president of Senegal Abdou Diouf had been informed and had discussed the issue with his Chadian counterpart, Hissein Habré.

After his release, Abdourahmane Gueye received medical care but was never compensated. Habré's regime had come to an end and Hissein Habré had taken refuge in Senegal. The new Chadian authorities refused to grant reparations and advised Abdourahmane Gueye to prosecute Hissein Habré in Senegal.

The defense lawyers later tried to show that the Chadian Ministry of the Interior, which had ordered the release of the Senegalese from the DDS prison, was indeed the government entity under which the DDS was placed, thus suggesting that President Hissein Habré did not control it and was in no way responsible for Abdourahmane Gueye's arrest, detention, or release. They pointed to the recklessness of the victim who had taken a foreign military aircraft into a foreign state that was in turmoil. They wondered whether, in this context, the Chadian state was not in its rightful role of defending its sovereignty by arresting him and carrying out checks. Abdourahmane Gueye agreed with the defense lawyers on the need for controls in such a context. But he added that the Chadian authorities should have released him after finding that there was nothing incriminating about him and that he was innocent.

From questions asked by the public prosecutor's office and the lawyers for the civil parties, it was learned that the Senegalese had been arrested by the services of the Office of the President of the Republic of Chad and that it was on the premises of the latter that he was interrogated before being placed in detention by the DDS. It was also learned that he was not a politician and had no contact with Libya, that DDS archives confirmed his revelations about his arrest and release, and that he was just an innocent victim of the regime, like so many others.

Ngarba Akhaye

Ngarba Akhaye, a Chadian who spoke in Arabic translated into French, told the Assize Chamber that he had also been arrested and detained in appalling conditions before being released.[9] The reasons for his arrest, which took place in 1986, were unclear. He was allegedly accused of stealing cows that belonged to a DDS agent. DDS agents also, allegedly, suspected him of holding information about certain opponents of the Habré regime. In order to obtain information, DDS agents subjected him to several methods of torture, which he described in detail: electric wires, blows with a rifle, attempted drowning. He did not say anything. He did not know anything. He had been detained successively in several of the regime's detention facilities, including at La piscine, Camp des martyrs, and Les locaux. In detention, the jailers had appointed him cook and gravedigger. Along with a few other designated detainees, he prepared food for the inmates during the day and, at night, buried those who had died.

He was released by a DDS agent in 1989 following a referendum organized by the Habré regime on the adoption of a new constitution. At the time of his release, the DDS officer made him swear on the Quran that he would never tell anyone about what he had experienced, heard, or seen during his detention. The defense lawyers reviewed his notes about the conditions of his release and noted that Hissein Habré did not personally decide on the release of prisoners, to which the victim replied that the DDS agent who had released him worked for President Hissein Habré. He was just another victim of a system set up by him.

Madina Fadoul Kitir

Madina Fadoul Kitir, a Zaghawa who was also a victim of the regime, told the Assize Chamber in Arabic translated into French that she had just had a baby when she was arrested as part of the repression against members of her ethnic group in April 1989.[10] She was taken to the DDS and interrogated. She was stunned and taken aback when a DDS officer asked her if she knew why she had been arrested. How could she know? The DDS agent accused her of helping her husband escape. Her husband, whom she had not seen again and who, according to her, had been executed, had escaped from a prison where he was being held as part of the repression against the enemies of the Habré regime. According to the DDS, her husband went to the marital home after the escape and she gave him clothes. She did not know about it and had not helped him, she told the DDS. The defense lawyers later insinuated that the victim's husband was part of the rebellion, a rebellion that justified the Chadian government's brutal reaction. The victim denied that her husband was a rebel.

After the first interrogation, she was released by the DDS. The next day, DDS agents came back and asked her to follow them. She accepted but wanted to follow them with her newborn child. The DDS officers ordered her to leave her child because they were taking her to a place unsuitable for a baby. She objected. They tried to tear the newborn from her arms.

After her description of this scene, Madina Fadoul Kitir was overwhelmed by emotion and started to cry. The courtroom was shrouded in compassionate silence. When she was able to pull herself together, she continued her testimony.

The DDS agents managed to snatch the baby from her. The baby was handed over to the people at her home. The agents blindfolded Madina Fadoul Kitir, put her in a car, and took her away. After driving for a while, the car stopped. She was taken out and a few minutes later she was thrown into a basement. Now she could see. It was dark. The next day, they came back to get her and, after allowing her to relieve herself, took her to the DDS agent Mahamat Djbrine known as "El Djonto." She shuddered with confidence and comfort at the sight of him.

She knew him. He was her brother's friend. She thought he was going to set her free. El Djonto asked her about her escaped husband, who was allegedly involved in the "Zaghawa rebellion." He had information that he had come to see her before he had fled and joined the rebellion. He wanted to know about it. She didn't know what he was talking about. He also questioned her about members of her family. Not satisfied with the answers of the victim, who tirelessly repeated that she knew nothing, he abandoned her to three other interrogators who transferred her to another room and beat her for a long time. She lost consciousness and no longer felt the pain that invaded her body with the rhythm of the blows. The DDS officers took her to another office and threw her on the floor. She was bleeding profusely from her wounds. The DDS agents wanted to feed her, but she couldn't eat. She remained at the DDS and, the next day, they took her to the prison named Les locaux and left her on a veranda of the detention facility.

There she found other women of the Zaghawa ethnic group like her, including the wife of Idriss Déby Itno, the man who would succeed Hissein Habré as Chadian head of state. Some of these women recognized her. She was in pain and did not want to talk or drink. A doctor consulted her and gave her medication for high blood pressure. She was taken to one of the cells by inmates. The cell was roomy. There was a barrel used as a urinal. In a corner of the cell, there was garbage piled up. The living conditions in the cell were miserable, the food insufficient.

After three months and a few days, a DDS officer came to read out a list of people released for the New Year. The regime, in its occasional leniency, released prisoners on the occasion of New Year's Day festivities. Her name was on the list. She was finally going to escape her nightmare. But one of the inmates named Fatimé, not having heard her name, had collapsed. The

DDS officer then ordered that the released women remain in the prison for three more days to assist the unfortunate non-releasable woman. Three days later, they were released after swearing that they would not talk about what they had experienced and not tell anyone about what they had seen or heard in prison.

Marabi Toudjibedjé

While most of those arrested, detained, and then released were suspected, rightly or wrongly, of opposing Habré's regime, the system sometimes turned brutally against its agents and placed them in the same repressive pattern.

For example, Marabi Toudjibedjé, an employee of the DDS, ended up on the other side of the prison bars. Telling his story to the judges of the Assize Chamber and later answering questions from the prosecutors, the lawyers for the civil parties, and the defense lawyers, he introduced himself as a former soldier in the Chadian army, a jailer in the DDS, and deputy registrar of Les locaux prison.[11] He described the prisons of the regime, torture of arrested persons, atrocious conditions of detention, detainees relieving themselves and defecating in front of co-detainees in half-barrels placed in cells, sick prisoners not being treated, death and burials. As deputy registrar, he wrote reports containing information on detainees, the number of detainees and deaths. He gave these reports to his boss.

When asked by the prosecutors and the lawyers for the civil parties about the fate of those reports, he replied that he did not know. However, he stated that in the course of his duties, he had seen Hissein Habré at the DDS. Hissein Habré came there often, twice a month, and spoke with the director of the DDS. Marabi Toudjibedjé seemed embarrassed by the questions he was asked about torture. Was he participating as an agent of the regime in the torture sessions? "No," he replied, he was one of the chiefs, he was present and supervising. He did not have the power to prevent these practices of torture. Later, he was suddenly turned into a victim.

In 1985, moved by the disastrous living conditions of the detainees, Marabi Toudjibedjé realized he had made a "mistake." He bought bread and meat and gave these to people in detention. His superior, the DDS director Saleh Younouss, noticed this. He reminded him that prisoners were destined to die. Saving them wasn't part of his job. Marabi Toudjibedjé was arrested and thrown into prison on the spot. In an instant, kindness and magnanimity had tipped him over to the other side of the bars, that of the opponents of the Habré regime who were believed to be deserving of punishment.

When asked by a lawyer for the civil parties why he had fed the detainees, Marabi Toudjibedjé remained silent for a moment. Then, he explained, full of weariness, that the prisoners were unhappy.

For the time he was in prison, he had been designated as a gravedigger. He participated in the removal of bodies from the cells and their burial on the orders of DDS agents. He was released in 1986 and returned to the Chadian army. Upon his release, Marabi Toudjibedjé swore that he would not say anything about what he had experienced, seen, and heard in prison. He was required to do so in front of a picture of the three monkeys who see no evil, hear no evil, and speak no evil. He described the picture in which the first monkey covers his eyes with his hands, the second covers his mouth, and the third covers his ears. The description of the picture triggered the general hilarity of the courtroom public. This ritual of being sworn to secrecy upon liberation by the DDS in front of this picture was to be repeated ad infinitum.

Indeed, several victims, such as Khadija Hassan Zidane, Hawa Brahim, and her mother, had also been released after swearing on the Quran and in front of a picture of three monkeys that they would not talk about their prison experience.[12] This ritual undoubtedly had the ambition to give DDS a mystical and spiritual dimension. It meant that beyond release, DDS intended to continue mentally imprisoning those released by maintaining terror, denial, and silence, using a religious book to frighten victims. In any event, by their testimony before the Assize Chamber, the victims who had sworn had chosen to tell the truth in the name of justice and the establishment of an individual's criminal responsibility. However, not all the victims were submitted to this ritual because they were not released by Habré's regime.

ARRESTED, DETAINED, AND RELEASED BY THE DOWNFALL OF THE HABRÉ REGIME

Several Chadian victims were not released until the fall of the Habré regime, but only after having been arrested and spending long periods in prison. This was the case, in particular, of Souleymane Guengueng.

Souleymane Guengueng

Souleymane Guengueng was undoubtedly one of the people without whom the trial of Hissein Habré would never have taken place. Before his testimony at trial, he had been expressing the distress of the victims and insisting on the serious crimes committed by the regime of Hissein Habré. His testimony was anticipated, even if his story and his struggle for justice had been published in a poignant book in 2012.[13]

Standing in front of the judges of the Assize Chamber and looking both proud and serious, Souleymane Guengueng revealed that he was 64 years old, a father of eight children, and lived in New York City in the United

States.[14] In a brief introduction, he stated that he had been unjustly accused and arrested in 1988. He lived through the painful experience of the prisons of the Habré regime for more than two years. He had seen fellow inmates suffer and die. While in prison, he had sworn that if he survived, he would fight for justice, for the dead and the disappeared, and above all prevent the repetition of such crimes. Souleymane Guengueng was convinced that God spared his life so that he could achieve what he had promised himself he would do. After the fall of the Habré regime, he pushed for the creation of the first organization AVCPR that sought the establishment of Hissein Habré's criminal responsibility. His quest for justice had brought him torment and threats. He lost his job. He went into exile in the United States, which had granted him the status of political refugee. But, visibly satisfied to finally be before judges charged with examining the criminal responsibility of Hissein Habré, Souleymane Guengueng noted that his efforts had been fruitful and invited the Assize Chamber to listen carefully to his testimony.

His problems started before 1988. He was based in Maroua, in the far north of Cameroon, and worked for the organization of the Lake Chad Commission, which brought together several states (Cameroon, Niger, Nigeria, and Chad); he traveled regularly in this capacity. The Cameroonian police had several times arrested and questioned him about weapons he had allegedly transported to help the opposition to the Habré regime. He had always denied any involvement. Having seen his photo at the Chadian presidential palace, a member of his family working for Hissein Habré had informed him of the risks he was running. He was advised not to return to Chad under any circumstances. However, Souleymane Guengueng's innocence had been proven. The Chadian authorities had assured him that he had nothing to worry about. His organization moved to Chad in 1987 after President Hissein Habré himself, he was told, had reassured them of their safety. Once settled in Chad, he freely continued his work and his travels in the countries of the Lake Chad Basin.

Everything changed on August 3, 1988. Returning to his organization's headquarters after a visit to the hospital where he had received treatment for an infection, he saw his wife get out of a taxi and join him. They talked and went into his office. With tears in her voice, she told him that DDS agents had come to the family home to arrest him. His cousin had been arrested. Souleymane Guengueng was listening to his wife's story when a tall man burst into his office. He informed Souleymane Guengueng that his director needed him for some information. The man promised him that the meeting would not last long. Souleymane Guengueng followed the man, assuring his pregnant wife that he would come back because he had nothing to hide.

Arriving at the place where he was to meet the director of the man he had followed, presumably a DDS agent, Souleymane Guengueng was placed in an interrogation room. His arrested cousin was next to him. A few minutes later, an agent came up to them. He asked Souleymane Guengueng if he knew why he was there. Souleymane Guengueng replied that he did not know anything about it. A man in battle dress, standing near the interrogator, rushed at him and hit him on the head with the butt of his rifle.

Souleymane Guengueng stopped at this point in his testimony to indicate to the Assize Chamber that he had still not healed from the after-effects of these blows. Despite being treated for several years after his release, he was very often afflicted by violent headaches.

After he had received these blows, Souleymane Guengueng lost consciousness for a brief moment. When he came to, the interrogator asked him the same question, did he know why he was there? He still did not know anything about it. The interrogator informed him that his cousin had stolen money that he had given him to recruit Codos cocotiers, an armed rebel group opposed to the Habré regime. Souleymane Guengueng denied this, replying that he had never taken a stand in the armed conflicts in Chad and that some of his family members or friends collaborated or had collaborated with the regime of Hissein Habré. The interrogator found that he was lying and had him sign a paper. Souleymane Guengueng signed the paper without reading it.

He was taken to the prison called Camp des Martyrs and locked in a cell. There was a lot of water in the cell and his feet were submerged. Under the water, the uneven surface of the rough floor, likely made of grotesquely striated or swept cement, cut into the soles of his feet and made standing uncomfortable. Mosquitoes were buzzing mercilessly in his ears. He saw a window on the heights of the cell and railings. He climbed up. He stretched out his legs and put them against the opposite wall. He stayed suspended to escape the wet and uneven ground below him. But the mosquitoes were relentless, and he came down when he was tired. He went up, then down. Several times. He thought he had sand in his eyes and his head was about to burst. That night, he did not sleep.

The next day, he was taken out of the cell for further questioning. The officer asked him if he had anything to add. "No," he replied. He was taken back to his torture cell where he spent three more days before being transferred to another cell. He found seven people there. This cell, which was 2.40 meters long, was very small for eight people. The inmates had to sit face to face, taking turns putting their legs on the shoulders of the detainee sitting in front of them.

Souleymane Guengueng wanted to show the Assize Chamber how the detainees did this. In order to do so, he wished to involve an outside person. The president of the Assize Chamber refused.

Souleymane Guengueng continued his story, describing the uncomfortable but necessary positions that prisoners adopted to survive. He went on to describe the conditions of life in prison. Returning to a point already made by another victim, Zakaria Fadoul Kitir,[15] he said that the food served to the detainees was probably sprinkled with sand. The first time he had tasted it, his teeth had crushed grains of sand instead of rice. The sauce that accompanied the rice had a blood-red color. Despite the foul state of the meals, the inmates ate. But, many fell ill, experiencing bad coughs, swollen gums, and decaying teeth.

One day, on the orders of a chief officer outraged by the state of the prisoners, the cells were opened, except for three cells in which newly arrested people were being tortured. The inmates found, for the first time, that there were about 50 of them. The cells of the Camp de martyrs were now to be open every day from 9 a.m. until lunchtime. Souleymane Guengueng invited some detainees to pray with him. A few people joined him and they prayed. Later, at the instigation of Souleymane Guengueng, the prayers were accompanied by fasts. The detainees prayed and fasted, hoping that God would deliver them from prison. A few days later, after the beginning of their religious practice, the jailers brought them mats and blankets. Souleymane Guengueng saw it as a sign that their prayers were being answered. God had come to their rescue.

But Souleymane Guengueng was sick. He vomited regularly, had malaria, and edema. His gums were slightly swollen. He sometimes lost consciousness, and it was fortunate that DDS officers and detainees designated as gravediggers had not taken him for a summary burial during their nightly visits. One day, worried about Souleymane Guengueng's health, the detainees had alerted a visiting commissioner. After spending more than six months in Camp des martyrs, Souleymane Guengueng was transferred to Les locaux prison because it had an infirmary.

When he arrived there, he was taken to a cell in front of the infirmary. A male nurse ordered onions to be fed to him to unclog his arteries. He was also given a light porridge of rice. In his new prison, he met people he knew, including his cousin who was arrested at the same time as him. He was put in cell D, the one reserved for the sick. Thanks to his cousin and a few accomplices within the prison, he managed to get medication that gradually helped him regain his health. Souleymane Guengueng was transferred to cell C. The cell was too small for the number of people the jailers put in it. There was a steady stream of inmates in that cell. Some detainees were being extracted, while others were arriving.

The daily life in the Les locaux was filled with revealing, insignificant or offbeat stories. The detainees questioned whether a group of detainees, apparently the family of Goukouni Weddeye,[16] was being treated better. This family was considered a noble family that deserved better treatment. Some inmates would kill rats and eat them after roasting them. Souleymane Guengueng pointed out that it was good flesh and that it was a luxury for those who ate it. A small disagreement arose when one inmate made fun of another inmate who was cleaning a rat that was about to be eaten. An inmate acting as a historian made a decision. He recalled that the first prey of African hunters was rats. In an interrogative statement, the historian asked what sins were committed by those who ate rats. Informed of the "historian's findings," the inmates set out the next day on a rat hunt. But they couldn't find rats anymore.

Souleymane Guengueng revealed that he was suspected, along with others, of being one of the leaders of the detainees who were planning an escape. DDS agents transferred them back to the Camp des martyrs where they locked them in a dark cell for almost three months. After being chained up, they were then transferred to La gendarmerie prison, another detention facility of the regime. They were confined in a cell where light bulbs were kept on for 24 hours a day, a situation that had lastingly affected his eyesight, Souleymane Guengueng later added. The conditions were difficult in La gendarmerie. As elsewhere, inmates were dying there.

Returning later to the conditions of detention, the defense lawyers wanted to know whether Souleymane Guengueng was a doctor because he had stated that, while in detention, he had helped a fellow prisoner to dispose of his feces. A detainee, who had been horribly tortured, was no longer able to defecate. To help him, Souleymane Guengueng reported that he had to help him by using his hand. To the question of the defense lawyers, Souleymane Guengueng answered that one did not need to be a doctor to perform such an act. The defense lawyers returned to this episode, demanding more and more details about how this had been accomplished. Souleymane Guengueng replied that he wanted to save his fellow man. His gesture had helped the detainee find some relief from his discomfort.

During this episode of his testimony, Souleymane Guengueng suddenly burst into tears. The public remained silent as the microphone echoed the sound of his sobbing voice from all four corners of the courtroom.

In September 1990, the jailers subjected Souleymane Guengueng and his fellow inmates to draconian conditions. The detainees received tea which sometimes was accompanied by rice porridge. They lived like this until the fall of Hissein Habré's regime in early December 1990, when Idriss Déby Itno's troops entered N'Djamena. The fall of Hissein Habré opened the prison doors to freedom.

Fatimé Hachim Saleh

Fatimé Hachim Saleh had also had to wait for the fall of the regime.[17] She arrived in front of the judges with a satisfied look and recited a few verses from the Quran before being interrupted by the president of the Extraordinary

African Assize Chamber. She told the judges that the DDS arrested her and her husband in 1989. Her husband was questioned about the help he had allegedly given Idriss Déby Itno, the opponent to Hissein Habré, to facilitate his escape. Her husband did not know anything. He was just a simple merchant. He was then taken away and she never saw him again.

The victim sobbed for a few seconds before continuing her testimony.

The DDS agents also interrogated her. They wanted information about the amounts of money she and her husband allegedly gave to help Zaghawa rebels against the Habré regime. She did not know anything. Although she was pregnant, the regime's agents took her to the Les locaux prison where she was detained.

Two days after her detention began, she was taken from her cell to a riverbank for interrogation. She was asked the same questions while her interrogators fired into the air with their guns to impress or frighten her. She still did not have anything to say. She was taken back to her cell to be extracted again, several times, for the same type of interrogation. She ended up delivering a seven-month premature baby in prison. In the absence of a doctor, a fellow inmate had rummaged through a pile of garbage, found a dirty but sharp object, and cut the placenta. The child, a boy, was alive. He died later. The jailers retrieved his tiny body and buried it.

She remained in custody. The cell was in pretty bad shape. The jailers would sometimes beat the inmates who, under the beatings, lost blood. Some of the inmates were sick. Food was scarce. There was a regular influx of new detainees whose physical condition would gradually deteriorate. She had served as a translator for the DDS officers for detainees who spoke Arabic, a language in which she was proficient. Her fellow inmates were pardoned by the Habré regime on the occasion of a New Year's Day. She was left alone in the cell.

She had met Hissein Habré in prison. She took the opportunity to ask him why, unlike her fellow inmates, she had not been pardoned. Hissein Habré had replied that he preferred to free a hundred men in her place. She was worth, all alone, a hundred men! She was only able to leave after Idriss Déby Itno's troops entered N'Djamena on December 1, 1990, and President Hissein Habré had fled.

Abakar Adoum

Abakar Adoum, another victim, revealed to the Extraordinary African Assize Chamber that he was one of the skeletal people just out of prison as seen in the video made by the Chadian National Commission of Inquiry.[18] He recounted that in 1990 he was a teacher in a provincial town in Chad. For reasons he said he did not know, DDS agents arrested him in front of his children, chained his arms and feet, and put him in a truck that drove to Iriba, a small town in Chad. Then, they transferred him to N'Djamena by plane with other prisoners. Taken to La piscine prison, he found himself in front of a DDS agent named Abakar Torbo. The DDS officer asked him why he was arrested. He did not know anything about it, he replied. The officer then asked him why he did not know anything. Obviously, he knew nothing about why he knew nothing. Locked in a cell, he was later removed for further questioning. He still did not know anything. He was locked up again.

He referred to the horrible living conditions in the cells, although he said that after his transfer to La gendarmerie prison, the conditions were better. He had only been freed after Hissein Habré had escaped in December 1990. He proudly noted that he had been filmed and all of Africa had been able to see his photo after his release.

Younous Mahadjir

In the same vein, Younous Mahadjir testified that he was arrested in 1990.[19] He was accused of committing acts that were detrimental to the Chadian Republic. He was suspected of having distributed leaflets hostile to the regime of Hissein Habré. He had indeed discussed it with a friend because they were concerned about the situation in Chad. But he had never seen these leaflets and had never distributed them. He knew only two people who had knowledge of the leafleting project. DDS agents wanted to learn more about his accomplices. He did not know anything else. DDS agents tortured him. They tied him up using the "arbatachar" binding method of torture, which was well presented in the Chadian National Commission's report.[20] This method involved tying a person's arms and feet behind his back, causing a sudden twisting of the chest and excruciating pain. They also put him through the ordeal of simulated drowning and he had choked. Afterward, they threw him into a cell, but extracted him several times for the same tortures. Detained after these acts of torture, he was not released until after the fall of Hissein Habré.

Lacoubou Mbaïnassoum

Lacoubou Mbaïnassoum had also been arrested in connection with the leaflet case.[21] He had typed up the contents of these leaflets. Tortured like Younous Mahadjir, he was only able to get out of prison after the fall of Hissein Habré.

Doungous Batil

As for Doungous Batil, he told the Assize Chamber that he had been arrested and taken to the Special Brigade for Rapid Intervention (BSIR).[22] The DDS agents accused him of having links with the Hajaraï rebellion and of recruiting for it. He said he had no connection with the rebels and knew nothing. He added, after questions from the defense lawyers, that they also accused him of fabricating *gris-gris*, fetishes that are attributed supernatural powers, for rebels to help them win their battles against Hissein Habré's regime.

The DDS agents promised to make him talk. They took him to the premises of the Chadian presidential palace. They interrogated him, chained him up, beat him on the head and hips, tortured him, and threw him into a gutter, presumably a place of detention within the presidential palace of the Republic of Chad.

A prosecutor asked Doungous Batil whether President Hissein Habré was there during his interrogation. President Hissein Habré was there, the victim answered firmly. Doungous Batil explained that there was a person dressed in a white boubou sitting a little higher. Fearful, he had not dared to look up at this person. He added that one of the torturers had told him that he was in front of Hissein Habré. Detained then in the regime's jails, Doungous Batil said that when the rebels entered N'Djamena during the fall of Hissein Habré, he could not flee because he was very weak. The fall, however, had set him free.

So, in Hissein Habré's Chad, agents of his regime arrested, detained people in deplorable conditions, and tortured them. As part of these reprehensible acts, some victims had also experienced sexual violence.

VICTIMS OF SEXUAL VIOLENCE

In the context of dictatorships and especially armed conflicts, acts of sexual violence are very often systematically committed. They are an expression of the sense of omnipotence and impunity of the perpetrators. They are used as instruments of terror and as weapons of war. When crimes committed during dictatorships and armed conflicts are brought before criminal courts, the issue of sexual violence cannot be avoided. Several women appearing before the Extraordinary African Assize Chamber reported sexual violence. Not without difficulty.

For example, Hawa Brahim had been transferred, like many other women, from a prison in N'Djamena to Ouadi-Doum, a locality in the Chadian desert.[23] This locality, occupied by Libya during the armed conflict, had been taken over by Habré's forces which had set up a military camp there.[24] When the president of the Extraordinary African Assize Chamber and the general prosecutor questioned Hawa Brahim about sexual violence in Ouadi-Doum, she was visibly embarrassed. She said she did not want to talk about it because there was television and children were watching.[25]

This attitude was understandable. Addressing sexual violence in the context of a trial is never easy. For this reason, closed sessions may be held to ensure the protection of victims. However, before the Extraordinary African Assize Chamber, some victims spoke publicly about sexual violence, usually in response to questions from judges, prosecutors, or lawyers.

This was the case for Haje Meremia Ali.[26] She testified that she was a merchant who often went to Libya to buy goods. She was arrested and tortured by agents of Habré's regime who suspected her of being in the pay of the Libyans for whom she had allegedly transported documents. As she refused to confess—she knew nothing anyway—the regime's agents tied her up, suspended her, beat her several times with a truncheon, electrocuted her, and detained her in Les locaux prison in N'Djamena before transferring her to Ouadi-Doum where, she noted, the women prisoners were literally used as sex slaves by the military.

Khadija Hassan Zidane, another victim of sexual violence, gave a striking testimony at the trial.[27] The facts she presented to the Extraordinary African Assize Chamber made her testimony appear to be one of the most intense moments in the trial of Hissein Habré.

In Arabic translated into French, Khadija Hassan Zidane presented herself as an Arab and a housewife and a victim of the repression of Hissein Habré's regime. She recounted that one day, Hissein Habré sent someone to get her. The messenger informed her that her brother, a professional pilot, had been arrested. He was in pain and she needed to see him. She followed the messenger who took her to the residence of Hissein Habré. There, she saw Libyans who had been arrested. She was ordered to serve them food. She did it for a fortnight.

Concerned that there was no clarification as to the date of the events she related, the president of the Assize Chamber put the question to her. She could not give an answer. She did not know when she experienced these events. She continued her testimony.

She was then tortured. The torturers wanted to know who freed the Libyans. There had likely been an escape of Libyan detainees. She did not know anything about it. Three months and 15 days later, she was released before being arrested again and tortured, notably by electrocution. She was asked about Libyans, but she knew nothing.

Khadija Hassan Zidane proposed to show the Assize Chamber judges, if they so wished, the traces that the acts of torture had left on her body. She was detained by DDS for a year before being transferred to Ouadi-Doum, where she continued to be detained. Members of her family, her mother and her little sister, had also been arrested. Her mother had been tortured.

Certainly because of the disjointed nature of Khadija Hassan Zidane's story, the president of the Assize Chamber sought clarification on what she had said, in order to ensure the consistency of her testimony. He wanted to know more about what happened to her. Replying to his question, Khadija Hassan Zidane explained that during one of her interrogations at the presidential palace, Hissein Habré was present. She had been questioned about the identity of those who had favored or played a role in the escape of the Libyans. She had suffered a lot of abuse. DDS officers had stuck a pipe in her mouth and turned on the water.

Suddenly, Khadija Hassan Zidane changed the course of the topic and talked about a woman who had been arrested and raped. Then she stopped the story and recalled that she was an old woman, and that an old woman could not talk about certain things. The president of the Assize Chamber wanted to know more about that story. He offered Khadija Hassan Zidane an *in camera* hearing to talk about these things. She refused, said she had nothing to hide. In a radical change of tone, she declared that she was ready to undress and revealed that her jailers raped her while she was in detention. Sometimes her jailers would come and take her out of her cell and rape her. At the time of her first arrest, she was taken to Hissein Habré, who raped her. The former president of the Republic of Chad had raped her four times, she said, referring to the accused, who was sitting a few feet away from her in the courtroom, as "the one who is there." A murmur of amazement seemed to pervade the courtroom. Khadija Hassan Zidane continued her testimony without really taking it into account.

She talked about the co-detainees and the transfer of several women, including herself, to Ouadi-Doum. In Ouadi-Doum, they looked after the soldiers, washed their clothes, and were often raped.

A prosecutor questioned her about the violence she suffered. Khadija Hassan Zidane went back to the rape of which she accused the former head of state. During the rape, she explained, she had tried to resist him without success. Hissein Habré stabbed her with a pen. She said that she was ashamed of what she was saying to the judges and that it was a humiliation to her. After a question about the scars left by the abuse she had suffered, the victim invited the prosecutor to come and see for himself the marks left by the pen used by Hissein Habré to stab her in her sexual area. The prosecutor replied that he relied on the president of the Assize Chamber to order action on the finding of the scars alleged by the victim.

The president of the Assize Chamber took back the floor without referring to the request of the prosecutor and was about to hand it over to the lawyers for the civil parties. He was interrupted by a defense lawyer who made a similar request. The defense lawyer stressed the need to establish in a closed session the scars of the victim in the face of the serious accusations against Hissein Habré, a former head of state. Another defense lawyer suggested that the findings be made by experts, because he personally would not be attending. The statements of the defense lawyers were translated to the victim. Very annoyed by the doubt that her account of the rape seemed to raise, she offered to undress in front of the Assize Chamber judges and the courtroom. She asserted firmly that she was not ashamed and she would undress. She would like everyone to see what she had been through. The president of the Assize Chamber took the floor and spoke quietly. He reserved the right to make a decision later to have an expert look at the scars of the victim, he then asked the lawyers of the civil parties to start their interrogation.

The lawyers for the civil parties wanted to know if the victim really knew Hissein Habré. Yes, she answered, she knew him. The lawyers for the civil parties questioned her about the rape allegedly committed by Hissein Habré and the fact that she had declared, during the investigation phase, that she would not talk about it and that she would wait until she was before the judges to do so. The victim explained her rapes, described the places and circumstances in which the rapes took place, went so far as to reveal details about the fourth rape, the clothes Hissein Habré wore during the rapes, the resistance she put up against him, the "liquid that came out" and that he made her swallow. After the rapes, Hissein Habré left her there, all alone. An agent of the regime of Hissein Habré used to pick her up and take her away. She had no water to use for washing herself after the rapes.

The defense lawyers then tried to question the credibility of the victim and the veracity of her accusations. She was asked questions about her date of birth, her age, and the date of her hearing before the Assize Chamber. The victim replied that she did not know, that she could not identify the years, but that she knew the facts she was reporting were 25 years old. The defense wanted to understand how she was able to know that the facts were 25 years old if she could not count the years, and why she testified that her little sister was 18 years old at the time of her arrest. The victim replied that her sister, unlike herself, had a birth certificate. Besides, everyone was talking about her sister's age.

The victim answered questions from the defense. But when asked about the rape allegedly committed by Hissein Habré, she expressed her dismay. Khadija Hassan Zidane no longer wished to repeat what she had already said about the rapes. She seemed overwhelmed by the repeated questions about these rapes. The defense insisted and went back to the details of the rapes. The victim finally responded and repeated her accusations. A defense lawyer asked her if she had consulted a psychiatrist. "No," she replied, she was not crazy and did not need to go to such a specialist. The defense lawyer continued, questioning the veracity of some of the information she reported. According to him, Saleh Younouss and Mahamat Djibrine, two DDS officials, had not worked in the DDS at the same time. The victim accused them both of being responsible for her arrest. "How was that possible?" he asked.

The defense lawyer called Khadija Hassan Zidane a liar, provoking an intervention by the president of the Assize Chamber who asked him to respect the victim. The defense lawyer responded and asked the president of the Assize Chamber to respect the accused as well. The president of the Assize Chamber strongly urged him to sit down. The defense lawyer refused. The president of the Assize Chamber insisted. The defense lawyer did not want to sit down, but at the insistence of two other defense lawyers, he ended up sitting down. The president of the Assize Chamber suspended the hearing.

Sometime later, on the resumption of the hearing, another defense lawyer asked questions. He wanted to know whether the victim had been heard elsewhere by other judicial authorities before the trial. The victim said she had been heard before. However, she repeated tirelessly that during the past hearings, she had deliberately omitted addressing certain facts, including rapes, which she had promised not to reveal until she confronted Hissein Habré. The lawyer tried to demonstrate through his questions that the victim had not told the whole truth before the other judicial authorities who had heard her. He insisted and noted that it was at the insistence of the president of the Extraordinary African Assize Chamber that she had decided to address the rapes she allegedly suffered. In particular, he wished to know more about the victim's position during the rape. After that question, Khadija Hassan Zidane got very angry. Suddenly, she got up, bent down, and put her hands on the table in front of her, turning her back to the lawyer. She looked defiantly at the lawyer and asked him loudly what more he wanted. She was tired of recounting the details of that rape. The president of the Assize Chamber intervened and told her that it was normal for her to be asked questions and that she should not get upset because all the parties in the trial are playing their part. She said she did not like to talk about all these details. The lawyer then indicated that she had stated that in the room in which she had been raped there were only three chairs. She had just said that there were three chairs and a table. The victim confirmed that there were three chairs and a table.

After further questions from the defense lawyer, the president of the Assize Chamber returned to the medical examination of the victim proposed by the prosecutors and the defense. He indicated that the Assize Chamber could not examine the scars left by the alleged rape because it did not have the competence to do so. According to the Assize Chamber, the evidence provided by the hearings and testimonies was sufficient and would allow the truth to be uncovered.

The testimony of Khadija Hassan Zidane was an illustration of the problems posed by the issue of sexual violence in the context of a hearing, of the difficulty for some women victims to talk about it, of the trauma they experienced when they decided to share their experience and discuss the details, the willingness of those involved in the trial to always know a little more in order to judge their credibility as well as the veracity of the facts reported, and the incomprehension of the victims, who could seem to be disconcerted and outraged that their allegations could be questioned. However, in the context of international criminal justice, the accusation against a former head of state for committing rape during his presidency was not common. This testimony was undoubtedly a key moment, and the tensions it has generated demonstrate this.

Other crimes, equally serious, fueled the hearings and debates in the trial of Hissein Habré. Over the course of more than three months of trial proceedings, victims and survivors seemed similar. The same horrors were recounted: arrest, torture, dispossession of property, distress of persons, summary executions, and so on. Several horrible acts of torture were reported: a car exhaust pipe put into a person's mouth, the car was then started and the accelerator was pressed down;[28] a person being tied up using the arbatachar binding method and whose bones cracked;[29] people thrown alive into barrels of boiling water;[30] and a soldier whose 10 fingernails were methodically torn out of his hands with pliers.[31] In the morbid silence of Courtroom No. 4 of the Palais de Justice in Dakar, listening was like hearing the screams of the torture victims. Thus, it was now certain that serious crimes were committed in Chad under the regime of Hissein Habré. And so was the fact that these crimes had consequences and sequels.

NOTES

1. EAC, Hearing of Clément Dokhot Abaifouta, November 9, 2015, https://www.youtube.com/watch?v=kuqNGt7RyWc, accessed 5/16/2021. EAC, Transcripts, November 9, 2015.
2. EAC, Hearing of Facho Balaam, September 10, 2015, Online Playlist of the *Forum interactif sur les CAE*. EAC, Transcripts, September 10, 2015.
3. Zakaria Fadoul Kitir, *Les moments difficiles dans les prisons d'Hissène Habré en 1989* (Editions Sépia, 1998).
4. See the section "Internal Repression from a Historical Perspective" (chapter 5).
5. EAC, Hearings of Zakaria Fadoul Kitir, September 30, 2015, and October 1, 2015, Online Playlist of the *Forum interactif sur les CAE*. EAC, Transcripts, September 30, 2015, and October 1, 2015.
6. EAC, Ordonnance de renvoi, 2015, 30-31.
7. Tchad, Rapport de la commission nationale d'enquête du ministère tchadien de la justice, *Les crimes et les détournements de l'ex-président Habré et de ses complices* (Paris: L'Harmattan, 1993), 43.
8. EAC, Hearing of Abdourahmane Gueye, November 23, 2015, Online Playlist of the *Forum interactif sur les CAE*. EAC Transcripts, November 23, 2015.

9. EAC, Hearing of Ngarba Akhaye, September 28, 2015, Online Playlist of the *Forum interactif sur les CAE.* EAC, Transcripts, September 28, 2015.

10. EAC, Hearing of Madina Fadoul Kitir, October 12, 2015, and October 13, 2015, Online Playlist of the *Forum interactif sur les CAE.* EAC Transcripts, October 12, 2015, and October 13, 2015.

11. EAC, Hearing of Marabi Toudjibedjé, September 30, 2015, Online Playlist of the *Forum interactif sur les CAE.* EAC, Transcripts, September 30, 2015.

12. EAC, Hearing of Hawa Brahim, October 21, 2015. EAC, Hearing of Khadija Hassan Zidane, October 20, 2015, Online Playlist of the *Forum interactif sur les CAE.* EAC Transcripts, October 21, 2015, and October 20, 2015.

13. Souleymane Guengueng, *Prisonnier de Hissene Habré. L'expérience d'un survivant des geôles tchadiennes et sa quête de justice* (Paris: L'Harmattan, 2012).

14. EAC, Hearing of Souleymane Guengueng, November 18 and 19, 2015, Online Playlist of the *Forum interactif sur les CAE.* EAC, Transcripts, November 18 and 19, 2015.

15. EAC, Hearing of Zakaria Fadoul Kitir, September 30, 2015, Online Playlist of the *Forum interactif sur les CAE.* EAC Transcripts, September 30, 2015.

16. Former president of Chad and brother-in-arms of Hissein Habré, who had become his opponent, See chapter 1 of the book.

17. EAC, Hearing of Fatimé Hachim Saleh, October 13 and 14, 2015, Online Playlist of the *Forum interactif sur les CAE.* EAC, Transcripts, October 13 and 14, 2015.

18. EAC, Hearing of Abakar Adoum, October 19, 2015, Online Playlist of the *Forum interactif sur les CAE.* EAC Transcripts, October 19, 2015.

19. EAC, Hearing of Younous Mahadjir, November 16, 2015, Online Playlist of the *Forum interactif sur les CAE.* EAC Transcripts, November 16, 2015.

20. Rapport de la commission nationale d'enquête du ministère tchadien de la justice, op. cit., note 7, 112.

21. EAC, Hearing of Lakoubou Mbainassen, November 17, 2015, Online Playlist of the *Forum interactif sur les CAE.* EAC, Transcripts, November 17, 2015.

22. EAC, Hearing of Doungous Batil, October 5, 2015, Online Playlist of the *Forum interactif sur les CAE.* EAC, Transcripts, October 5, 2015.

23. EAC, Hearing of Hawa Brahim, October 21, 2015, Online Playlist of the *Forum interactif sur les CAE.* EAC, Transcripts, October 21, 2015.

24. Mario J. Azevedo, *The Roots of Violence: A History of War in Chad* (London-New York: Routledge, 2005) 89.

25. EAC, Hearing of Hawa Brahim, op. cit., note 23.

26. EAC, Hearings of Hadjé Mérami Ali, October 21 and 22, 2015, Online Playlist of the *Forum interactif sur les CAE.* EAC, Transcripts, October 21 and 22, 2015.

27. EAC, Hearing of Khadija Hassan Zidane, October 19 and 20, 2015, Online Playlist of the *Forum interactif sur les CAE.* EAC, Transcripts, October 19 and 20, 2015.

28. EAC, Hearing of Brahim Tassi, October 13, 2015, Online Playlist of the *Forum interactif sur les CAE.* EAC, Transcripts, October 13, 2015.

29. EAC, Hearing of Mahamat Nour Dadji, September 29, 2015, Online Playlist of the *Forum interactif sur les CAE*. EAC, Transcripts, September 29, 2015.

30. EAC, Hearing of Brahim Tassi, October 13, 2015, Online Playlist of the *Forum interactif sur les CAE*. EAC, Transcripts, October 13, 2015.

31. EAC, Hearing of Mahamat Nour Dadji, op. cit., note 29.

Chapter 8

Consequences and Sequels of Crimes

DIRECT VICTIMS

Serious crimes have the particularity that they have equally serious consequences for the direct victims, for those who have individually suffered crimes. Obviously, a significant number of victims lost their lives during the repression of Hissein Habré's regime. Patrick Ball, an American statistician who had worked for several international criminal tribunals and truth commissions, was designated by the EAC to conduct a statistical analysis on the mortality rate in Chadian prisons during the regime of Hissein Habré. He testified before the Assize Chamber after the submission of his report to the tribunal.[1] He explained to a visibly stunned Assize Chamber that between 1985 and 1988, the mortality rate in detention centers in Chad was extremely high, compared to the mortality rate of American soldiers in Japanese detention centers and the mortality rate of German soldiers at the hands of Soviet soldiers during the Second World War. In the same vein, the Chadian National Commission of Inquiry set up after the fall of Hissein Habré had noted in its report that 40,000 people had been victims of the Habré regime crimes.[2] Although the defense lawyers challenged the Chadian Commission of Inquiry's conclusion that 40,000 people had died because of the repression, the former chairman of the commission, Mahamat Hassan Abakar, testified that this number was only an estimate, a minimum figure based on the commission's findings mainly in capital city of N'Djamena, which had several jails.[3] The number of victims who died was probably, in his view, much higher than 40,000.[4]

Many other victims survived the crimes. They rarely came out of it unscathed. Most of the direct victims who testified before the Extraordinary African Assize Chamber reported physical or mental sequela.

To cite just a few examples, Clément Abaifouta stated that he was prone to memory lapses and general fatigue and had become insensitive to death and was unable to cry when his father and mother died.[5] Souleymane Guengueng's eyesight was permanently affected after he was exposed to light 24 hours a day in a cell.[6] Since he had been beaten and tortured, Doungous Batil had not been able to get rid of pain in his testicles.[7] Djété Kourtou Gamar, who had testified that Habré's agents had attempted to execute him, was disabled for life; his leg had been torn apart by bullets and had to be amputated to save him.[8] Some of the aftereffects of the survivors of Habré's regime were presented to the Assize Chamber by a health professional who treated them.

Hélène Jaffé, a doctor of French nationality, had treated several people alleging to have been victims of torture in Chad. During her testimony, she sometimes acted as a spokesperson for the victims, reported on what they had said and presented the physical and mental aftereffects of torture.[9] Speaking in a quiet and soft voice, she seemed to be holding the courtroom public's hand and leading them into the room where she met with victims.

The courtroom could imagine her sitting, listening, consulting, examining, prescribing treatment, and trying to comfort the torture survivors. A victim explained that he was tied up using "arbatachar" binding. The agents of the Habré regime who had tied him up had abandoned him in this atrocious position. It was the hour of the breaking of the Ramadan fast, and they had left. Found the next day, the man had gangrene in his arms, a condition that left doctors with no choice but to amputate both arms to save him. Another patient recounted being arrested, placed in a cell, tied up, and tortured with electric wires that the DDS agents had placed on his nipples and genitals. The man had discharged urine and stool. These torture victims told Hélène Jaffé their stories one after the other, each one sharing their own individual and particular experience of torture.

In her testimony before the Assize Chamber, Hélène Jaffé presented the aftereffects of the abuses suffered: traces of fractures and burn marks; scared abrasions left on skin from being whiplashed; and burn marks on ankles and wrists where victims had been tied during torture. There were also broken jaws and cheekbones and faces deformed after being shot; shoulders that had been demolished or torn off; hands that were no longer usable; dizziness that appeared suddenly; and depression that caused victims to scream at night and who could no longer look at themselves in the mirror because they were horrified by a body that reminded them of those terrible moments.

The testimony of Hélène Jaffé was a litany of horrors.

Hélène Jaffé asked her patients what she could do for them. Many said they wanted to sleep. Because, explained the doctor, sleeping when you have been tortured is difficult. The tortured person is afraid to sleep because sleep is a place of despair and pain, filled with traumatic nightmares, scary images, and fears of seeing the past reappear. Several victims also wanted relief from the pain that, since the acts of torture they had suffered, had settled in various parts of their bodies without anything being able to dislodge it. Sleep and no more pain, this was summarized in a few words what most of the survivors wished for when they were examined by Dr. Hélène Jaffé.

During the interrogation phase of the Hélène Jaffé hearing, the lawyers for the civil parties and the prosecutors asked questions insisting on the practice of torture by Habré's regime. The defense lawyers attacked the credibility of the doctor's testimony and, in particular, sought to show that she had not herself experienced the facts reported by her patients. Hélène Jaffé sometimes lost her composure, seeming to wonder how anyone could doubt her. She had seen those abuses on those damaged bodies. She had been able to read the pain in the eyes of the survivors of these abject crimes, which had also produced, as part of an inevitable causal link, indirect victims.

INDIRECT VICTIMS

International crimes committed on a large scale have the peculiarity of producing innumerable indirect victims, people who are indirectly affected by the repression because they are close to the persons being targeted. For example, Fatime Toumle, Zenaba Bassou Ngolo, and Mariam Hassan Bagueri each told the Assize Chamber about the disappearance and probable death of their husbands who belonged to the Hajaraï ethnic group.[10]

Satta Gaye, the sister of Demba Gaye, who was arrested by Habré's regime at the same time as the Senegalese Abdourahmane Gueye was arrested, testified about the difficulties she encountered when she sought to obtain a death certificate for her brother who died on the premises of the DDS.[11]

Mahamat Nour Dadji—the son of a former high-ranking official of the Habré's regime, Ahmat Dadji, director of Chad's national sugar company, and a member of the Hajaraï ethnic group—testified about the effects his father's arrest had on his family in 1987.[12] DDS agents had entered the family home and said to his father: "The President needs you." His father had followed them. Later, he and some members of his family were arrested several times and questioned by the DDS about his father's activities: What were his activities? Where did he hide the weapons? He did not have an answer. He had met his father at the BSIR, seated and now a prisoner of the regime he had served. Mahamat Nour Dadji had been released after a short detention. His father had not. The family home had been looted by DDS agents and his entire family had been driven out. He and his family had taken refuge in another house belonging to his father. They had also been expelled from it, and they were now destitute and unable to have three meals a day as before.

Mahamat Nour Dadji spoke, his throat tight with emotion, of his mother being forced to live without resources. He seemed to address the judges and the public when he asked them to imagine the situation. His mother often cried, he added. He had tried to find his father, had solicited agents of the state and the president of the Republic of Chad. Unsuccessfully, he could not explain the sudden enmity between Hissein Habré and his father. Both had been students in Paris. His father had worked abroad for his country. He had held positions within the regime of Hissein Habré. Mahamat Nour Dadji knew children of Hissein Habré and attended the same school as them.

During the interrogation phase of the hearing of Mahamat Nour Dadji, the prosecutors pointed out that Hissein Habré's regime arrested people suspected of rebellion while systematically extending the repression to their relatives, considered ipso facto as supporters of the rebellion or holders of information.

In the same vein, Mahamat Hassan Abakar, the former chairman of the National Commission of Inquiry, also spoke of indirect victims, of many children and women, excluded from family homes, becoming collateral victims of the arrest of a father suspected of opposition to the regime.[13] The Commission of Inquiry he led had reported that there were more than 80,000 orphans and 30,000 widows in Chad as a consequence of the Habré regime's repression.[14]

Chad had thus experienced a human tragedy and serious crimes under the regime of Hissein Habré. But, at the end of this tragic suffering that had been reported in great detail, at the end of the aftereffects and consequences being endured by the victims, it was the criminal responsibility of Hissein Habré that must be established. Was Hissein Habré, the former head of state of Chad, who was impassively attending his trial and keeping his head and face partly concealed under a white turban and sunglasses, criminally responsible for international crimes?

NOTES

1. EAC, Hearing of Patrick Ball, September 18, 2015, Online Playlist of the *Forum interactif sur les CAE*. EAC, Transcripts, September 18, 2015.
2. Tchad, Rapport de la commission nationale d'enquête du ministère tchadien de la justice, *Les crimes et les détournements de l'ex-président Habré et de ses complices* (Paris: L'Harmattan, 1993), 97.
3. EAC, Hearing of Mahamat Hassan Abakar, September 16, 2015, Online Playlist of the *Forum interactif sur les CAE*. EAC, Transcripts, September 16, 2015.
4. Ibid.

5. EAC, Hearing of Clément Dokhot Abaifouta, November 9, 2015, Online Playlist of the *Forum interactif sur les CAE.* EAC, Transcripts, November 9, 2015.

6. EAC, Hearing of Souleymane Guengueng, November 18, 2015, Online Playlist of the *Forum interactif sur les CAE.* EAC, Transcripts, November 18, 2015.

7. EAC, Hearing of Doungous Batil, October 5, 2015, Online Playlist of the *Forum interactif sur les CAE.* EAC, Transcripts, October 5, 2015.

8. EAC, Hearing of Djété Kourtou Gamar, October 6, 2015, Online Playlist of the *Forum interactif sur les CAE.* EAC, Transcripts, October 6, 2015.

9. EAC, Hearing of Hélène Jaffé, October 12, 2015, Online Playlist of the *Forum interactif sur les CAE.* EAC, Transcripts, October 12, 2015.

10. EAC, Hearing of Fatime Toumle, October 5, 2015, Online Playlist of the *Forum interactif sur les CAE.* EAC, Transcripts, October 5, 2015. EAC, Hearing of Mariam Hassan Bagueri, October 29, 2015, Online Playlist of the *Forum interactif sur les CAE.* EAC, Transcripts, October 29, 2015. EAC, Hearings of Zenaba Bassou Ngolo and Service Brahim, October 6, 2015, Online Playlist of the *Forum interactif sur les CAE.*

11. EAC, Hearing of Satta Gaye, November 23, 2015, as cited by *Ministère public v. Hissein Habré*, Judgment, May 30, 2016, para. 867.

12. EAC, Hearing of Mahamat Nour Dadji, September 29, 2015, Online Playlist of the *Forum interactif sur les CAE.* EAC, Transcripts, September 29, 2015.

13. EAC, Hearing of Mahamat Hassan Abakar, September 15, 2015, Online Playlist of the *Forum interactif sur les CAE.* EAC, Transcripts, September 15, 2015.

14. Rapport de la commission nationale d'enquête du ministère tchadien de la justice, op. cit., note 2, 97.

Chapter 9

Was Hissein Habré Criminally Responsible?

During the trial, several witnesses and victims named Hissein Habré as the person responsible for the crimes committed, the most significant of these accusations coming, for example, from Khadija Hassan Zidane, who accused the former president of having raped her, and from Doungous Batil, who testified that the president was present when he was interrogated and tortured.[1] The testimony of Bandjim Bandoum, the repentant who presented Hissein Habré as the real leader of the DDS, was in line with this logic, as was the testimony of those who claimed that Hissein Habré visited the DDS.[2] If, over and above the individual responsibility thus alleged in the testimonies, one added the accusations against Habré's regime, its military and its repressive organs established that through the testimonies and the documents collected during the investigating phase, one could wonder whether the former head of state might not have been aware of what was happening in his country, especially since witnesses had pointed out that he knew.

Michael Dottridge, a British national and former Amnesty International staff member researching violations of civil and political rights in Central Africa—and therefore in Chad—testified that during the Habré regime, thousands of cards and letters had been sent to the Chadian authorities by Amnesty International, expressing concern about the situation of political prisoners in Chad.[3] These cards and letters were later found in the DDS archives. Hissein Habré's regime failed to respond to Amnesty International's calls for the release of prisoners or the end to torture. Invited to react by the general prosecutor after the broadcast of an audio document in which Hissein Habré was heard denying the accusations of human rights violations made by Amnesty International, "Mike" Dottridge explained to the Assize Chamber that he could only conclude that the Chadian president was aware of the cards and letters sent by Amnesty International. In others words, the former president knew that serious human rights violations were being committed in Chad.

Professor at the University of San Francisco and former member of Human Rights Watch, Olivier Bercault, who testified before the Extraordinary African Assize Chamber, went in the same direction.[4] In collaboration with Reed Brody, he wrote a voluminous book of more than 700 pages, a work entitled *La plaine des morts* (The Plain of the Dead) in reference to the name given to a wasteland in the suburbs of N'Djamena where the victims of Habré's regime were allegedly secretly and summarily buried for years.[5] In this document, serious crimes committed in Chad under Habré's regime were reported, testimonies of individuals and victims were presented, and Hissein Habré's personal involvement in the commission of the crimes was highlighted.

In the same vein, the former president of the National Commission of Inquiry presented, inter alia, the report which, after the fall of Hissein Habré, had concluded that the latter was personally responsible for the crimes committed under his regime.[6] Daniel Fransen, the Belgian investigating judge who had investigated the case of Hissein Habré, told the Assize Chamber that the incriminating and exculpatory evidence collected had led to the conclusion that Hissein Habré could be tried for the crimes alleged by the Chadian plaintiffs.[7] In his view, the body of evidence incriminating Hissein Habré was voluminous and important.

It was clear from the record of the testimonies that they were rather damning for the former Chadian president. However, the inconsistencies and contradictions sometimes noted by the defense lawyers, including differences between the statements made by the victims during the investigation phase and those made before the Assize Chamber could not be overlooked. The defense sought to question the objectivity of NGOs defending the victims of Hissein Habré's regime, considering that they were the visible element of a cabal carried out against Hissein Habré in the name of Western and foreign governments that may have infiltrated them.

Therefore, based on the documents and the testimonies collected, the judges of the Assize Chamber had to establish the judicial truth, the guilt, or the innocence of the accused. But before that, the parties to the trial still had to present their closing arguments in order to guide the judges in establishing the truth. On the basis of the hearings and other documents, the presentation of the closing arguments of the prosecutors, of the lawyers for the civil parties, and of the defense lawyers started in February 2016.[8]

THE PROSECUTION'S CASE: BEYOND THE TESTIMONY, OVERWHELMING EVIDENCE AGAINST HISSEIN HABRÉ

Prosecutors of the EAC delivered closing arguments of relentless severity.[9] Referring to the history of Chad and the repression that this state experienced under the presidency of Hissein Habré, they insisted that the accused was criminally responsible for crimes of torture, crimes against humanity, and war crimes. They considered that he must be individually and directly responsible for these crimes, responsible as an accomplice, as a participant in a joint criminal enterprise, and as a superior.

For the prosecutors, Hissein Habré was individually and directly responsible for having participated and contributed to the commission of the crime of torture against Khadija Hassan Zidane, the victim alleging that she was raped four times by the former head of state. For these same facts, the prosecutors considered that Hissein Habré must be found guilty of crimes against humanity. He must be convicted of war crimes and for failure to act under the rules of international humanitarian law. Prosecutors referred in particular to the ill-treatment of POWs in Chadian armed conflicts and the failure to implement the procedures provided for in international law. Hissein Habré, warlord, head of state and army, did not protect these prisoners. Prosecutors noted in particular a written message attributed to Hissein Habré. The author of the message ordered that no prisoner of war should leave prison except in the event of death. He pointed to the responsibility of the International Committee of the Red Cross (ICRC) for the escape of POWs and did not want this type of situation to happen again. The prosecutors recalled that the expert Tobin Tanaka, a forensic document examiner commissioned by the EAC to analyze handwritten documents, had attributed to the same person this written instruction and other documents deemed to have been written by Hissein Habré. Therefore, for the prosecution, Hissein Habré knew the situation which the POWs were in and had simply failed to act.

Prosecutors demonstrated that, by virtue of developments in international criminal law, Hissein Habré participated jointly in the commission of crimes. Prosecutors referred to this as a joint criminal enterprise. Under this mode of criminal responsibility developed by the ICTY, a person can be held responsible for a crime even if he or she did not directly participate in it, the important element here being the carrying out of a common criminal act by several persons, including the accused.[10] According to the prosecutors, Hissein Habré and his collaborators participated in such an enterprise and intentionally committed crimes of torture and crimes against humanity. Reviewing the testimony of several witnesses, they pointed out that Hissein Habré participated in this joint criminal enterprise by setting up a repressive system, creating secret prisons, and giving orders of arrest, interrogation, execution, or release to his subordinates.

According to the prosecutors, Hissein Habré must be found guilty of complicity in the commission of the crimes because he incited and encouraged their perpetration by, inter alia, establishing a cult of his personality and engaging in inflammatory rhetoric against his enemies while knowing that such rhetoric could have effects in the context of repression. His presence and words on the battlefield also encouraged the commission of war crimes against POWs. The gifts offered to members of the regime's secret police after dispossessing its enemies encouraged the commission of crimes against humanity.

The criminal responsibility of Hissein Habré as a superior was also defended by the prosecutors. Taking up the many developments in international criminal law since the Nuremberg Trials, prosecutors stated that war crimes, such as the execution of POWs committed by the Chadian army, must be attributed to Hissein Habré who was the chief and commander of his troops. Hissein Habré had effective control over his troops. He knew that elements under his command were committing crimes and did not punish them. In the same vein, Hissein Habré was responsible, as a superior, for crimes against humanity. Reiterating the numerous massacres, summary executions, kidnappings, and disappearances reported by victims, the prosecutors demonstrated that there was a common element of subordination between the bodies of repression on the one hand and the presidency of the Republic of Chad and Hissein Habré on the other. Hissein Habré had knowledge of these crimes. He knew and did nothing to stop them.

At the end of the closing arguments, the general prosecutor asked the Assize Chamber to sentence Hissein Habré to life imprisonment and to confiscate his property and objects that had been seized during the proceedings.

THE PLEADING OF THE LAWYERS FOR THE CIVIL PARTIES: HISSEIN HABRÉ, GUILTY OF CRIMES ACCORDING TO THE VICTIMS

Like the prosecutors, the two groups of civil parties' lawyers representing the victims pleaded for Hissein Habré to be found criminally responsible.[11] The first group of lawyers, defending the interests of Clément Abaifouta et al. insisted on Hissein Habré's direct participation in the crimes. These lawyers explained that Hissein Habré had set up a repressive system that had the goal of getting all the enemies of the regime out of the way. The commission of the crimes was part of that goal. Hissein Habré had given orders to commit crimes and had himself committed the crime of rape, torture, and sexual violence against Khadija Hassan Zidane. The lawyers also pointed out, as the prosecution, Hissein Habré's involvement in a joint criminal enterprise and dwelt on the assistance and encouragement he provided in the commission of the crimes. Finally, they pointed to the criminal responsibility of Hissein Habré as a superior exercising effective control over the actors of repression while being aware of the crimes committed and refraining from punishing the perpetrators.

The second group of civil party lawyers representing the organizations RADHT and AVCRP insisted on the criminal responsibility of Hissein Habré in the framework of a joint criminal enterprise, recalling the repressive bodies created by Hissein Habré, and noting his effective control over them. These lawyers also underlined the responsibility of Hissein Habré in the commission of war crimes.

All in all, the lawyers for the civil parties agreed on the need to find Hissein Habré guilty of crimes against humanity, war crimes, and torture.

THE PLEADING OF THE DEFENSE LAWYERS: HISSEIN HABRÉ, DEFENDER OF HIS COUNTRY AND AN INNOCENT MAN

The defense lawyers' closing arguments were eagerly awaited. Because they were particularly formidable during the hearings of victims and witnesses, there were questions about how they would defend the accused Hissein Habré, establish contradictions, and perhaps reveal a truth different from the one claimed for years by the victims. The lines of defense of Hissein Habré's lawyers revolved around a few essential points: on the one hand, the particular context in which Hissein Habré led his country and the efforts he made in a difficult situation; on the other hand, the illegitimate nature of the trial and the lack of evidence to conclude that Hissein Habré was responsible of crimes.[12]

With regard to the context in which Hissein Habré led Chad, the defense lawyers presented some elements on the history of Chad before Hissein Habré came to power through a coup d'état, a situation which, in their view, was no exception in Africa during that period. They recalled that the regime of Hissein Habré had been recognized as a legitimate one by the United Nations and the Organization of African Unity (now the African Union). After coming to power, Hissein Habré had been confronted with Libya's expansionist ambitions to destabilize his country by attacking it and supporting opponents of his regime. Hissein Habré had militarily defended his country while pursuing a policy of national reconciliation. He had worked to pacify Chad, which was plagued by many internal divisions. Chadians, under the influence of foreign powers, had wanted to overthrow the regime of Hissein Habré, who had defeated the Libyan invader and safeguarded the territorial integrity of Chad.

The defense lawyers explained and justified certain acts committed under Hissein Habré's regime. The arrests of certain individuals were necessitated by the context. These persons were carrying out activities that could undermine Chadian state security. The defense lawyers pointed to the fact that not all Chadians belonging to the allegedly repressed ethnic groups had been systematically arrested. Some members of these ethnic groups had continued to occupy their positions in the Chadian state apparatus without being disturbed. In the same vein, the defense lawyers noted that the detention of persons was a common practice in all countries of the world and that Chad was no exception. With regard to the conditions of detention of persons in Chad, they explained that the general situation of the majority of the Chadian population was difficult in view of the country's economic problems. One could therefore not expect more favorable treatment of prisoners in such a country.

The illegitimacy of the trial and the lack of evidence were also noted. In a veritable diatribe, the defense lawyers argued that the trial of Hissein Habré actually had a political objective. The trial was taking place only because Idriss Déby Itno, the then president of Chad, wanted to definitively keep Hissein Habré away from the conquest of power. They cited as proof the fact that Hissein Habré was the only person on trial while the alleged perpetrators of the crimes allegedly committed were not being tried by the Extraordinary African Assize Chamber. They added that the testimonies of the victims were not acceptable evidence. These alleged victims were supported and coached by organizations such as Human Rights Watch. Against the idea that crimes against humanity were committed in Chad, the defense lawyers insisted that there was no evidence of a widespread or systematic attack in Chad. They systematically questioned the credibility of victims and witnesses and went back over the many errors noted in the minutes of their hearings during the investigation. They highlighted the contradictions established during their hearings before the Extraordinary African Assize Chamber.

They considered that Hissein Habré was not aware of everything that was happening in his country. The DDS, the body considered to be the central element of the repression he allegedly carried out, was, they recalled, legally placed under the authority of the Chadian Ministry of the Interior. For them, Hissein Habré could not be held responsible for what was happening at the DDS, as this body was under the supervision of the Ministry of the Interior. Acts of torture at the DDS were only alleged and the consequences of these alleged methods of torture could never be proven. Even if acts of torture had been committed at the DDS, DDS agents were responsible for them. Not

Hissein Habré. The discovery at the DDS of thousands of letters and cards sent by Amnesty International, which was concerned about the disappearance of people and human rights violations, was, according to them, proof that Hissein Habré was unaware of what was happening in the DDS. These letters would have been discovered in the archives of the presidency of the Chadian Republic if the former president knew what was happening.

With regard to the war crimes allegedly committed, the defense lawyers considered that the deaths recorded could only have been the consequence of the armed fighting. The report of the Chadian National Commission of Inquiry was also being questioned. The defense lawyers raised the lack of neutrality of the members of this commission of inquiry appointed by new Chadian authorities after the fall of Hissein Habré.

In conclusion, the defense lawyers rejected any criminal responsibility of Hissein Habré, whether envisaged directly, as part of the joint criminal enterprise, or as a superior. Logically, they called for the acquittal of Hissein Habré for crimes against humanity, war crimes, and torture in the upcoming judgment.

NOTES

1. EAC, Hearing of Khadija Hassan Zidane, October 20, 2015, Online Playlist of the *Forum interactif sur les CAE.* EAC Transcripts, October 20 and 21, 2015; EAC, Hearing of Doungous Batil, October 5, 2015, Online Playlist of the *Forum interactif sur les CAE.* EAC, Transcripts, October 5, 2015.

2. EAC, Hearing of Bandjim Bandoum, September 22 and 23, 2015, Online Playlist of the *Forum interactif sur les CAE.* EAC, Transcripts, September 22 and 23, 2015.

3. EAC, Hearing of Mike Dottridge, September 14, 2015, Online Playlist of the *Forum interactif sur les CAE.* EAC, Transcripts, September 14, 2015.

4. EAC, Hearing of Olivier Bercault, September 21, 2015, quoted by EAC, *Ministère public v. Hissein Habré*, Judgment, May 30, 2016, para. 233.

5. Olivier Bercault (Écrit en collaboration avec Reed Brody), *La Plaine des Morts. Le Tchad de Hissène Habré 1982-1990* (Black Print Cpi Ibérica, Human Rights Watch), 2013.

6. EAC, Hearing of Mahamat Hassan Abakar, September 15, 2015, Online Playlist of the *Forum interactif sur les CAE.* EAC, Transcripts, September 15, 2015.

7. EAC, Hearing of Daniel Fransen, September 17, 2015, Online Playlist of the *Forum interactif sur les CAE.* EAC, Transcripts, September 17, 2015.

8. The documents on the closing arguments of prosecutors, lawyers for the civil parties, and defense lawyers were available online: http://forumchambresafricaines.org/actes-judiciaires-cae/, accessed 9/30/2018. The most part of the recordings and videos of these closing arguments are available on the Online Playlist of the *Forum interactif sur les CAE.* Another video of the closing arguments of a defense lawyer

is available online: https://www.youtube.com/watch?v=VCaQ6zEIXoY, accessed 5/16/2021.

9. Réquisitoire du parquet, February 10, 2016, Online Playlist of the *Forum interactif sur les CAE. Réquisitions finales devant la chambre africaine extraordinaire d'assises*, January 2016, http://forumchambresafricaines.org/actes-judiciaires-cae/, accessed 9/30/2018.

10. See, for example, ICTY, *The Prosecutor v. Mitar Vasiljevié*, no. fT-98-32-A, February 25, 2004, paras. 87–111.

11. For the videos of their final arguments, Online Playlist of the *Forum interactif sur les CAE*. Also see *Conclusions pour: les victimes regroupées au sein de deux associations que sont RADHT et ACVRP*, January 2016, and *Conclusions finales. Déposé par: avocats des parties civiles (Clément Abaifouta et al.)*, January 2016. http://forumchambresafricaines.org/actes-judiciaires-cae/, accessed 9/30/2018.

12. Recordings and videos of the EAC, Procès Hissein Habré - Plaidoirie de la Défense - Me Mounir Ballal, February 11, 2016, Online Playlist of the *Forum interactif sur les CAE*. See also, Procès Hissein Habré - Plaidoirie de la Défense - Me Mbaye SENE, February 11, 2016), https://www.youtube.com/watch?v=VCaQ6zEIXoY, accessed 5/16/2021.

Chapter 10

The Judgment

On May 30, 2016, Courtroom No. 4 of the Dakar Palais de justice was lively, unlike on some days when, as the monotony set in as the trial unfolded, it seemed weary and almost empty.[1] That day, the judges of the Extraordinary African Assize Chamber, who had been deliberating the Habré case since the end of the closing arguments in February 2016, were set to deliver their verdict.

Many in the courtroom, the victims, and the organizations that supported them certainly hoped that Hissein Habré was about to be sentenced to life imprisonment, in accordance with the prosecutors' final arguments. With a smile poorly masking relief and the taste of having finally had their revenge against a man whom they felt was responsible for having shattered their lives forever, the victims relied on the judges of the Assize Chamber to restore their dignity.

Hissein Habré's supporters, some of them seated in part of the courtroom and massed behind the former president, who remained imperturbable in his seat, wanted to believe in his acquittal. For them, the former head of state was innocent. They certainly anticipated an unconditional release of their champion. For them, the trial was just a farce orchestrated by the West against Hissein Habré, an anti-imperialist, freedom-fighting Africanist who disturbed the West and its henchmen.[2]

The press, both national and international, were also in the courtroom, as were many curious people and personalities who did not want to miss this event in African criminal history.

THE CONVICTION OF HISSEIN HABRÉ

The judges of the Extraordinary African Assize Chamber entered the courtroom. Its president, Gustave Kam, sat in his big chair. He looked both serious and good-natured, a particular characteristic of his attitude throughout the trial. He announced that he would read a summary of the decision of the Assize Chamber.[3] The full written judgment was made available to the public on July 31, 2016.[4]

The president of the Assize Chamber began by recalling very briefly the procedure in the Habré case before the Chamber. He thanked those who had participated in the implementation of the procedure. These introductory remarks were followed by a development on the case. He summarized the investigation phase and the referral of Hissein Habré to the Assize Chamber. He recalled the main and final arguments of the prosecutors and the lawyers for the civil parties and the defense.

The president of the Assize Chamber said that acts amounting to crimes against humanity, war crimes, and torture had certainly been committed in Chad. In a long and sometimes tedious development, because most of the elements presented had been the subject of arduous debate during months of hearings and testimonies, the president talked about victims, populations of southern Chad, members of the Hajaraï and Zaghawa ethnic groups, women victims of sexual violence, political opponents, and so on. However, the questions that arose when listening to the sometimes disjointed monologue of the president of the Assize Chamber were whether Hissein Habré was responsible for the crimes whose content was spelled out and, if he was, how many years in prison was he sentenced to.

Finally, the president attacked the question of the criminal responsibility of Hissein Habré. Throughout his presentation on the issue, he drew parallels between the facts reported during the hearings and the alleged crimes committed by Hissein Habré, before using the relevant provisions of the EAC Statute to characterize the crimes and draw consequences for criminal responsibility.

The emblematic case of Khadija Hassan Zidane, who claimed to have been raped by Hissein Habré, was used as the first element in the demonstration of Hissein Habré's criminal responsibility. The president of the Assize Chamber stated that there was no reason to doubt the statements of the victim. The former head of state of Chad raped her and was guilty, on the one hand, of crimes against humanity with rape and torture as underlying acts and, on the other hand, of the autonomous crime of torture. There was the sound of whispering in the courtroom, presumably coming from the victims. The president continued.

Hissein Habré was responsible for intentional homicide, an act constituting crimes against humanity, for ordering the execution of two soldiers in Ngalo, Chad. With regard to the joint criminal enterprise, the president of the Assize Chamber noted that Hissein Habré exercised direct control over repressive bodies, including the DDS and BSIR, which were mentioned many times by victims and witnesses. Several individuals, Hissein Habré and individuals working in repressive bodies, participated in this joint criminal enterprise. As such, Hissein Habré was responsible for the autonomous crime of torture and a series of acts constituting crimes against humanity such as homicide, the massive and systematic practice of summary executions, the abduction of persons followed by their disappearance, torture, and inhuman acts, rape, and sexual slavery. As a superior who exercised control over the Chadian national armed forces, Hissein Habré was also held responsible for acts constituting war crimes such as willful killing, murder, inhuman and cruel treatment, and torture and illegal detention.

In short, the president of the Assize Chamber stated that Hissein Habré was responsible for crimes against humanity, war crimes, and torture, the crimes for which he was being prosecuted. The verdict then delivered by the president of the Assize Chamber, who looked briefly at the accused when he spoke his name, was only a logical conclusion: "Hissein Habré, the Chamber finds you guilty," he proclaimed, before listing the war crimes, crimes against humanity, and acts relating to the crime of torture attributed to the former head of state of Chad.

Hissein Habré was nevertheless acquitted of the specific charge of the war crime of illegally transferring POWs. However, this incidental acquittal only attracted attention for a few seconds.

The president of the Assize Chamber quickly embarked on the sentence. While an immediate indication of the sentence was expected, he held the courtroom in suspense. He first gave an explanation of the reasons for the sentence and the elements taken into account in its determination. The courtroom public learned that the Chamber took into consideration the seriousness of the crimes over a period of eight long years, the involvement of Hissein Habré in the commission of the crimes, the rape he committed on several occasions, and his insulting attitude toward the Assize Chamber before which he presented himself with his head partially hidden in a turban and a large part of his face sheltered behind glasses and he never stood up for the judges when they entered the courtroom or when they left it. It was also learned, and it was a little surprise after the presentation of the long list of criminal acts committed by Hissein Habré, that the Assize Chamber took into account extenuating circumstances, including the fact that Hissein Habré was allegedly a good father and helped his family.

For the observer of these extenuating circumstances, they could simply mean that Hissein Habré was ultimately a human being capable of the worst, committing heinous international crimes, but also of the best, taking care of his family and showing kindness and generosity.

However, the president of the Assize Chamber was quick to point out that these extenuating circumstances had only a very limited impact. They were clearly outweighed by the aggravating circumstances identified. In a solemn moment, the president of the tribunal ruled: "Hissein Habré, the Chamber sentences you to life imprisonment."

The Assize Chamber thus followed the prosecutors' closing arguments. However, the president of the Assize Chamber also stated that there was no need for confiscation of the seized property. No one seemed to notice that last element, as the life sentence triggered victim satisfaction. In the following days, the national and international press echoed the sentencing of Hissein Habré to life imprisonment and salutes a historic moment and a victory for the fight against impunity in Africa.

After sentencing, the president of the Assize Chamber declared that the accused had 15 days to appeal the judgment. The defense lawyers appealed a few days later.

Before adjourning the hearing, the president of the Assize Chamber convened a status conference to hear the parties' submissions on civil interests. Indeed, once a conviction has been handed down, the Assize Chamber must rule on the civil interests. This was a specific feature of the EAC procedure that allowed the criminal judge to rule on civil interests, that is, to examine civil claims for damages.

REPARATIONS TO VICTIMS

Under the EAC proceedings, victims could bring civil actions and, as such, claim reparations for the harm they had suffered. In the area of reparations, as we have seen, the EAC Statute was in line with the Statute of the ICC, which provided for similar forms of reparations and a victims' fund.[5] Article 27(1) of the EAC Statute provided that the EAC may award three forms of reparation: restitution, compensation, and rehabilitation. Article 28 of the EAC Statute provided for the establishment of a Trust Fund for Victims. The fund was set to be financed by states, NGOs, international institutions, and other interested sources. Article 27(2) stated that the EAC may decide that the fund is the source of financing for compensation allowed to victims. Based on the opportunity offered by the mechanism of the EAC Statute, the two groups of civil parties filed applications for reparations with the African Extraordinary Assize Chambers.

The Claims of Civil Parties

The first group of 4,733 direct and indirect victims, the civil party group *Clément Abaifouta et al.*, demanded that the Assize Chamber award financial reparations to all victims.[6] The group detailed precisely the elements that must be taken into account in granting compensation. It determined the sums to be allocated according to the categories of victims and the violations suffered. Moving away from the forms of reparation proposed by the EAC Statute, it also called for collective and symbolic reparations such as a day of commemoration, the construction of training centers, teaching about the period when crimes were committed, and the erection of monuments. For this group of victims, a part of the money spent on compensation should be used for the development of income-generating projects. In total, the group of victims requested that a sum of 168,385,000,000 CFA francs (approximately more than 256 million euros) be allocated to the victims. It added that Hissein Habré must be ordered to pay the said sum and the costs.

The second group of 3,798 direct and indirect victims, the group of the organizations ACVRP and RADH, demanded that the Assize Chamber award a compensation of 150,000,000 CFA francs (approximately more than 228,000 euros) to each victim, that is, a total sum of 569,700,000,000 CFA francs (approximately more than 868 million euros).[7] This group asked the Assize Chamber to force Hissein Habré to pay the said sum and to declare the Chadian state civilly responsible. Such a declaration would oblige Chad to pay reparations to the victims.

Informed of the initiatives of the civil parties, the prosecutors and the defense lawyers made observations on their requests for reparation.

The prosecutors noted that the Assize Chamber must rule on the reparations to be granted and on the admissibility of applications for the "constitution of civil parties," that is, the applications of those who wished to be recognized as victims.[8] It must declare admissible applications for the constitution of civil parties when they appear reasonably based on detailed and probable elements. The reparations requested by the groups of victims were well-founded and it was for the Assize Chamber to assess and award them. With regard to the implementation of certain forms of symbolic and collective reparation requiring the intervention or assent of the Chadian state, the prosecutors considered that the Assize Chamber should seek the observations of that state. However, they opposed the request for a declaration of the Chadian state as civilly responsible. In their view, such a declaration would violate the rights of a state which was not a party to the proceedings and whose defense had not been ensured. For the prosecutors, the reparations were to be financed by the fund created by the Statute of the EAC; the proceeds from the seizure of

Hissein Habré's property as a conservatory measure were to be paid to the civil parties through this fund.

In its observations on victims' applications, the defense lawyers moved away from the issue of civil interests and reparations.[9] They challenged the composition of the Assize Chamber which was to make the decision on reparations. According to the defense lawyers, while the EAC Statute required that the judges appointed be judges with at least 10 years' experience, one of the judges of the Assize Chamber, Amady Diouf, had never served as a judge prior to his appointment to the EAC. Hissein Habré was convicted by an Assize Chamber whose composition was irregular and so he must be released. According to the lawyers of the defense, the same Assize Chamber could not continue to rule on civil claims because of the irregularity of its composition. The Assize Chamber declared the defense application inadmissible on July 5, 2016,[10] and continued the examination of the civil interests.

The Decision of the Assize Chamber

In its decision of July 29, 2016, on civil interests and reparations, the Assize Chamber found admissible the constitutions as civil parties of victims who had proven or substantiated their identity.[11] It drew up a list of victims whose applications for civil action were admissible. It awarded victims a compensation of several million CFA francs. It reduced the amounts proposed and sometimes considered them exorbitant. Thus, it granted 20 million CFA francs (about 30,000 euros) to victims of rape and sexual slavery; 15 million CFA francs (about 22,000 euros) to those who had suffered arbitrary detention and torture, to those who had been POWs, and to survivors of massacres; and 10 million CFA francs (about 15,000 euros) to indirect victims. The Assize Chamber ordered Hissein Habré to pay the sums awarded to the victims and validated the protective measures related to the seizure of some of his bank accounts and a building that belonged to him.

Collective reparations proposed by one of the civil party groups were rejected. The Assize Chamber considered that the group of victims did not provide sufficient information to assess the feasibility of applications relating to development projects, the construction of monuments and training centers. In the same vein, it concluded that ordering Chad to teach its history would be contrary to the sovereignty of that state. The nonparticipation of that state in the proceedings was also a ground for the rejection of the claim for the establishment of its civil liability. Not satisfied with this decision on civil interests, the lawyers for the civil parties appealed to the Extraordinary African Assize Appeals Chamber.

NOTES

1. The record and video of what happened on May 30, 2016, is online, Video Verdict Procès Hissene Habré, May 30, 2016, Online Playlist of the *Forum interactif sur les CAE.*

2. Many comments and articles have been published in favor of Hissein Habré on his website: http://hisseinhabre.com/-soutiens-temoignages-.html, accessed 5/16/2021.

3. See, the summary of the judgment, EAC, *Prononcé et résumé du jugement dans l'affaire Le parquet général contre Hissein Habré*, May 30, 2016, and Video Verdict. Procès Hissene Habré, May 30, 2016, Online Playlist of the *Forum interactif sur les CAE.*

4. EAC, *Ministère public v. Hissein Habré*, Jugdment, May 30, 2016.

5. Articles 75 and 79 of the ICC Statute.

6. For the claims of the group of victims, see the document, Chambres Africaines Extraordinaires Chambre d'Assises pour parties civiles, *Abaïfouta Clément et autres* (no date in the document), http://forumchambresafricaines.org/actes-judiciaires-cae/, accessed 9/30/2018. See also EAC (Extraordinary African Assize Chamber), *Ministère Public v. Hissein Habré*, Jugement sur les intérêts civils, July 29, 2016, paras. 2–20.

7. For the claims of the group of victims, see the document, *Mémoire aux fins d'indemnisation*, June 10, 2016, http://forumchambresafricaines.org/actes-judiciaires-cae/, accessed 9/30/2018. See also EAC (Extraordinary African Assize Chamber), *Ministère Public v. Hissein Habré*, ibid., paras. 21–26.

8. For the observations of the prosecutors, see the document, Observations du Parquet général sur les demandes de réparations des parties civiles, June 15, 2016, http://forumchambresafricaines.org/actes-judiciaires-cae/, accessed 9/30/2018. EAC (Extraordinary African Assize Chamber), *Ministère Public v. Hissein Habré*, ibid., paras. 32–38.

9. For the observations of the defense lawyers, see *Ministère public v. Hissein Habré*, ibid., paras. 27–31.

10. EAC (Extraordinary African Assize Chamber), Ordonnance déclarant irrecevable le « mémoire en défense (sur intérêts civils) » déposé par les conseils de l'accusé Hissein Habré, July 5, 2016.

11. All the details of the civil claim decision of the EAC are in EAC (Extraordinary African Assize Chamber), *Ministère Public v. Hissein Habré*, Judgment sur les intérêts civils, op. cit., note 6.

Chapter 11

The Appeal

As for international criminal courts or tribunals,[1] the possibilities for the parties to appeal a decision to the Extraordinary African Assize Appeals Chamber were limited. Article 25 of the EAC Statute restricted appeals to cases of "procedural error," "error on a question of substantive law which invalidates the decision; including an error as to jurisdiction," and "error of fact which resulted in a denial of justice." On the basis of these provisions, the defense lawyers and the civil parties appealed the decisions of the Extraordinary African Assize Chamber on different grounds.

GROUNDS FOR THE DEFENSE LAWYERS APPEAL

In their appeal, the defense lawyers first pointed to alleged procedural errors by the Assize Chamber, citing, for example, the refusal to rule on its request for a nullity of the proceedings, the reading of a summary of the judgment and not its entirety, and the failure to check the identity cards of witnesses and victims prior to their hearing.[2] They noted errors of fact that allegedly led to a denial of justice, including the "corruption" of witnesses and civil parties, some of whom had attended the hearings of the Assize Chamber prior to their own hearing, the public broadcast of the trial that allegedly compromised the credibility of testimonies, and the calling as a witness for the prosecution of a former Belgian investigating judge who had investigated the case. Finally, the Assize Chamber allegedly committed several errors of law: refusing to recognize that the DDS was placed under the supervision of the Chadian Ministry of the Interior; taking into consideration a case of rape that was not reported during the investigation phase and that was reported under "pressure" from the president of the Assize Chamber; and refraining, during the appeal period, from making available the entire judgment.

To these main grounds of appeal, the defense lawyers added the challenge to the decision declaring inadmissible its application relating to the irregularity of the composition of the Extraordinary African Assize Chamber.

GROUNDS FOR THE CIVIL PARTIES' APPEAL

For their part, the two groups of civil parties challenged the decision on civil interests on specific grounds.[3] The group defending the interests of the two victims' organizations, ACVRP and RADHT, protested against the rejection of the constitution of civil parties for certain victims and the amount allocated to the victims. The civil party group representing *Clément Abaïfouta et al.* also underlined this rejection. However, this group noted the Assize Chamber's lack of reasoning; a lack of reasoning which, in its view, extended to the refusal to grant collective reparations. The Assize Chamber also allegedly forgot to include victims in an annex to its decision and was mistaken about the groups to which they belonged. The Extraordinary African Assize Chamber of Appeal was therefore called upon to correct these errors.

At the time when the defense and the lawyers for the civil parties were scrambling to file their motions, the members of this Appeals Chamber were not yet officially known.

THE ESTABLISHMENT OF THE EXTRAORDINARY AFRICAN ASSIZE APPEALS CHAMBER

Certainly for financial reasons, since they would have had to be paid if they had been appointed, the members of the Appeals Chamber had not yet been appointed during the trial phase. It was necessary to await the end of the proceedings before the Assize Chamber, the certainty of an appeal, and the need to constitute an Appeals Chamber before appointing its members. Article 31, paragraph 1(c), of the EAC Statute provided that the Appeals Chamber would sit "at the time when an appeal is filed against the decision rendered" by the Assize Chamber. It can be stated without hesitation that if none of the parties had appealed the Assize Chamber's judgment, the members of the Appeals Chamber would not have been appointed.

Appeals by the defense lawyers and the civil parties therefore put the African Union and Senegal under an obligation to appoint judges of appeal. Article 11(3) of the EAC Statute provided that these judges were to be appointed, after a proposal of the minister of justice of Senegal, by the chairperson of the African Union Commission. The Appeals Chamber was to be composed of three judges, including a president. As mentioned previously, the judges must be of Senegalese nationality, with the exception of the president of the Chamber, who must be "a national of another State of the African Union." Appointments took place at the end of September 2016.[4] A Malian judge, Wafi Ougadeye, working for the Supreme Court of Mali, was appointed president of the Appeals Chamber. Two Senegalese judges were appointed: Matar Ndiaye and Bara Gueye. An alternate judge of Senegalese nationality, Amadou Tidiane Sy, was also appointed. The end date of the term of office of the judges was April 30, 2017. They therefore had seven months to complete the appeal procedures and issue their final judgment.

PROCEEDINGS BEFORE THE APPEALS CHAMBER

The judges of the Appeals Chamber took office on October 3, 2016.[5] The Chamber then exchanged with the parties: documents sent by the parties, requests for clarification by the Appeals Chamber, filing of final arguments, filing of requests by the defense, and so on. At this stage, the Appeals Chamber rejected requests from the defense lawyers and civil parties for the production of evidence at the appeals stage.

The Appeals Chamber hearings did not commence until January 9, 2017. The defense lawyers filed a motion challenging the composition of the Appeals Chamber. According to them, one of the judges of the Appeals Chamber, Bara Gueye, had considered or known of a case in which Hissein Habré was involved. For this reason, this judge should be discharged or abstained. The Appeals Chamber decided on the defense lawyers' motion. The challenged judge did not participate in the decision concerning him. The alternate judge replaced him. The Appeals Chamber thus composed rejected the defense application, suspended the hearing, and returned composed of the three judges of the Appeals Chamber, including the contested and now reinstated judge.

The judges also ruled on the defense lawyers' motion requesting the nonappearance of Hissein Habré, who had refused to be brought into the courtroom. Unlike the president of the Assize Chamber, the president of the Appeals Chamber, using his discretionary power under the Senegalese Code of Criminal Procedure, did not order the appearance of Hissein Habré. He required the accused to be read the minutes of the hearings and to be informed of all the proceedings and decisions taken with respect to him.

The decision not to forcibly compel Hissein Habré to appear in court during the Appeals Chamber's proceedings was questionable. Was it a decision aimed at avoiding the chaotic disorder experienced during the hearing on

September 7, 2015, when the trial began? Was it a "compassionate" decision that took into account Hissein Habré's former position as head of the Chadian state? Was it a decision suggesting that Hissein Habré had already been sufficiently humiliated? Was there another reason? It was difficult to answer these questions, as the president of the Appeals Chamber used his discretionary power and did not need to give clear reasons for his decision.

It was therefore without Hissein Habré in the courtroom that the hearings of the Appeals Chamber took place. These hearings consisted of verbal jousting between the prosecutors, the lawyers for the civil parties, and the defense lawyers. Nothing surprising was raised. The defense detailed the points on which it had appealed. The prosecutors and the civil parties rejected the claims of the defense lawyers. The civil parties wanted the decision on the civil claims to be reviewed.

APPEAL JUDGMENT

The African Extraordinary Assize Appeals Chamber reiterated all the arguments of the parties in its Judgment of April 27, 2017. With one exception, it rejected all grounds for appeal by the defense lawyers, citing elements of international criminal law and the Senegalese Code of Criminal Procedure.

It ruled in favor of a single request by the defense lawyers concerning Khadija Hassan Zidane's rape allegedly committed by Hissein Habré. With regard to this rape, the defense lawyers had argued that it had been alleged for the first time before the Assize Chamber and at the "instigation" of its president. According to them, this was only an attempt to humiliate Hissein Habré, as the victim's testimony was riddled with inconsistencies. However, this argument was not part of the evidence relied upon by the Appeals Chamber to grant the defense its motion.

The Appeals Chamber noted that international criminal law and the Senegalese Code of Criminal Procedure recognized the power of the trial courts, in this case, the Assize Chamber, to recharacterize facts, that is, to give the facts a new legal consideration. The Assize Chamber was not bound by the characterization of facts adopted by the Investigative Chamber during the investigation phase. However, the Appeals Chamber noted that in the case of the alleged rape of Khadija Hassan Zidane, this was not a recharacterization of facts, but new facts presented during the trial phase. The power of recharacterization is limited to the facts established in the pre-trial investigation. According to the Appeals Chamber, by deciding to take into account facts not identified by the Investigative Chamber in its order for the referral of Hissein Habré, the Assize Chamber violated procedural rules. The Appeals Chamber therefore acquitted Hissein Habré of the crime of rape committed directly against Khadija Hassan Zidane. It hastened to state, however, that this acquittal had no consequence on the sentence imposed on Hissein Habré because of the magnitude of the crimes perpetrated.

With regard to the civil claims, the Appeals Chamber partially reversed the Assize Chamber's judgment. It corrected factual and material errors relating, inter alia, to the admissibility of the civil parties applications of several victims and to the group to which some civil parties belonged. Several victims were thus recognized as civil parties and added to the list of victims annexed to the judgment. With regard to collective and moral reparations, the Appeals Chamber followed the Assize Chamber and pointed out Chad's sovereignty. Contacted by the Appeals Chamber, Chad did not promise to make collective reparations effective. However, the Appeals Chamber encouraged the implementation of collective reparations through the Trust Fund for Victims. With respect to victims whose applications were found inadmissible, the Appeals Chamber indicated that they could seek reparations from the Trust Fund for Victims, which was not limited to victims whose applications were found admissible by the EAC.

The Appeals Chamber set the amount of reparations to be awarded to victims at 82,290,000,000 CFA francs (more than 125 million euros). Hissein Habré would be forced to pay the reparations. However, it noted that Hissein Habré's assets could not cover the financial reparations granted. Accordingly, it indicated that the Trust Fund for Victims would have to finance reparations, with the proceeds of any assets and property of Hissein Habré that might be discovered to be paid into the fund. In January 2018, setting in motion the operationalization of reparations funding, the African Union adopted the *Statute of a Trust Fund for the Benefit of Victims of the Crimes of Hissène Habré*.[6] Article 15 of this document, in accordance with the EAC Statute and the Appeals Chamber's judgment, provided that the fund was to be financed by the recovery of the convicted person's property and by voluntary contributions.

The judgment of the Extraordinary African Assize Appeals Chamber rendered on April 27, 2017, brought the trial of Hissein Habré to an end. The appeal judgment decision could not be subject to appeal according to Article 25(4) of the EAC Statute. Hissein Habré was to stay in prison for the rest of his life. Article 26, paragraph 4, provided that Senegalese courts were to have jurisdiction over procedural matters, including detention, that could arise after the dissolution of the EAC. In 2019 and 2020, proceedings related to the detention of Hissein Habré emerged and appeared to call into question the life sentence confirmed by the Appeals Chamber.

HISSEIN HABRÉ SERVING HIS LIFE IMPRISONMENT SENTENCE AND THE PROBLEMATIC FIGHT FOR A RELEASE

Attempts by Hissein Habré supporters to secure his release by the Senegalese authorities had been reported.[7] His supporters said he should be released, sometimes arguing that he was ill.[8] Concerned by these new developments, victims of Hissein Habré's regime filed a complaint with the UN CAT and relied on the follow-up to the 2006 ruling against Senegal.[9] The CAT found in December 2019 that Senegal's release of Hissein Habré would violate the 1984 Convention against Torture. According to the Committee, the early release of perpetrators of international crimes was not compatible with international obligations under the Convention against Torture.[10] The decision of the CAT did not prevent Hissein Habré from applying for a release from prison.

In 2020, in the context of the COVID-19 pandemic, Hissein Habré requested a 60-day release from prison. Through his lawyer, he argued that he was subject to health risk and that he was particularly vulnerable to COVID-19 because of his advanced age.[11] On April 6, 2020, a Senegalese judge granted Hissein Habré permission to leave prison for 60 days.[12] The Senegalese authorities insisted that this was not a release, that Hissein Habré had only been granted a 60-day leave with permission, that he was still under the escort of prison guards, and that due to the COVID-19 pandemic, the Cap Manuel prison where Hissein Habré was being held had been completely emptied in order to accommodate the new inmates who would be quarantined.[13] Despite fears that the 60 days could be renewed and later become a definitive release, Hissein Habré was returned to prison on June 7, 2020,[14] a date that strangely coincided with the anniversary of his seizure of power in Chad, which took place on June 7, 1982.

Thus, in accordance with the judgment of the Appeals Chamber, Hissein Habré served his life sentence in Cap Manuel prison in Dakar, Senegal, until his death on August 24, 2021.[15]

On April 30, 2017, the EAC closed. They had only tried Hissein Habré for particularly serious crimes committed in Chad under his presidency. The proceedings, from the pre-trial stage to the Appeals Chamber's judgment (2013–2017), lasted just over four years. A rather reasonable length of time compared, for example, to the seven years (2006–2013) of the proceedings of the SCSL in the case of Charles Taylor, the former president of Liberia, or the nine years (2012–2021) of the proceedings of the ICC in the case of Charles Blé Goudé and Laurent Gbagbo, the latter a former head of state of Côte d'Ivoire. The silence of the accused, who refused to fight despite the presence of particularly committed court-appointed defense lawyers, may explain this reduced duration. This may also be the result of the inquisitorial procedure adopted by the EAC and marked in particular by extensive files constituted during the investigation phase, an important role of the judges, whether during the investigation, trial, and appeal phases.

The trial of Hissein Habré had been welcomed by human rights defenders and those campaigning for the fight against impunity for international crimes. However, this condemnation, beyond the symbolic satisfaction of the victims who finally saw the harm they experienced being recognized by the criminal justice system, left open the question of the impact of the trial on social peace and reconciliation in Chad.

NOTES

1. See, for example, Article 25 of the ICTY Statute, Article 24 of the ICTR Statute, and Article 81 of ICC Statute.
2. All the grounds of appeal of the defense lawyers are detailed throughout the Appeal judgement: EAC (Extraordinary African Assize Appeals Chamber), *Le Procureur général v. Hissein Habré*, Arrêt, April 27, 2017, 22 ff.
3. Ibid., 143 ff.
4. Ibid., para. 38.
5. This element and all the elements that will follow are a summary of the judgment: EAC (Extraordinary African Assize Appeals Chamber), *Le Procureur général v. Hissein Habré*, op. cit., note 2.
6. AU, *Statute of a Trust Fund for the Benefit of Victims of the Crimes of Hissène Habré*, Doc. EX.CL/1040(XXXI) Annex, 2018.
7. Human Rights Watch, *Senegal/Chad: No Reparations for Ex-Dictator's Victims. Four Years After Hissène Habré's Conviction, African Union and Chad Fail Victims*, May 29, 2020, online: https://www.hrw.org/news/2020/05/29/senegal/chad-no-reparations-ex-dictators-victims, accessed 5/16/2021.
8. RFI, "Santé d'Hissène Habré: ses victimes s'inquiètent d'une possible grâce", December 2, 2019, https://www.rfi.fr/fr/afrique/20191202-senegal-tchad-hissene-habre-victime-proces-sante-grace, accessed 5/16/2021.
9. CAT, *Suleymane Guengueng, et al. v. Senegal*, Communication No. 181/2001, Craintes de libération d'Hissène Habré, doc. G/SO 229/31 SEN(1) Follow-up, December 23, 2019.
10. Ibid.
11. Senegal, Tribunal de Grande Instance Hors Classe de Dakar, Cabinet du juge d'application des peines, Ordonnance accordant une permission de sortir au détenu Hissène Habré, April 6, 2020.
12. Ibid.
13. Senegal, Ministère de la justice, Direction de l'administration pénitentiaire, Communiqué de presse, April 6, 2020.
14. Jeune Afrique, "Sénégal : le Tchadien Hissène Habré regagne sa prison, Jeune Afrique," June 7, 2020, online: https://www.jeuneafrique.com/996420/societe/senegal-le-tchadien-hissene-habre-regagne-sa-prison/, accessed 5/16/2021.
15. Emediasn, "Décès de Hissène Habré," August 24, 2021, http://emedia.sn/DECES-DE-HISSENE-HABRE.html, accessed August 31, 2021.

Chapter 12

Beyond Individual Responsibility

Was the Hissein Habré Trial a Contribution to Social Peace and Reconciliation in Chad?

Trials for international crimes are sometimes seen as a way for a society to come together in spite of past conflicts. There are traditional ideas about the social and peacemaking function of criminal justice and its positive effects. For example, in his book *Mass Atrocity, Collective Memory, and the Law*, Mark Osiel developed the idea of a didactic function of international trials, the idea that these trials are a forum in which competing versions of history are offered, and in which, despite their differences, the parties learn about each other.[1] International criminal tribunals may be a step toward social peace and living together without vindictive ambition, a step toward reconciliation. Because of the scale of international crimes, the theme of reconciliation is sometimes at the center of debates on the potential effects of the trials that examine them. These trials have become important mechanisms of transitional justice, defined by the UN secretary-general as "the full range of processes and mechanisms associated with a societies attempts to come to terms with a legacy of large-scale past abuses, in order to ensure accountability, serve justice and achieve reconciliation."[2]

During the trial of Hissein Habré, it appeared that the Chadian social fabric had been torn apart. Internal armed clashes and repression based on ethnicity, political opposition, or simply on difference and suspicion were indicative of a social fabric and the Chadian people being damaged. In this context, is it possible to consider that the trial contributed to the reconciliation of Chadians and enabled the country to turn the page of a painful history?

THE ERUPTION OF RECONCILIATION AND FORGIVENESS IN THE TRIAL

Although the theme of reconciliation between Chadians was not the objective of the trial, it sometimes erupted into the debates before the Extraordinary African Assize Chamber. The hearing and testimony of Bandjim Bandoum, the former DDS agent, went beyond the strict framework of the trial and the search for the truth for a moment to become part of the framework of reconciliation and forgiveness.[3]

A lawyer for the civil parties, William Bourdon, had asked the repentant if he had anything to say to Hissein Habré, who was comfortably seated in his chair and looking away. Bandjim Bandoum had addressed the former president directly. He asked him to speak, not to remain silent because Chad needed reconciliation. He noted that he had done his part by taking responsibility for his own actions. The former president also had to take responsibility. After another question from the lawyer who wanted to know if he had anything to say to the victims, the civil parties, and his family, Bandjim Bandoum, in a situation that was as unpredictable as it was unprecedented, confessed to having covered up atrocities and asked the victims for forgiveness: "This forgiveness is not enough, I know, but at least I say it publicly. I ask their forgiveness."[4] The approach of the former DDS agent was undoubtedly a first step toward reconciliation between him and the victims. Indeed, there can be no true reconciliation without at least an acknowledgment of fault by the perpetrator, an expression of remorse, and a request for forgiveness.

THE UNCERTAIN NATURE OF SOCIAL PEACE AND RECONCILIATION IN CHAD AFTER THE TRIAL

But the surprising scene of Bandjim Bandoum asking for forgiveness cannot be considered as proof or as a sign of reconciliation between Chadians. At this stage, it is difficult to state whether the trial of Hissein Habré had had any effect on social peace and reconciliation in Chad. Social peace and reconciliation continue to face many obstacles. First, the convicted person, Hissein Habré, did not acknowledge the crimes of which he was accused. He expressed neither regret nor remorse. Second, even if Hissein Habré was found guilty, the criminal responsibility of several of his collaborators, who participated in the repression, had not been established by the EAC. More worryingly, in a March 2018 statement, Human Rights Watch revealed the release of several of Hissein Habré's collaborators,[5] who were convicted in 2015 by a Chadian criminal court.[6] One can imagine the humiliating scenes and the frightened look of the victims when they meet the people against whom they had testified. Third, with regard to reparations, as of early 2021, the victims had still not received the financial compensation granted by the EAC and the 2015 decision of a Chadian criminal court.[7] The execution of this court's judgment, which also ordered the erection of a monument in memory of the victims and the transformation of the DDS headquarters into a museum, remains uncertain. The organization of public demonstrations by victims of Hissein Habré's regime to denounce the non-execution of the judgment is proof that frustrations remain strong and accompany social demands.[8] Victims have been complaining that most of them, those who have not yet died, live in deplorable conditions of poverty, unable to meet their basic needs, and unable to heal from the pain caused by the repression of the Habré regime. The Trust Fund for Victims of the Crimes of Hissène Habré set up by the African Union, which in May 2021 was still not operational, could contribute to healing if voluntary contributions were to flow in and financial compensation was finally paid to the victims.

To these elements that are directly related to the repression of Habré's regime and its consequences, one must add the regular social protests directed against the government of Idriss Déby Itno, who, in the context of an armed rebellion against his regime, was reportedly shot and later died of his injuries in April 2021.[9] After this death, a transitional military council chaired by Idriss Déby Itno's son, Mahamat Idriss Déby, took power in Chad.[10] These regimes, like that of Hissein Habré's, faced recurrent armed rebellions, attempts at overthrow, and accusations of human rights violations.[11] Reconciliation and lasting peace in Chad, therefore, remain a long way off. Faced with this situation, should another solution be devised and adopted in order to foster lasting peace and reconciliation?

A TRUTH AND RECONCILIATION COMMISSION IN CHAD TO PURGE THE PAST?

Truth commissions are temporary, nonjudicial official bodies charged with examining abuses that are generally committed on a large scale and, in some cases, with promoting peace and reconciliation.[12] A commission fulfilling some of these characteristics, the Chadian National Commission of Inquiry, had already been created after the fall of Hissein Habré's regime. However, this commission had focused mainly on telling the truth about the crimes committed under his regime. Reconciliation among Chadians was not part of its mandate. Is it therefore time to create a new truth commission to settle the past, to contribute to reconciliation, and to stop the cycle of social disputes against the backdrop of regular armed conflicts which inevitably leave resentments and fuel future conflicts?

It could be a good idea to set up a new truth commission in Chad. However, it should first be borne in mind that truth commissions are not a panacea for solving all the problems caused by serious international crimes within a state.

They are only one element among others, including criminal accountability of perpetrators, reparations, and good governance, which make it possible to reestablish the rule of law and ensure social peace and reconciliation over the long term. Second, the mandate of such a commission would have to be objectively defined. It should not be limited to an investigation into the crimes committed under the regime of Hissein Habré, crimes whose extent is now known, at least in part. It would investigate the crimes committed in Chad since the country's independence while bringing together different communities and social groups in a reconciliatory process. It would establish responsibilities from a historical point of view and make recommendations to the Chadian state that could be implemented to help avoid the repetition of such tragedies. These recommendations could, for example, include proposals for institutional reforms, the development of a comprehensive reparations program that would include already known measures such as financial compensation, but also symbolic measures such as an official apology from the Chadian state and collective reparations proposed by a group of civil parties during the trial of Hissein Habré. Finally, it is to be hoped that the Chadian authorities will agree to establish such a commission, provide the means to ensure it can function, and implement any recommendation it may make.

For the time being, it is risky to bet on the establishment and effectiveness of such an institution in Chad after the trial of Hissein Habré. The will of the political actors, the Chadian authorities, and the opponents engaged in armed struggle is uncertain. Chad governments, which in recent years have become major actors in the fight against terrorism in Africa,[13] do not seem ready to embark on such a path. For example, delays in the implementation of a judicial decision granting reparations to the victims of the Habré regime create skepticism. Would a government that does not swiftly implement a binding judicial decision be more willing to implement the recommendations of a truth commission? The answer should be negative, although a potential evolution cannot be completely excluded. The real challenge therefore remains the enforcement of court decisions and the effectiveness of reparations granted to victims.

Therefore, at this posttrial stage, social peace, reconciliation, and guarantees of non-repetition of such crimes in Chad remain very uncertain despite the conviction of Hissein Habré for international crimes. However, the trial of Hissein Habré raises questions about its significance in the global fight against impunity in Africa.

NOTES

1. Mark Osiel, *Mass Atrocity, Collective Memory, and the Law* (New Brunswick: NJ: Transaction Publishers, 1997).

2. United Nations Secretary General, *The Rule of Law and Transitional Justice in Conflict and Post-Conflict Societies*, UN Doc. S/2004/616, 2004, para. 8.

3. See EAC, Hearing of Bandjim Bandoum, September 22 and 23, 2015, Online Playlist of the *Forum interactif sur les CAE.* EAC Transcripts, September 22 and 23, 2015.

4. Ibid.

5. Human Rights Watch, *Chad: Government Fails Ex-Dictator's Victims. 3 Years On, No Action on Habré-Era Reparation*, March 22, 2018.

6. Cour d'appel de N'Djamena, *Ministère Public et Ismael Hachim et autres v. Saleh Younous Ali, Waroun Fadoul ali et autres*, Répertoire n°01/15, March 25, 2015.

7. Reed Brody, "Hissène Habré's Victims Continue Fight for Reparations. Five Years After Chadian Dictator's Guilty Verdict, Victims Still Await Justice," Dispatches, *Human Rights Watch*, May 26, 2021, online : https://www.hrw.org/news/2021/05/26/hissene-habres-victims-continue-fight-reparations, accessed 5/26/2021.

8. See, for example, Moussa Nguedmbaye, "Tchad : encore une manifestation des victimes de l'ancien président Habré," October 14, 2019, online: https://tchadinfos.com/politique/tchad-encore-une-manifestation-des-victimes-de-lancien-president-habre/, accessed 5/16/2021; RFI Afrique, "Tchad: « sit-in » d'artistes en soutien aux victimes d'Hissène Habré," July 20, 2019, online: http://www.rfi.f.r/fr/afrique/20190720-tchad-justice-sit-in-artistes-soutien-victimes-hissene-habre, accessed 5/16/2021; RFI Afrique, "Tchad: les victimes d'Hissène Habré réclament toujours le versement des indemnisations," February 5, 2020, online: http://www.rfi.fr/fr/afrique/20200205-tchad-victimes-hiss%C3%A8-habr%C3%A9-r%C3%A9clament-versement-indemnisations, accessed 5/16/2021.

9. Chad, Déclaration du conseil militaire de transition, online: https://presidence.td/galleries/declaration-du-conseil-militaire-de-transition/?fbclid=IwAR0vg9vVr_5pI9kL_Jbq10hJpvBik3nbw5ec49PNOQFqqeQs8E7oBcIJA0g, accessed 5/16/2021.

10. Ibid.

11. See inter alia, United Nations News, "Chad: UN rights office profoundly disturbed over violence against protesters," April 30, 2021, online: https://news.un.org/en/story/2021/04/1091082, accessed 5/16/2021; Human Rights Council (Working Group on the Universal Periodic Review), *Compilation on Chad. Report of the Office of the United Nations High Commissioner for Human Rights.* UN Doc. A/HRC/WG.6/31/TCD/2, August 31, 2018; Human Rights Council (Working Group on the Universal Periodic Review), Summary of Stakeholders' submissions on Chad. Report of the Office of the United Nations High Commissioner for Human Rights, UN Doc. A/HRC/WG.6/31/TCD/3, August 24, 2018; Mohamed Tétémadi Bangoura, *Violence politique et conflits en Afrique : le cas du Tchad* (Paris: L'Harmattan, 2006).

12. On Truth commissions, see Priscilla B. Hayner, *Unspeakable Truths : Transitional Justice and the Challenge of Truth Commissions* (New York: Routledge, 2011). Office of the United Nations High Commissioner for Human Rights, *Rule-of-Law Tools For Post-Conflict States. Truth commissions*, UN Doc. HR/PUB/06/1, 2006.

13. Nick Ridley, *Terrorism in East and West Africa: The Under-focused Dimension* (Cheltenham: Edward Elgard Publishing, 2014), 120–121.

Chapter 13

The Hissein Habré Trial's Significance in the Global Fight against Impunity in Africa

African Justice or Foreigners' Justice

In Africa, the conviction of a former head of state for international crimes in a continental criminal proceeding was unprecedented. Of course, this was not the first time that senior state officials had been tried in this continent. Before Hissein Habré, several former African heads of state faced legal proceedings. In 2009, *Prosecuting Heads of State* was published detailing a research project that had brought together many experts and scholars to investigate the cases of heads of state who had been the subject of legal proceedings for various reasons between 1990 and 2008.[1] Some of these heads of state had been prosecuted in Africa under national procedures relating to human rights violations committed while in power. For example, this was the case of Mengistu Haile Mariam, the former president of Ethiopia sentenced to death in absentia; Moussa Traoré, the former president of Mali sentenced to death and finally pardoned after his sentence was commuted to life imprisonment; Pascal Lissouba, the former president of the Republic of Congo sentenced to death in absentia; Pasteur Bizimungu, the former president of Rwanda sentenced to 15 years in prison before being pardoned; and Hastings Kamuzu Banda, the former head of state of Malawi, acquitted. To this list can be added African heads of state indicted by international or hybrid tribunals: Charles Taylor, the former president of Liberia, sentenced to 50 years in prison by the SCSL;[2] Laurent Gbagbo, the former president of Côte d'Ivoire, tried by the ICC and later acquitted;[3] Muammar Gaddafi, the former Libyan head of state, indicted by the ICC and dead before the trial;[4] and Omar al-Bashir, the former president of Sudan, tried by his country for corruption and against whom the ICC issued an arrest warrant, still outstanding in May 2021.[5]

The EAC were the first regional criminal tribunal created by Africans in Africa to try a former African head of state accused of international crimes. Yet some claimed that the West, sometimes understood in the African perception as Western Europe and North America, was lurking in the shadows and was controlling the proceedings against Hissein Habré.[6] A suspicion of bias, fueled by debates in the media and, above all, comments on the Internet, had weighed on the proceedings against Hissein Habré.

In the context of the mistrust of some Africans toward the ICC,[7] for those who defend the "African solution" for perpetrators of international crimes in Africa, the trial of Hissein Habré in Africa proves that Africans have the capacity and the will to try their leaders who perpetrate these crimes. They do not need foreigners or non-African states. They have even less need of international criminal courts established by the West. In the context of this promotion of an African criminal court, the condemnation of Hissein Habré in Africa by African judges sounded like the awakening of Africa. Africa has shown the world what it can do. The success of Hissein Habré's trial restored the dignity and criminal sovereignty of Africans.

The admiration and celebration of a landmark African trial, however, leaves open some questions that seem to have been overshadowed by the surrounding enthusiasm: What was the real share of "Africans" in this trial? Could the trial have taken place without the help and intervention of "Westerners"?

AFRICAN JUSTICE: AFRICANS AT THE HEART OF THE HISSEIN HABRÉ CASE

Africans were at the heart of the process that led to the establishment of Hissein Habré's criminal responsibility. From the beginning to the end of the process that led to Hissein Habré's conviction, there have been Africans who have worked for the fight against impunity. The commission that investigated the crimes committed by Habré's regime was a national commission set up by Chad and composed of Chadians. After the fall of Habré's regime, Chadian victims organized themselves and decided to seek to establish his criminal responsibility in Africa and Belgium.[8] Because of Hissein Habré's exile in Senegal, this African state was at the center of the process that led to the trial. It was before the Senegalese courts that the first complaints were filed. It was during these complaints that the case took shape and developed. While it is true that developments in the case have temporarily shifted to Belgium, and that the decisions of the CAT and the ICJ have exerted pressure,[9] it is in Africa that the proposal to try Hissein Habré under an ad hoc procedure was officially made, that is, when the ECOWAS Court of Justice suggested the organization of a trial in the framework of an ad hoc court of an international character. The African Union, an African regional organization, took up this proposal and engaged in collaboration and negotiations with Senegal that led to the establishment of the EAC.

The tribunal established by the African Union and Senegal was the result of an agreement between these two entities. The court that tried Hissein Habré was undoubtedly African. The addition of the adjective "African" to its name reflects the desire to give it a symbolic and continental dimension. It can be seen as an explicit affirmation of the criminal sovereignty of a continent confronted with international crimes. The judges of the EAC were Africans, mostly Senegalese, one from Burkina Faso and one from Mali who served as presidents of the Assize Chamber and the Assize Appeals Chamber, respectively. All the prosecutors and clerks were nationals of Senegal. The lawyers were mostly Africans. Similarly, Africa contributed financially to the trial. Chad's contribution amounted to 2 billion CFA francs (approximately 3 million euros) and that of the African Union to US$1 million.[10] However, if this African participation appears to be proof of an African leap forward in the fight against impunity for international crimes, some points are still subject to discussion.

First, the analysis of Chad's financial contribution cannot, objectively, be limited to a discourse on the state's willingness to fight impunity. As it is often the case in the fight against impunity at the international level, there are troubled links between politics and the judiciary. An examination of the conflictual relations between Hissein Habré and the leaders of Chad raises the following question: Was Chad's financing of the trial of Hissein Habré a means for Idriss Déby Itno, the then Chadian head of state, to get revenge on the former Chadian president, who allegedly planned to assassinate him in 1989 as part of the repression of members of his Zaghawa ethnic group? It should not be forgotten that in 2008 an attempted coup d'état in Chad failed to overthrow Idriss Déby Itno. Hissein Habré had been suspected of being the hand behind the coup attempt. The Chadian courts had sentenced him to death in absentia for his alleged participation in this coup de force.[11] A paradoxical observation must be made of what took place after the closure of the EAC: the conviction of Hissein Habré for real international crimes—the criminal responsibility of Hissein Habré being confirmed after months of the trial—had the effect of keeping a political opponent of Idriss Déby Itno away from Chad until his death in prison. One may therefore wonder whether Chad's financial contribution was not a way for the Chadian leaders in office to work toward this removal, while this time taking definitive revenge on Hissein Habré. After having contributed resolutely to the financing of the trial of Hissein Habré, Chad, which was led by Idriss Déby Itno until April 2021, was less inclined to participate just as readily in the financing of reparations granted by the EAC and Chadian justice to the thousands of victims. Similarly, as we have seen, according to a report by Human Rights Watch, some people that the EAC had wanted to put on trial, Saleh Younouss and Mahamat Djibrine, and who were sentenced by the Criminal Court of N'Djamena in 2015 for crimes committed under the regime of Hissein Habré, have been released.[12]

Second, while the financial participation of the African Union in an African trial is to be commended, this pan-African organization, so much vaunted and celebrated for its African roots and its vision of a positive developing Africa, would not have worked efficiently in recent years without funding from the European Union and other donors.[13] There is a certain paradox in the behavior of several African states that loudly proclaim their independence and sovereignty, but do not seem to lose their pride when they do not pay their financial contribution to the African Union and when the pan-African institution is financed largely by funds from "partners." The African Union has recently begun to reflect on the operationalization and sustainability of its financial autonomy. In an act that made people laugh a lot, but was no less symbolic, the former head of state of Zimbabwe, a state where the poverty rate is moreover constantly decried, offered the African Union Foundation 1 million dollars from the sale of cows and said that the institution's financial autonomy had to be built up.[14] During his presidency of the African Union in 2018, the head of state of Rwanda, a state that has recovered economically thanks to international aid, also stressed building up the financial autonomy of the African Union.[15] Efforts have been made and the awareness of some African states is real. However, much remains to be done to ensure the financial independence of the African Union. Therefore, on a strictly institutional level, one may legitimately wonder whether the financial contribution of the African Union to Hissein Habré's trial was not a form of indirect contributions by the donors and development partners, at least in part.

Third, the financial contribution of Chad and the African Union was insufficient for the extraordinary trial of a former Chadian head of state residing in Senegal and accused of crimes committed in Chad against mostly Chadian victims. Indeed, the funding for international proceedings and/or trials against current or former rulers is crucial. No money, no trial for international crimes. Money is here the lifeblood of justice. The barely 4 million euros proposed by Africa seemed insignificant when compared to the tens or even hundreds of millions of euros often involved in international criminal proceedings.[16] For that reason and others, the decisive participation of the West in the success of the trial of Hissein Habré cannot be overlooked.

THE WEST: DECISIVE ACTOR IN THE TRIAL OF HISSEIN HABRÉ

Despite the certainty about the crimes committed in Chad and the criminal responsibility of Hissein Habré, his trial before the EAC would hardly have taken place without the help and involvement of the West, the NGOs headquartered there, and several states outside Africa.

Support from Western NGOs

Although the Chadian victims had begun to organize after the fall of Hissein Habré, their mobilization had not led to anything concrete before Reed Brody and Human Rights Watch, an organization based in the United States, and other NGO activists took up the case. The support of Human Rights Watch, the network of International Federation for Human Rights, and the UK-based Amnesty International, which had already well-documented the massive human rights violations in Chad, made it possible to make the criminal proceedings against Hissein Habré effective. It is no exaggeration to write that, and this will not detract from the necessity and legitimacy of the proceedings that led to the conviction of Hissein Habré, the trial would probably not have taken place without their commitment. Sometimes in the shadows, sometimes in the light, it is in fact these organizations that knocked on the doors of states, including the most powerful ones, and found funding. They have exerted pressure through lobbying, press releases, conferences on the crimes committed in Chad, and helping victims mount their proceedings in Belgium and Senegal before the United Nations and the CAT. In a report published in 2017, Reed Brody discusses in detail the support provided to victims by donors and human rights organizations.[17] Without this help, the will to pursue Hissein Habré would have been quickly buried. Indeed, all those working on international crimes know how difficult it is to envisage the implementation of international criminal responsibility of former leaders. Even after they have left power, they often continue to benefit from strong national or international networks built while in power. In the face of this formidable power, victims can be very quickly disarmed and discouraged if they are not helped, carried, and supported. The assistance and support of NGOs for the holding of the trial of Hissein Habré appears to be an implementation of the defense of human rights at the heart of their mandate. However, in international criminal proceedings, the support of NGOs is never enough. The success of the procedures also depends on the support of the states.

Support from Western States

Western states have also contributed logistically and financially to the establishment and operation of the EAC. The list of participants in the round table that defined the budget of the EAC is edifying. While the African Union, Chad, and the host state, Senegal, had participated, the European Union, Belgium, Canada, France, Germany, Luxembourg, the Netherlands, Spain, Switzerland, the United Kingdom, the United States of America, the Office of the United Nations High Commissioner for Human Rights, and the United Nations Office for Project Services had also participated.[18] At the end of the round table, the estimated budget of approximately 8.6 million euros was retained for the financing of the EAC. The contributions were as follows: European Union (2 million euros), Germany (500,000 euros), Belgium (500,000 euros), France (300,000 euros), Luxembourg (100,000 euros), the Netherlands (1 million euros), United States (US$1 million).[19] An addition of these sums leads to the conclusion that more than half of the financing of the EAC came from states or institutions outside Africa. These contributions inevitably attract curiosity, leading to questions about the motivations for making such contributions.

In most Western states, there is no shortage of rhetoric about the will to combat impunity. Several states and institutions have taken a stand in favor of the fight against impunity for the perpetrators of serious international crimes. Their logistical or financial support to international criminal tribunals appears to be an extension of this stand. But, when these states finance or support the fight against impunity, don't they have other interests? Was the financing of the trial of Hissein Habré part of this logic and, if so, what interest would the West have had in partially financing the trial of a former African head of state?

These questions are not always easy to answer. On the one hand, the claims of critics of the Hissein Habré trial that Westerners wanted to "shoot" Hissein Habré are not always explicitly based on concrete and verifiable evidence. On the other hand, by targeting the West and considering the existence of other interests under the guise of the fight against impunity, there is a conscious or unconscious risk of discrediting the facts and the victims who have experienced such crimes.

However, an examination of issues related to international crimes and the trial of perpetrators very often leads to the observation of the coexistence of a plurality of truths in which politics and the judiciary inevitably intersect.[20] Of course, the relationship between politics and the judiciary does not constitute a denial of the reality of the international crimes committed nor does it constitute a denial of the individual international criminal responsibility of the perpetrators. The Habré case is no exception to this observation.

An examination of Chad's history, Hissein Habré's career, and available documents reveals troubled links between Chad, its former president, and certain Western powers. As we have seen, Hissein Habré had done part of his studies in France before returning to Chad.[21] When he defined himself in the 1970s as an opponent of the regime of François Tombalbaye, the former president of Chad, allying himself with Goukouni Weddeye to fight against this regime, Hissein Habré proved particularly effective in the media coverage of kidnappings and other acts of rebellion.

In April 1974, Hissein Habré and his rebel acolytes had kidnapped a German doctor, Christophe Staewen, and two French nationals—Marc Combe and Françoise Claustre, an ethnologist. The kidnappings and their aftermath, as recounted by Goukouni Weddeye, were allegedly proposed by Hissein Habré and motivated by requests for ransoms and weapons.[22] During the German hostage-taking, the German's wife had been killed, as had two Chadian officers present. The German doctor was freed after negotiations between his country and the rebels. The French remained captive. A French commander seconded to the Chadian government, Commander Galopin, was sent to negotiate with the rebels. He was sequestered and then executed by the rebels in circumstances that have remained unclear to this day.

According to Goukouni Weddeye, the rebels attributed responsibility for their cleavages to the French commander, who reportedly worked tirelessly to undermine the unity of the forces fighting against the then Chadian government. In addition, the rebels made Commander Galopin's release conditional on the handing over of arms by the Chadian government. They were not given the weapons. A threatening message, whose sender had not been clearly identified (France or the Chadian government?) and which ordered the rebels to release the French commander under pain of reprisals, pushed the rebels to execute Commander Galopin. Obviously, this part of the account by the former rebel leader Goukouni Weddeye is not verifiable. However, it is certain that the French commander sent to negotiate the release of the hostages was taken hostage and executed by Chadian rebels.[23]

Marc Combe, who managed to escape, told the story of his detention in a book.[24] As for Françoise Claustre, she remained captive. Efforts were made to secure her release. Her abduction became an affair of state in France. French politicians and journalists became interested in the case. Parliamentarians raised it in the French National Assembly. This was, for example, the case during an extraordinary session in 1975 when the Member of French Parliament Michel Boscher asked a question on this subject.[25] France began negotiations with the rebels. On the radio, Georges Vedel, a famous French law professor, appealed to Hissein Habré, his former student, for the release of Françoise Claustre.[26] He begged him. Hissein Habré remained inflexible, did not free the Frenchwoman despite negotiations and a promise of liberation. Françoise Claustre's husband, Pierre Claustre, negotiated with Hissein Habré and the rebels.[27] But the negotiations failed and he in turn was taken hostage. The Claustre couple were not released until 1977 after Hissein Habré had distanced himself from Goukouni Weddeye who, after final negotiations with Libya, allegedly gave Françoise Claustre and her husband back their freedom.[28]

Thus, Western nationals, French and German, had been victims of rebels, one of whose leaders was Hissein Habré, the future Chadian head of state. France had been the most exposed and targeted.

Several questions arise from the evocation of these acts of Hissein Habré, the former rebel leader. Had these acts returned to the memory of France and prompted it to finance the trial? Had France remembered a report by Raymond Depardon on the captivity of Françoise Claustre surrounded by rebels in a dry and arid Chadian desert?[29] Had it remembered this unknown African, referred to as Hissène Habré, described as the leader of the rebels and appearing on French television screens with sunglasses on his face, a revolutionary cap on his head, his moustache tightened, his clothes loosely wrapped around a thin and dry body? The report had moved the whole of France. In 1987, in *Le Nouvel Observateur*, Jean-Paul Mari wrote on this subject:

> Remember, the image of Françoise Claustre recorded by Raymond Depardon's camera. France has a tight throat when it listened to the complaint of the young French ethnologist. Taken hostage on 21 April 1974 in Bardaï, she was not released until 30 January 1977. Three years. Old white anguish in front of cruel and mysterious Africa, ancient theme of the beautiful young woman reduced to the mercy of her torturer in an inaccessible castle, symbol of the tormented relationship between France and its former colony, challenge of a "famished puppet" to the French state, brutal discovery of terrorism taking innocent hostages. . . . France is delirious, lost in obscure negotiations where we see plenipotentiaries dragging their briefcases and their dignity in the rock of Tibesti.[30]

Had not France, relieved of this quasi humiliation and national trauma, forgotten? Did the trial of the former terrorist and hostage-taker allow France these many decades later to take revenge on this rebel who had attacked the French? If so, the trial of Hissein Habré, beyond the international crimes reported by the victims, would also be a way of washing away the past affront. Germany's participation in the financing of the trial would follow the same logic.

However, the history of Chad under the presidency of Hissein Habré shows that, putting aside its resentments toward the desert rebel and favoring its interests in the region, France was a strong supporter of Habré's regime when he came to power in 1982. France was concerned about the instability in Chad and Libya's intrusion into part of Chad's territory. It actively supported the maintenance of the territorial integrity of Chad and thus supported the maintenance of Hissein Habré in power.[31] The public records of the French Parliament confirm the assertions concerning the civil and military aid provided by France to the regime of Hissein Habré who was fighting against Muammar Gaddafi's Libya.[32] Hissein Habré and his troops had succeeded in repelling the Libyan forces. France succeeded in preserving stability in the region by supporting Habré's armed forces.

But later, France did not come to the aid of Hissein Habré when the latter's power was attacked by the armed rebellion that put an end to his regime. After the fall of Hissein Habré, a French Senator referred to Chad as the place "where France has not lifted a finger [. . .] to keep the no less sinister Hissène Habré in power."[33] France had therefore supported Hissein Habré's regime and had later stopped its support. Why? Because of the acts of kidnapping and sequestration of French nationals a few years earlier? It seems that France's interests had evolved over time and that the abduction of French nationals did not adequately explain this turnaround. Although other elements cannot be excluded, some elements of explanation have been put forward.

On the one hand, Human Rights Watch published a report during the trial of Hissein Habré which stated that France's resentment toward Hissein Habré arose from the latter's concealed collaboration with the Americans.[34] The NGO relied on revelations made by Claude Silberzahn, a Frenchman appointed in 1989 as director of the Direction Générale de la Sécurité Extérieure (French secret service),[35] in a book published in 1995 and containing extensive information on the relationship between France and Hissein Habré.[36] It was reported that Hissein Habré was collaborating with the United States, participating in the creation of an anti-Muammar Gaddafi force—that of Colonel Haftar—trained by the CIA on the Chadian territory, without informing France, which had been supporting him for years. Hissein Habré made the French understand that he no longer needed them. That is where the disenchantment allegedly came from. What might have appeared to be one of the attributes of Chad's sovereignty, a state being free to maintain relations with whomever it wished without informing other states, had become an act of ingratitude and an act of treason.

On the other hand, it was reported that Hissein Habré had sharply criticized the speech delivered by French president François Mitterrand at La Baule in June 1990.[37] In that speech, a plea for democracy in Africa, the French president had insisted that his country's aid to African states would henceforth be conditional on the democratization of those states' regimes, respect for human rights, and multiparty politics. To this speech, Hissein Habré allegedly replied that there was no lesson to be learned from a formerly colonizing state, vilifying a Western thought and ideal which, according to him, was not in line with African specificities.[38]

These episodes in Chad's history were also noted during the trial of Hissein Habré for international crimes. Referring to Hissein Habré's reply to François Mitterrand's La Baule speech, a lawyer for the civil parties questioned the fact that Hissein Habré, after having been helped by France, had spit "somehow in the soup."[39] The historian Arnaud

Dingammadji recalled that Hissein Habré had been supported by foreign powers, including France and the United States.[40] He stressed that despite the support given to the regime of Hissein Habré by France, Hissein Habré intended to remain independent. The consequence of this breakdown in relations between France and the Habré regime was the lack of support offered when Hissein Habré was facing the rebels led by Idriss Déby Itno. The former colonial power did not support Hissein Habré, nor did the United States.

The relationship between Hissein Habré and the United States, which participated in the financing of his trial, is equally peculiar and complex. Hissein Habré's regime between 1982 and 1990 was certainly the Americans' unexpected bulwark against the expansionist Libyan policy of Muammar Gaddafi, their enemy. The Americans had also supported Hissein Habré and his regime. Hissein Habré had been received in 1987, as we saw, at the White House by then-American president Ronald Reagan. The United States had even acknowledged, in a letter to the secretary-general of the United Nations, the support to Hissein Habré's Chad and the supply of arms, including anti-aircraft missiles.[41] According to the United States, the aid provided in no way violated international rules.[42] It was part of cooperation with Chad, which, in the face of the Libyan invasion, was exercising its right of self-defense in accordance with the Charter of the United Nations.[43] A 1987 US State Department document clearly summarized the support given to the Chadian government:

> The US supports the Chadian Government in resisting Libyan aggression, restoring its territorial integrity, and pursuing reconstruction and internal political reconciliation. The US believes that resistance to Libyan domination of Chad is important for regional security, and is concerned about the threat posed to Chad and its neighbors by the continued Libyan occupation of parts of northern Chad.[44]

The document also detailed the substantial military equipment assistance provided to Chad under Hissein Habré regime.

A Human Rights Watch report published during Hissein Habré's trial examined US foreign aid to the former Chadian head of state.[45] Prior to the NGO's report, the National Commission of Inquiry set up after Hissein Habré's fall had shed a striking light on US support for the repressive regime. It found that the United States was "at the top of the list" of states that had "actively supported the DDS," the regime's political police.[46] The Americans advised the DDS, supported it financially and logistically. The commission had indicated that aid had allegedly become more substantial toward the end of the Habré presidency,[47] when Hissein Habré, according to the Human

Rights Watch report, began to move away from France and toward the United States. On the other hand, like France, the United States did not support Hissein Habré when he was confronted with the rebels. Were they certainly no longer interested in it, since the expansionist plans of the Libyan enemy had since been stopped? Or, did not they sense a fall of Hissein Habré? In any case, it remains difficult to establish a link between these elements of Chadian-American relations under the Habré regime and the decision of the United States to finance his trial.

Due to the complex political relations of Hissein Habré with France and the United States, there is no clear indication as to whether there was a will for revenge in the context of the trial. Reed Brody even revealed that France resisted to get involved in the process of bringing Hissein Habré to justice.[48] It was after discussions with Reed Brody and a leading Chadian lawyer, Jacqueline Moudeïna, that Senegalese-born Rama Yade, a member of the French government in charge of human rights, convinced French president Nicolas Sarkozy to support the case.[49]

In any case, the existence of Western or other state interests explaining the financing of Hissein Habré's trial would not call into question the reality of the international crimes committed and the painful experience of the victims of his regime. The financing of the trial should therefore be placed in an international framework where, unlike during the Cold War, the fight against impunity in Africa has been gaining momentum. The financing of the trial by Western powers, and even by the African Union, can be seen as a desire on their part to position themselves as human rights defenders, to make up for lost time, and to restore their image after having been silent in the face of serious human rights violations in Chad. In this sense, the trial of Hissein Habré has been an opportunity for several states, which have a collective and historical responsibility because of their silence, to purge the past.

THE COLLECTIVE RESPONSIBILITY OF STATES AND THE INTERNATIONAL COMMUNITY

At the time the international crimes were committed in Chad, several states had not denounced and strongly acted against the repressive and macabre machine revealed by the trial. As suggested by the image of the three monkeys before which the detainees of Habré's regime had to swear upon their release that they had seen nothing, heard nothing, and would say nothing about what they had experienced in the regime's jails, several states closed their ears, mouths, and eyes as a brutal crackdown on Hissein Habré's victims took place.

In the context of relations between Chad and certain Western states such as France and the United States, it now appears that at the time, the fight against impunity was not on the international agenda. Hissein Habré could act as he wished in his country as long as he protected the interests of the West, in particular by blocking Libya's expansionist ambitions. In this regard, one of the most astonishing pieces of information, already known but disseminated by the trial, was the reference to the offices of USAID, an American agency that provides development aid to foreign states, which were located near the DDS and its torture centers.[50] This proximity raises the question of whether the Americans who worked there could not hear the shrill cries of those being tortured. In the same vein, reports submitted by the US State Department to the US Senate and House of Representatives from 1983 to 1990, during Hissein Habré's regime, contained information on the many gross human rights violations committed in Chad.[51]

The lack of action of foreign states on the atrocities committed in Chad cannot, however, be reduced to the French and American cases. One may wonder about the attitude of other Western states involved in financing the trial, at least because of Amnesty International's denunciation of serious human rights violations revealed in the report of the Chadian National Commission of Inquiry.[52] In this regard, Amnesty International sent thousands of letters and cards to Habré's regime that expressed concern about massive human rights violations. The cards and letters came from Amnesty International branches in several of the states, including those that funded the trial. Thus, apart from France and the United States from which several thousand letters and cards were sent, more than 7,000 letters and cards were sent from Germany and the Netherlands, more than 2,000 from Belgium, around 30 from Luxembourg, and several thousand from other current Member States of the European Union such as Sweden, Finland, and Italy.[53] Although NGOs are not, in principle, state organs, one wonders whether these state authorities were not aware of this activity of sending letters and cards drawing attention to serious human rights violations in an African state, albeit a distant one.

Africa also turned a blind eye to the commission of crimes in Chad under Hissein Habré. Zaire (now the Democratic Republic of Congo) was even named by the expert historian who testified at the trial as one of the major supporters of Habré's regime.[54] The historian pointed out some initiatives for peace talks and some agreements between the regime and the rebel groups.[55] However, African states did not collectively and energetically denounce the human rights violations and international crimes uncovered by the trial. The Organization of African Unity, which has since become the African Union, did not prevent the commission of crimes in Chad. Could it have been otherwise? In the 1980s when serious crimes were being committed in Chad, the same types of crimes were certainly being committed in several African states headed by dictators. One could not have expected criticism or denunciation from such regimes.

So the international community had done nothing. The finding of such inaction leads to the conclusion that all states of the international community undoubtedly have a historical and collective responsibility for the perpetration of international crimes in Chad. This historical and collective responsibility should always be invoked in the event of the commission of international crimes and of silence and lack of action of states and the international community. This responsibility and the need for reconciliation in order to avoid international crimes lead to positioning the trial of Hissein Habré not in the reduced framework of an Africa that is finally bringing Africans to justice, or the West without which the trial would not have taken place, but in the framework of human criminal justice.

NOTES

1. Ellen L. Lutz and Caitlin Reiger, ed., *Prosecuting Heads of State* (Cambridge: Cambridge University Press, 2009), 301–303.

2. SCSL (Trial Chamber), *The Prosecutor v. Charles Ghankay Taylor*, no. SCSL-03-01-T, Judgment, May 18, 2012.

3. ICC (Appeals Chamber). *The Prosecutor v. Laurent Gbagbo and Charles Blé Goudé*. Judgment in the appeal of the Prosecutor against Trial Chamber I's decision on the no case to answer motions. no. ICC-02/11-01/15-1400, March 31, 2021.

4. ICC, Situation in Libya, *The Prosecutor v. Saif Al-Islam Gaddafi*, no. ICC-01/11-01/11, Case Information Sheet, November 2009.

5. ICC, Situation in Darfur, Sudan, *The Prosecutor v. Omar Hassan Ahmad Al Bashir*, no. ICC-02/05-01/09, Case Information Sheet, April 2018. Sudarsan Raghavan, "Former Sudanese Ruler Omar Hassan al-Bashir is Convicted of Corruption, Money Laundering," *Washington Post*, December 14, 2019.

6. La cellule de communication avec la collaboration des Avocats. *Le Sénégal « juge » le Président Hissein Habré*, June 2015, 42, 101–102.

7. On International Criminal Court in Africa, see chapter 2.

8. For another account on that topic, see, for example, Celeste Hicks, *The Trial of Hissène Habré : How the People of Chad brought a Tyrant to Justice* (London: Zedbooks, 2018).

9. See chapter 1.

10. Table ronde des donateurs pour le financement du procès d'Hissène Habré, Document final, Dakar, November 24, 2010, para. 15; Reed Brody, *The Hissène Habré case. The Victims' Struggle to Bring their Dictator to Justice*, Brot für Welt, April 2017, 14.

11. See chapter 1.

12. Human Rights Watch, *Chad: Government Fails Ex-Dictator's Victims. 3 Years On, No Action on Habré-Era Reparation*, March 22, 2018.

13. See some of the available financial report (not all of them are available for public), for example, Financial Report and Audited Financial Statements of the African Union Commission (AUC) for the Year Ended December 31, 2014, 18; Financial Report and Audited Financial Statements of the African Union Commission (AUC) For the Year Ended December 31, 2015, 16; African Union Annual Report and Consolidated Financial Statements for the Financial Year Ended December 2017, 8–9.

14. African Union, *President Mugabe hands over 300 Head of Cattle to the African Union Foundation*, Press Release, February 26, 2016; see also the video of the Speech of the president of Zimbabwe the day of the donation: SABC Digital News, "Mugabe donates $1 million to African Union," July 4, 2017, online: https://www.youtube.com/watch?v=FOrQ86PjoJM, accessed 5/16/2021.

15. See for example, Remarks by President Paul Kagame Launch of the African Union Peace Fund, Addis Ababa, November 17, 2018.

16. See, for example, David Wippman, "The Costs of International Justice," *The American Journal of International Law* 100, no. 4 (2006): 861; ICC-ASP, Resolution of the Assembly of States Parties on the proposed program budget for 2020, the Working Capital Fund for 2020, the scale of assessment for the apportionment of expenses of the International Criminal Court, financing appropriations for 2020 and the Contingency Fund, Resolution ICC-ASP/18/Res.1, December 6, 2019.

17. Reed Brody, *The Hissène Habré case*, op. cit., note 10.

18. Table ronde des donateurs, op. cit. note 10.

19. Ibid., para. 15; Reed Brody, *The Hissène Habré case*. op. cit., note 10, 14.

20. See for example on that matter, regarding ICTY, Florence Hartmann, *Paix et châtiment. Les guerres secrètes de la politique et de la justice internationales* (Paris: Flammarion, 2007).

21. See chapter 1.

22. For this information and those that follow, see the document, Entretiens de Goukouni Weddeye avec Laurent Correau, *Témoignage pour l'histoire du Tchad*, Document Radio France Internationale, September 23, 2008, 57 ff. For more on Goukouni Weddeye, see Goukouni Weddeye, *Combattant, une vie pour le Tchad* (Paris: Espaces & Signes, 2019).

23. See the document, Citation à l'ordre de l'armée, lu par monsieur Yvon Bourges ministre de la défense, avril 20, 1976; and Archives, Le Commandant Galopin est cité à l'ordre de l'armée, *Le Monde*, 22 avril 1976, online: https://www.lemonde.fr/archives/article/1976/04/22/le-commandant-galopin-est-cite-a-l-ordre-de-l-armee_2967685_1819218.html, accessed 5/16/2021.

24. Marc Combe, *Otage au Tibesti* (Paris: Flammarion, 1976).

25. France, Assemblée nationale Session extraordinaire 1974-1975-Compte rendu intégral - 3° séance-Séance du Mercredi 10 Septembre 1975, 143.

26. The call of the law professor is available in the audio document, Alain Foca (Radio France internationale), *Hissène Habré, l'affaire Claustre (1 et 2/6)*, September 1, 2015, 49:30 mn.

27. Pierre Claustre, *L'affaire Claustre. Autopsie d'une prise d'otages* (Paris: Karthala, 1990).

28. Entretiens de Goukouni Weddeye, op. cit., note 22, 63; Alain Foca (Radio France internationale), *Hissène Habré, l'affaire Claustre (1 et 2/6)*, op. cit., note 26.

29. Archives Video Document, IT1 20H, "Raymond Depardon filme Françoise Claustre," September 27, 1975, online: https://m.ina.fr/video/CAA7501083501/raymond-depardon-filme-francoise-claustre-video.html, accessed 5/16/2021.

30. Jean-Paul Mari, *Le Nouvel Observateur Monde*, July 10–16, 1987, 52 (Translation from French).

31. See Assemblée Nationale française, *Rapport d'information déposé par la commission des affaires étrangères en conclusion des travaux d'une mission d'information constituée le 14 novembre 2012, sur « engagement et diplomatie : quelle doctrine pour nos interventions militaires ? » et présenté par M. Guy-Michel Chauveau et M. Hervé Gaymard*, 2015, 117–118; Conférence de presse conjointe de M. François Mitterrand, Président de la République, et de M. Hissène Habré, Président de la République du Tchad, sur les relations franco-tchadiennes et l'aide militaire française. Paris, lundi 13 juillet 1987, online: https://www.vie-publique.fr/discours/139665-conference-de-presse-conjointe-de-m-francois-mitterrand-president-de-l, accessed 5/16/2021; Robert Buijtenhuijs. "L'art de ménager la chèvre et le chou: la politique tchadienne de François Mitterrand," *Politique Africaine*, no. 16 (1984): 110–111; Colonel Spartacus. *Les documents secrets. Opération Manta. 1983–1984* (Plon, 1985).

32. Assemblée nationale, Questions écrites remises à la Présidence de l'Assemblée nationale et réponses des ministres, 9 décembre 1985, JO 1985- n°48 A.N. (Q), 5655–5656; Sénat, compte rendu intégral 33e séance, séance du 4 juin 1987, JO 1987-n°33 S. (C.R.), 1531 and 1544; Sénat, compte rendu intégral, 39e séance, séance du 6 décembre 1988, JO 1988-n° 55 S. (C. R.), 2332.

33. Sénat, Compte rendu de séance, séance du 5 décembre 1991, JO 1991, n° 100 S. (C. R.), 4895 (Translated from French).

34. Human Rights Watch, *Allié de la France, condamné par l'Afrique. Les relations entre la France et le régime tchadien de Hissène Habré (1982–1990)*, June 2016. See also the summary of the Report in English, Human Rights Watch, *Supported by France, Convicted by Africa France-Chad Relations during the Hissène Habré's Rule (1982–1990)*, June 2016.

35. France, Conseil des ministres du 22 Mars 1989, Mesures d'ordre individuel, Texte intégral, March 22, 1989.

36. Claude Silberzahn (avec Jean Guisnel), *Au cœur du secret : 1500 jours aux commandes de la DGSE (1989–1993)* (Paris: Fayard, 1995).

37. François Mitterrand (French President), Le discours de La Baule (1990) La Baule, June 20, 1990.

38. H. Sada, "Habré: connais pas," *Jeune Afrique*, no. 1563, December 12–18 1990; Robert Buijtenhuijs, "Hissein Habré Seigneur de la guerre jusqu'au bout," *Politique africaine* (1991), online: http://www.politique-africaine.com/numeros/pdf/041135.pdf, accessed 5/16/2021.

39. EAC, Hearing of Arnaud Dingammadji, September 9, 2015, Online Playlist of the *Forum interactif sur les CAE*. EAC, Transcripts, September 9, 2015.

40. Ibid.

41. UN Doc. S/19271, November 13, 1987.

42. Ibid.

43. Ibid.

44. US Department of State, Bureau of Public Affairs, *Chad, US Policy* (Washington, DC: Bureau of Public Affairs, Dept. of State), July 1987.

45. Human Rights Watch, *Enabling a Dictator The United States and Chad's Hissène Habré 1982–1990*, June 2016.

46. Tchad, Rapport de la commission nationale d'enquête du ministère tchadien de la justice, *Les crimes et les détournements de l'ex-président Habré et de ses complices* (Paris: L'Harmattan, 1993), 29.

47. Ibid.

48. Reed Brody, *The Hissène Habré case*, op. cit., note 10, 27.

49. Ibid.

50. See EAC, Hearing of Mahamat Hassan Abakar, September 15, 2015, Online Playlist of the *Forum interactif sur les CAE*. EAC Transcripts, September 15 and 16, 2015.

51. Country Reports on Human Rights Practices for 1983, Submitted to the Committee on Foreign Affairs U.S. House of Representatives and the Committee on Foreign Relations U.S. Senate by the Department of State (Washington, U.S. Printing Government Office), February 1984, 82–89; Country Reports on Human Rights Practices for 1984, Submitted to the Committee on Foreign Relations U.S. Senate and the Committee on Foreign Affairs U.S. House of Representatives by the Department of State (Washington, U.S. Printing Government Office), February 1985, 73–76; Country Reports on Human Rights Practices for 1985, Submitted to the Committee on Foreign Affairs U.S. House of Representatives and the Committee on Foreign Relations U.S. Senate by the Department of State (Washington, U.S. Printing Government Office), February 1986, 67–75; Country Reports on Human Rights Practices for 1986, Submitted to the Committee on Foreign Relations U.S. Senate and the Committee on Foreign Affairs U.S. House of Representatives by the Department of State (Washington, U.S. Printing Government Office), February 1987, 62–69; Country Reports on Human Rights Practices for 1987, Submitted to the Committee on Foreign Affairs U.S. House of Representatives and the Committee on Foreign Relations U.S. Senate by the Department of State (Washington, U.S. Printing Government Office), February 1988, 57–63; Country Reports on Human Rights Practices for 1988, Submitted to the Committee on Foreign Relations U.S. Senate and the Committee on Foreign Affairs U.S. House of Representatives by the Department of State (Washington, U.S. Printing Government Office), February 1989, 66–73; Country Reports on Human Rights Practices for 1989, Submitted to the Committee on Foreign Affairs U.S. House of Representatives and the Committee on Foreign Relations U.S. Senate by the Department of State (Washington, U.S. Printing Government Office), February 1990, 69–76; Country Reports on Human Rights Practices for 1990, Submitted to the Committee on Foreign Relations U.S. Senate and the Committee on Foreign Affairs U.S. House of Representatives by the Department of State (Washington, U.S. Printing Government Office), February 1991, 70–78;

52. Tchad, Rapport de la commission nationale d'enquête du ministère tchadien de la justice, op. cit., note 46, 92–93.

53. Ibid.

54. See the testimony of Arnaud Dingammadji, op. cit., note 39.

55. Ibid.

Conclusion

Human Criminal Justice

Hissein Habré, a former head of state of Chad, was tried and convicted for the commission of international crimes by the Extraordinary African Chambers after an unprecedented mobilization of victims, human rights organizations, states, international organizations, and others. Whenever the interests of victims, many individuals, several states, international bodies, and nongovernmental and international organizations converge in the fight against impunity for international crimes, the justice implemented is human criminal justice. Here, human beings confronted with horror purge the evil in front of a court of law and remind us of humanist values. Whenever international crimes are committed, as the Preamble of the International Criminal Court Statute recalls, it is the international community as a whole that is affected. We are no longer Africans, Europeans, Americans, Asians, or Oceanians; we are the whole of humanity whose values have been undermined by the commission of such crimes; we are human beings affected by these serious crimes. In these situations where individuals and communities have been seriously affected, the international community must question itself, stand by the victims, and ensure that the perpetrators of crimes are brought to justice. This justice can be carried out anywhere, although it is preferable, when conditions are met, that it be located as close as possible to the victims—as it was in Africa.

The trial of Hissein Habré was the implementation of this human criminal justice. It was a trial that was certainly localized in Africa and that reaffirmed the fight against impunity on this continent, but it was also a trial that was an opportunity for human beings to recall humanist values. This trial was part of a general movement in favor of the fight against impunity. It was evidence that no matter where the crime was committed, no matter where the perpetrator took refuge, no matter what the perpetrator's former status was, no matter how many years went by, justice was still possible. It was also an appeal to leaders to avoid pursuing policies of terror, to avoid committing international crimes for which they may sooner or later be held accountable, crimes for which they may be held criminally responsible.

This human criminal justice is certainly not perfect. It is sometimes, rather very often, selective. It should be noted, for example, that only Hissein Habré was tried and sentenced by the EAC. Of course, he was not the only person responsible for this tragedy that had been going on for almost a decade in Chad. Several of his collaborators have escaped this justice. Nevertheless, the justice system has taken a step forward in the fight against impunity. This step should be followed by other steps. Human criminal justice must continue to hold perpetrators accountable, to restore the dignity of victims, to provide reparations, and to prevent the commission of international crimes. Human criminal justice must continue to advance everywhere.

Bibliography

Abdul-Haq Al-Ani. *The Trial of Saddam Hussein.* Atlanta: Clarity Press, 2008.

Accord de coopération judiciaire entre la République du Sénégal et la République du Tchad pour la poursuite des crimes internationaux commis au Tchad durant la période du 7 juin 1982 au 1er décembre 1990, May 3, 2013.

ACtHPR. *Michelot Yogogombaye c. République du Sénégal*, Req. 001/2008, Arrêt, December 15, 2009.

AFP. *Abdoulaye Wade va renvoyer l'ex-président Hissène Habré au Tchad*, Dépêche, July 8, 2011.

African Commission on Human and Peoples' Rights. *Commission nationale des droits de l'homme et des libertés c. Tchad*, Communication n° 74/92, October 1995.

Agreement Between the Government of the Republic of Senegal and the African Union on the Establishment of the Extraordinary African Chambers Within the Courts of Senegal, August 22, 2012.

Agreement Between the Kingdom of the Netherlands and the Republic of Kosovo Concerning the Hosting of the Kosovo Relocated Specialist Judicial Institution in the Netherlands, February 15, 2016.

Agreement Between the Kingdom of the Netherlands and the United Nations Concerning the Headquarters of the Special Tribunal for Lebanon, December 21, 2007.

Agreement Between the United Nations and Cambodia for the Prosecution of Crimes Committed During the Period of Democratic Kampuchea, 2003.

Agreement Between the United Nations and the Government of Sierra Leone on the Establishment of a Special Court for Sierra Leone, January 16, 2002.

Ahmad Allam-Mi. *Autour du Tchad en Guerre. Tractations politiques et diplomatiques 1975–1990.* Paris: L'Harmattan, 2014.

Arendt, Hannah. *Eichmann in Jerusalem: A Report on the Banality of Evil.* Rev. and enl. ed. New York: Viking Press, 1964.

Arrest Warrant of 11 April 2000 (*Democratic Republic of the Congo v. Belgium*), Judgment, I.C.J. Reports 2002.

Assemblée nationale française. *Rapport d'information déposé par la commission des affaires étrangères en conclusion des travaux d'une mission d'information constituée le 14 novembre 2012, sur « engagement et diplomatie: quelle doctrine pour nos interventions militaires? » et présenté par M. Guy-Michel Chauveau et M. Hervé Gaymard*, 2012, 2015.

AU. Decision on the Abuse of the Principle of Universal Jurisdiction. Doc. Assembly/AU/11(XIII), July 3, 2009.

AU. Decision on the Abuse of the Principle of Universal Jurisdiction. Doc. EX.CL/606(XVII), July 27, 2010.

AU. Decision on the Application by the International Criminal Court (ICC) Prosecutor for the Indictment of the President of the Republic of the Sudan. Doc. Assembly/AU/Dec.221(XII), February 3, 2009.

AU. Decision on the Hissene Habre Case. Doc. Assembly/Au/9(Xvi), 2011.

AU. Decision on the Hissene Habre Case. Doc. Assembly/Au/12(Xviii), 2011.

AU. Decision on the Hissene Habre Case. Doc. Assembly/Au/8(Xvii), 2011.

AU. Decision on the Hissene Habre Case and the African Union. Doc. Assembly/Au/8(Vi) Add.9, January 23–24, 2006.

AU. Decision on the Hissene Habre Case and the African Union. Doc. Assembly/Au/3(Vii), July 2, 2006.

AU. Decision on the Implementation of the Assembly Decision on the Abuse of the Principle of Universal Jurisdiction. Doc. Assembly/AU/3(XII), February 1–3, 2009.

AU. Decision on the Implementation of the Assembly Decisions on the International Criminal Court. Doc. EX.CL/670(XIX), July 1, 2011.

AU. Decision on the Implementation of the Decisions on the International Criminal Court. Doc. EX.CL/639(XVIII), January 31, 2011.

AU. Decision on the Meeting of African States Parties to the Rome Statute of the International Criminal Court (ICC). Doc. Assembly/AU/13(XIII), July 3, 2009.

AU. Decision on the Progress Report of the Commission on the Implementation of Decision Assembly/Au/Dec.270(XIV) on the Second Ministerial Meeting on the Rome Statute of the International Criminal Court (ICC). Doc. Assembly/AU/10(XV), July 27, 2010.

AU. Decision on the Progress Report of the Commission on the Implementation of the Assembly Decisions on the International Criminal Court (ICC). Doc. EX.CL/710(XX), January 30, 2012.

AU. Decision on the Report of the Commission on the Abuse of the Principle of Universal Jurisdiction. Doc. Assembly/AU/14 (XI), 2008.

AU. Directorate of Information and Communication, Press Release N° 089/2015, April 6, 2015.

AU. Doc. Min/Legal/ACJHR-PAP/3(II) Rev. 1.5.

AU. Progress Report of the Commission on the Hissene Habre Case (In the Implementation of Decision Assembly/Au/Dec.297(XV)). Doc. Assembly/AU/9(XVI) Rev.1, January 30–31, 2011.

AU. Report of the Committee of Eminent African Jurists on the Case of Hissene Habré, July 2, 2006.

AU. Statute of a Trust Fund for the Benefit of Victims of the Crimes of Hissène Habré. Doc. EX.CL/1040(XXXI) Annex, 2018.

Azevedo, Mario J. *The Roots of Violence: A History of War in Chad.* London and New York: Routledge, 2005.

Azevedo, Mario J., and Samuel Decalo. *Historical Dictionary of Chad.* 4th ed. Lanham: Rowman and Littlefield, 2018.

Bangoura, Mohamed Tétémadi. *Violence politique et conflits en Afrique: le cas du Tchad.* Paris: L'Harmattan, 2006.

Banks, S. Arthur, and Thomas C. Muller, eds. *Political Handbook of the World: 1998: Governments and Intergovernmental Organizations as of January 1, 1998.* New York: CSA Publications, 1998.

Bartrop, Paul R. *A Biographical Encyclopedia of Contemporary Genocide. Portraits of Evil and Good.* Santa-Barbara: ABC-CLIO, 2012.

Belgium. *Loi du 5 août 2003 relative aux violations graves du droit international humanitaire.*

Belgium. *Loi relative à la répression des infractions graves aux Conventions de Genève du 12 août 1949 aux Protocoles I et II du 8 juin 1977*, June 16, 1993.

Belgium. *Loi relative à la répression des violations graves du droit international humanitaire*, February 10, 1999.

Bercault, Olivier (Écrit par en collaboration avec Reed Brody). *La Plaine des Morts Le Tchad de Hissène Habré 1982–1990.* Black Print Cpi Ibérica, Human Rights Watch, 2013.

Bramstedt, Ernest Kohn. *Dictatorship and Political Police: The Technique of Control by Fear.* New York: Oxford University Press, 1945.

Brody, Reed. *Contra Terror in Nicaragua: Report of a Fact-Finding Mission: Sept. 1984 - Jan. 1985.* Boston, MA: South End Press, 1985.

Brody, Reed. 'Contra' Terrorism Is, Unfortunately, True. *New York Times*, April 26, 1985.

Brody, Reed. Prosecution of Hissène Habré. An 'African Pinochet'. In *Livre noir: Terrorisme et responsabilité pénale internationale: recueil des contributions préparatoires au Colloque du 5 février 2002, organisé par SOS attentats*, 307–324. Paris: Assemblée Nationale, 2002.

Brody, Reed. *The Hissène Habré case*: *The Victims' Struggle to Bring their Dictator to Justice.* Brot für Welt, April 2017.

Brody, Reed. The Prosecution of Hissène Habré: International Accountability, National Impunity. In *Transitional Justice in the Twenty-First Century: Beyond Truth Versus Justice*, edited by Naomi Roht-Arriaza and Javier Mariezcurrena, 278–300. Cambridge: Cambridge University Press, 2014.

Brody, Reed, and Michael Ratner, eds. *The Pinochet Papers: The Case of Augusto Pinochet in Spain and Britain.* The Hague: Kluwer Law International, 2000.

Buijtenhuijs, Robert. Hissein Habré Seigneur de la guerre jusqu'au bout. http://www.politique-africaine.com/numeros/pdf/041135.pdf (accessed 16 May 2021).

Buijtenhuijs, Robert. L'art de ménager la chèvre et le chou: la politique tchadienne de François Mitterrand. *Politique Africaine* 16, 1984.

Burundi. *Withdrawal*, C.N.805.2016.treaties-xviii.10, October 28, 2016.

Carayol, Rémi. Tchad: Bandoum Bandjim, le repenti du système Habré. *Jeune Afrique*, July 27, 2015. https://www.jeuneafrique.com/mag/250203/societe/tchad-bandoum-bandjim-le-repenti-du-systeme-habre/ (accessed 16 May 2021).

CAT. *Suleymane Guengueng and others vs. Senegal.* Communication No. 181/2001, May 17, 2006.

CAT. *Suleymane Guengueng et autres c/Sénégal.* Communication Présentée au Comité contre la torture (Article 22 de la Convention) pour violation des Articles 5 et 7 de la Convention, April 18, 2001.

CAT. *Suleymane Guengueng, et al. v. Senegal.* Communication No. 181/2001, Craintes de libération d'Hissène Habré. Doc. G/SO 229/31 SEN(1) Follow-up, December 23, 2019.

Chad. Commission nationale d'enquête du ministère tchadien de la justice. *Les crimes et les détournements de l'ex-président Habré et de ses complices.* Video, 52 minutes, 1992.

Chad. Cour d'appel de N'Djamena. *Ministère Public et Ismael Hachim et autres contre Saleh Younous Ali, Waroun Fadoul ali et autres.* Répertoire n°01/15, March 25, 2015.

Chad. Déclaration du conseil militaire de transition. https://presidence.td/galleries/declaration-du-conseil-militaire-de-transition/?fbclid=IwAR0vg9vVr_5pI9kL_Jbq10hJpvBik3nbw5ec49PNOQFqqeQs8E7oBcIJA0g (accessed 16 May 2021).

Chad. Decree Creating the Commission of Inquiry into the Crimes and the Misappropriations Committed by Ex-President Habré, His Accomplices and/or Accessories. Decree no. 014/P. CE/CJ/90, December 29, 1990.

Chad. *Lettre du ministre de la justice du Tchad levant l'immunité dont M. H. Habré pourrait se prévaloir*, October 7, 2002.

Chad. Rapport de la commission nationale d'enquête du ministère tchadien de la justice. In *Les crimes et les détournements de l'ex-président Habré et de ses complices*. Paris: L'Harmattan, 1993.

Chevolleau, Florent. *Hissène Habré: la traque d'un dictateur*, 2009, 57 mn.

Citation à l'ordre de l'armée, lu par monsieur Yvon Bourges ministre de la défense, April 20, 1976.

Claustre, Pierre. *L'affaire Claustre. Autopsie d'une prise d'otages.* Paris: Karthala, 1990.

Combe, Marc. *Otage au Tibesti.* Paris: Flammarion, 1976.

Comité de Pilotage du Comité International pour le Jugement Equitable de Hissène Habré. *Lettre ouverte à la communauté internationale et africaine*, April 15, 2008. https://www.hrw.org/fr/news/2008/04/15/lettre-ouverte-la-communaute-internationale-et-africaine (accessed 16 May 2021).

Conclusions pour: les victimes regroupées au sein de deux associations que sont RADHT et ACVRP, January 2016, and Conclusions finales. Déposé par: avocats des parties civiles (Clément Abaifouta et al.), January 2016.

Conférence de presse conjointe de M. François Mitterrand, Président de la République, et de M. Hissène Habré, Président de la République du Tchad, sur les relations franco-tchadiennes et l'aide militaire française, Paris, lundi 13 juillet 1987. https://www.vie-publique.fr/discours/139665-conference-de-presse-conjointe-de-m-francois-mitterrand-president-de-l (accessed 16 May 2021).

Council of the European Union. *The AU-EU Expert Report on the Principle of Universal Jurisdiction.* Doc. 8672/1/09 REV 1, April 16, 2009.

Cour d'appel de Dakar (Chambre d'accusation). Arrêt no. 138, November 25, 2005.

Criminal Procedure Code of Senegal.

Cryer, Robert, Darryl Robinson, and Sergey Vasiliev. *An Introduction to International Criminal Law and Procedure.* 4th ed. Cambridge: Cambridge University Press, 2019.

Debos, Marielle. *Le métier des armes au Tchad: le gouvernement de l'entre-guerres.* Paris: Karthala, 2013.

Del Ponte, Carla. Difficulties for the Participants Indictment Correct, Trial Impossible. In *The Milosevic Trial: An Autopsy*, edited by Timothy William Waters, 136–149. New York: Oxford University Press, 2013.

Dingammadji, Arnaud. *Les gouvernements du Tchad: de Gabriel Lisette à Idriss Déby Itno, 1957–2010.* Paris: L'Harmattan, 2011.

Dingammadji, Arnaud. *Ngalta Tombalbaye: parcours et rôle dans la vie politique du Tchad, 1959–1975.* Paris: L'Harmattan, 2007.

Diouf, Abdou. *Mémoires.* Paris: Editions du Seuil, 2014.

EAC. Cérémonie d'ouverture officielle du procès de Hisséne Habré, July 20, 2015. https://www.youtube.com/watch?v=D_Ys8grgcpI (accessed 16 May 2021).

EAC. Chambres Africaines Extraordinaires Chambre d'Assises pour Parties civiles. *Abaïfouta Clément et autres*, n.d.

EAC. Hearing of Abakar Adoum, October 19, 2015.

EAC. Hearing of Abdourahmane Gueye, November 23, 2015.

EAC. Hearing of Alifa Gaston, October 14, 2015.

EAC. Hearing of Arnaud Dingammadji, September 9, 2015.

EAC. Hearing of Bandjim Bandoum, September 22 and 23, 2015.

EAC. Hearing of Bichara Djibrine Ahmat, December 8, 2015.

EAC. Hearing of Brahim Tassi, October 13, 2015.

EAC. Hearing of Clément Dokhot Abaifouta, November 9, 2015.

EAC. Hearing of Daniel Fransen, September 17, 2015.

EAC. Hearing of Djede Kourtou Gamar, October 6, 2015.

EAC. Hearing of Djimingaye Halta, November 16, 2015.

EAC. Hearing of Djokota Prosper Kladoumngué, October 27, 2015.

EAC. Hearing of Doungous Batil, October 5, 2015.

EAC. Hearing of Facho Balaam, September 10, 2015.

EAC. Hearing of Fatimé Hachim Saleh, October 13 and 14, 2015.

EAC. Hearing of Fatime Toumle, October 5, 2015.

EAC. Hearing of Ginette Ngarbaye, November 19, 2015.

EAC. Hearing of Hawa Brahim, October 21, 2015.

EAC. Hearing of Hélène Jaffé, October 12, 2015.

EAC. Hearing of Khadidja Hassan Zidane, October 19 and 20, 2015.
EAC. Hearing of Lakoubou Mbainassen, November 17, 2015.
EAC. Hearing of Madina Fadoul Kitir, October 12 and 13, 2015.
EAC. Hearing of Mahamat Nour Dadji, September 29, 2015.
EAC. Hearing of Mahamat-Hassan Abakar, September 15 and 16, 2015.
EAC. Hearing of Mallah Ngabouli, October 27, 2015.
EAC. Hearing of Marabi Toudjibedjé, September 30, 2015.
EAC. Hearing of Mariam Hassan Bagueri, October 29, 2015.
EAC. Hearing of Mbaïssouroum Manda René, November 12, 2015.
EAC. Hearing of Mike Dottridge, September 14, 2015.
EAC. Hearing of Nahor Ngawara, November 17, 2015.
EAC. Hearing of Ngarba Akhaye, September 28, 2015.
EAC. Hearing of Olivier Bercault, September 21, 2015.
EAC. Hearing of Oumar Déby Itno, October 19, 2015.
EAC. Hearing of Patrick Ball, September 18, 2015.
EAC. Hearing of Satta Gaye, November 23, 2015.
EAC. Hearing of Souleymane Abdoulaye Taher, November 10, 2015.
EAC. Hearing of Souleymane Guengueng, November 18 and 19, 2015.
EAC. Hearing of Yakhara Diop Gassama, September 10, 2015.
EAC. Hearing of Younous Mahadjir, November 16, 2015.
EAC. Hearing of Zakaria Fadoul Kitir, September 30, 2015 and October 1, 2015.
EAC. Hearings of Facho Balaam, September 10, 2015.
EAC. Hearings of Hadjé Mérami Ali, October 21 and 22, 2015.
EAC. Hearings of Zenaba Bassou Ngolo and Service Brahim, October 6, 2015.
EAC. Le Parquet. Réquisitions finales devant la chambre africaine extraordinaire d'assises, January 2016.
EAC. Observations du Parquet général sur les demandes de réparations des parties civiles, June 15, 2015. http://forumchambresafricaines.org (accessed 30 September 2018).
EAC. Procès Hissein Habré - Plaidoirie de la Défense - Me Mbaye SENE (11/02/2016). https://www.youtube.com/watch?v=VCaQ6zEIXoY (accessed 16 May 2021).
EAC. Procès Hissein Habré - Plaidoirie de la Défense - Me Mounir BALLAL (11/02/2016). https://www.youtube.com/watch?v=X5CvDuvkRaw&list=PLdiYVTzvsPWFD8s9yATKcapYT7keDWIb4&index=9 (accessed 16 May 2021).
EAC. Prononcé et résumé du jugement dans l'affaire *Le parquet général contre Hissein Habré*, May 30, 2016.
EAC. Video Verdict-Procès Hissene Habré, May 30, 2016. https://www.youtube.com/watch?v=T74_bGLTWaQ (accessed 16 May 2021).
EAC (Extraordinary African Assize Appeals Chamber). *Le Procureur général v. Hissein Habré*. Arrêt, April 27, 2017.
EAC (Extraordinary African Assize Chamber). *Ministère public v. Hissein Habré*. Judgment, May 30, 2016.
EAC (Extraordinary African Assize Chamber). *Ministère Public v. Hissein Habré*. Jugement sur les intérêts civils, July 29, 2016.

EAC (Extraordinary African Assize Chamber). Ordonnance déclarant irrecevable le « mémoire en défense (sur intérêts civils) » déposé par les conseils de l'accusé Hissein Habré, July 5, 2016.

EAC (Extraordinary African Investigative Chamber). Ordonnance de non-lieu partiel, de mise en accusation et de renvoi devant la Chambre africaine extraordinaire d'assises, February 13, 2015.

ECCC. *Kaing Guek Eav alias Duch*. Case File/Dossier no. 001/18-07-2007/ECCC/TC. Judgment, July 26, 2010.

ECHR. *Marguš vs Croatie*. No. 4455/10, May 27, 2014.

ECOWAS Court of Justice. *Hissein Habré v. Republic of Senegal*. No. ECW/CCJ/RUL/05/13, November 5, 2013.

ECOWAS Court of Justice. *Hissein Habré v. République du Sénégal*. Doc. No. ECW/CCJ/APP/07/08. Arret no. ECW/CCJ/JUD/06/10, November 18, 2010.

Entretiens de Goukouni Weddeye avec Laurent Correau. *Témoignage pour l'histoire du Tchad*. Document Radio France Internationale, September 23, 2008.

Eudes, Marina, and Emmanuel Guematcha. Quels apports des Chambres africaines extraordinaires? *Revue belge de droit international*, no. 1 (2017): 93–214.

Fichtelberg, Aaron. *Hybrid Tribunals: A Comparative Examination*. New York: Springer, Series on International Justice and Human Rights, 2015.

FIDH. *Le Sénégal devrait extrader Hissène Habré en Belgique pour un procès équitable plutôt que de l'envoyer au Tchad où il risque sa vie*, Communiqué, July 10, 2011.

Foca, Alain (Radio France internationale). *Hissène Habré, l'affaire Claustre (1 et 2/6)*, September 1, 2015, 49:30 mn.France. Assemblée nationale Session extraordinaire 1974–1975-Compte rendu intégral - 3° séance-Séance du Mercredi 10 Septembre 1975.

France. Conseil des ministres du 22 Mars 1989 Mesures d'ordre individuel, Texte intégral, March 22, 1989.

France, Assemblée Nationale. *Proposition de résolution de M. André GERIN et plusieurs de ses collègues tendant à la création d'une commission d'enquête sur l'engagement de la France dans le conflit tchadien*. Doc. no. 782, April 4, 2008.

François Mitterrand (French President). Le discours de La Baule (1990) La Baule, June 20, 1990.

Gambia. *Withdrawal of Notification of Withdrawal*. C.N.62.2017.treaties-xviii.10, February 16, 2017.

Garner, Bryan A., ed. *Black's Law Dictionary*. 9th ed., Saint Paul, MN: West, 2009.

Greitens, Sheena Chestnut. *Dictators and Their Secret Police : Coercive Institutions and State Violence*. Cambridge : Cambridge University Press, 2016.

Guengueng, Souleymane. *Prisonnier de Hissene Habré. L'expérience d'un survivant des geôles tchadiennes et sa quête de justice*. Paris: L'Harmattan, 2012.

Harold, D. Nelson. *Area Handbook for Chad*. Vol. 550, Issue 159. Washington, D.C.: Foreign Areas Studies Division, American University, 1972.

Hartmann, Florence. *Paix et châtiment. Les guerres secrètes de la politique et de la justice internationales*. Paris: Flammarion, 2007.

Hayner, Priscilla B. *Unspeakable Truths: Transitional Justice and the Challenge of Truth Commissions*. New York: Routledge, 2011.

Hicks, Celeste. *The Trial of Hissène Habré: How the People of Chad Brought a Tyrant to Justice*. London: Zed Books, 2018.

Human Rights Council (Working Group on the Universal Periodic Review). Compilation on Chad. Report of the Office of the United Nations High Commissioner for Human Rights. UN Doc A/HRC/WG.6/31/TCD/2, August 31, 2018.

Human Rights Council (Working Group on the Universal Periodic Review). Summary of Stakeholders' Submissions on Chad. Report of the Office of the United Nations High Commissioner for Human Rights. UN Doc A/HRC/WG.6/31/TCD/3, August 24, 2018.

Human Rights News. *Les victimes accusent Hissène Habré de crimes contre l'humanité. Plaintes déposées au Sénégal contre l'ex-dictateur du Tchad*, September 16, 2008. https://www.hrw.org/legacy/french/docs/2008/09/15/senegal19817.htm (accessed 16 May 2021).

Human Rights Watch. *Allié de la France, condamné par l'Afrique. Les relations entre la France et le régime tchadien de Hissène Habré (1982–1990)*, June 2016.

Human Rights Watch. *Blog, Le procès de Hissène Habré*, September 7, 2015. https://www.hrw.org/fr/content/280858 (accessed 28 October 2021).

Human Rights Watch. *Chad: Government Fails Ex-Dictator's Victims. 3 Years On, No Action on Habré-Era Reparation*, March 22, 2018.

Human Rights Watch. *Chad: The Victims of Hissène Habré Still Waiting for Justice*, July 2005.

Human Rights Watch. *Enabling a Dictator the United States and Chad's Hissène Habré 1982–1990*, June 2016.

Human Rights Watch. *Ex-Chad Dictator Indicted in Senegal*, News Release, February 3, 2000.

Human Rights Watch. *Hissène Habré, les archives de l'horreur, les archives de la police politique*, 2003.

Human Rights Watch. *Les Agissements Déplorables du Sénégal*, July 4, 2000.

Human Rights Watch. *Le Sénégal a compétence sur les crimes commis par Hissène Habré*, May 10, 2000.

Human Rights Watch. *Senegal/Chad: No Reparations for Ex-Dictator's Victims: Four Years After Hissène Habré's Conviction, African Union and Chad Fail Victims*, 2020.

Human Rights Watch. *Supported by France, Convicted by Africa France-Chad Relations During the Hissène Habré's Rule (1982–1990)*, June 2016.

Human Rights Watch. *Tchad: Les victimes de Hissène Habré toujours en attente de justice*, July 2005.

IACDH. *"Las Dos Erres" Massacre vs Guatemala*, Judgment, November 24, 2009, Series C no. 211.

ICC. Situation in Libya, *The Prosecutor v. Saif Al-Islam Gaddafi*. No. ICC-01/11-01/11. Case Information Sheet, November 2009.

ICC. *The Prosecutor v. Laurent Gbagbo and Charles Blé Goudé*. Judgment in the Appeal of the Prosecutor Against Trial Chamber I's Decision on the No Case to Answer Motions. No. ICC-02/11-01/15-1400, March 31, 2021.

ICC. *The Prosecutor v. Laurent Gbagbo and Charles Blé Goudé*. No. ICC-02/11-01/15. Case Information Sheet, July 2021.

ICC. *The Prosecutor v. Laurent Gbagbo and Charles Blé Goudé*. Reasons for Oral Decision of 15 January 2019 on the Requête de la Défense de Laurent Gbagbo afin qu'un jugement d'acquittement portant sur toutes les charges soit prononcé en faveur de Laurent Gbagbo et que sa mise en liberté immédiate soit ordonnée. No. ICC-02/11-01/15-1263, July 16, 2019.

ICC. *The Prosecutor v. Laurent Gbagbo*. Warrant of Arrest for Laurent Koudou Gbagbo. No. ICC-02/11-01/11-1, November 23, 2011.

ICC. *The Prosecutor v. Laurent Koudou Gbagbo*. No. ICC-02/11-01/11, Transcripts, December 5, 2011.

ICC. *The Prosecutor v. Omar Hassan Ahmad Al Bashir*. No. ICC-02/05-01/09, Case Information Sheet, April 2018.

ICC. *The Prosecutor v. Omar Hassan Ahmad Al Bashir*. Second Warrant of Arrest for Omar Hassan Ahmad Al Bashir. No. ICC-02/05-01/09-95, July 12, 2010.

ICC. *The Prosecutor v. Omar Hassan Ahmad Al Bashir*. Warrant of Arrest for Omar Hassan Ahmad Al Bashir. No. ICC-02/05-01/09-1, March 4, 2009.

ICC. *The Prosecutor v. Saif Al-Islam Gaddafi*. Case Information Sheet. No. ICC-01/11-01/11, November 2009.

ICC. *The Prosecutor v. Thomas Lubanga Dyilo*. Judgment Pursuant to Article 74 of the Statute. No. ICC-01/04-01/06, March 14, 2012.

ICC. *Trial Chamber I decides to release Laurent Gbagbo and Charles Blé Goudé following acquittal*. No. ICC-CPI-20190116-PR1428, Press Release, January 16, 2019.

ICJ. Application Instituting Proceedings, Questions Relating to the Obligation to Prosecute or Extradite (*Belgium v. Senegal*), Filed in the Registry of the Court on 19 February 2009.

ICJ. Questions Relating to the Obligation to Prosecute or Extradite (*Belgium v. Senegal*), Judgment, I.C.J. Reports 2012.

ICJ. Questions Relating to the Obligation to Prosecute or Extradite (*Belgium v. Senegal*). Request for the Indication of Provisional Measures, Order, May 28, 2009.

ICJ. Request for the Indication of Provisional Measures submitted by the Government of the Kingdom of Belgium, February 19, 2009.

ICTR. *Le Procureur C. Jean-Bosco Barayagwiza*, Décision sur la requête des conseils de la défense en retrait de leur commission d'office. No. ICTR–97–19–T, November 2, 2000.

ICTR. *The Prosecutor v. Jean-Paul Akayesu*. No. ICTR-96-4-T, September 2, 1998.

ICTY. *Prosecutor v. Slobqdan Milosevic*, Transcripts, July 3, 2001.

ICTY. *The Prosecutor v. Dusko Tadiç*. No. IT-94-1-T, Judgment, May 7, 1997.

ICTY. *The Prosecutor v. Mitar Vasiljevié*. No. fT-98-32-A, February 25, 2004.

Interview of a Member of the Working Group on the Creation of the EAC.

Interview of Goukouni Weddeye in Alain Foca (Radio France International). Hissène Habré, l'affaire Claustre (1 et 2/6). Raymond Depardon filme Françoise Claustre. *IT1 20H*, September 27, 1975. https://m.ina.fr/video/CAA7501083501/raymond-depardon-filme-francoise-claustre-video.html (accessed 16 May 2021).

Kioko, Ben. Creating the EAC in Senegal. Perspectives From the African Union. In *The President on Trial: Prosecuting Hissene Habré*, edited by Sharon Weill, Kim Thuy Seelinger, and Kerstin Bree Carlson, 69–76. New York: Oxford University Press, 2020.

Kitir, Zakaria Fadoul. *Les moments difficiles dans les prisons d'Hissène Habré en 1989*. Editions Sépia, 1998.

Kritz, Neil J., ed. *Transitional Justice: How Emerging Democracies Reckon With Former Regimes.* 3 Vol. Washington, D.C.: United States Institute of Peace Press, 1995.

La cellule de communication avec la collaboration des Avocats. *Le Sénégal « juge » le Président Hissein Habré*, June 2015.

La cellule de communication du Président HH. "L'audience du mardi 9 septembre: Arnaud Dingammadji, prétendu Expert tchadien des Chambres africaines, ignore tout de son pays", Publication on Facebook « non au procès de Hissein Habré par le Sénégal », September 15, 2015. https://www.facebook.com/notes/non-au-proc%C3%A8s-de-hissein-habr%C3%A9-par-le-s%C3%A9n%C3%A9gal/laudience-du-mardi-9-septembre-arnaud-dingammadji-pr%C3%A9tendu-expert-tchadien-des-c/891584697595460/?__xts__[0]=68.ARDdK_M0U8YrI-rLvJm337tijCT6TrteUbdAkDjlLP2q0cPutSLXMQjph6Tx5pIn6cOvU2m6ZKkFDPOMY4VBWUVqvkryjIwAwWy7XFqM8TdSml0a-d3qNdeiSjT7pUQM2cDjNwTEM00YHmou4po0UdO7pRp_kajZsWohgENDvvLoKGHI1WG2DDijngWA2k5ypU-81p7jKRuQXoHZajLWKX8SPYoeuT5e2wiRZ7hrXkaxIx23dAUGSGBY-tOucpsmKxXM9BVYU7mlTDylbFwCWaiIxSO79OBUwYm0NQCbpUQ8QB-j_6QY0hGxeu0p_IAHFhGhA7uzN9tccxccdk53U1hg&__tn__=HH-R (accessed 16 May 2021).

Law No. 04/L-274 on Ratification of the International Agreement Between the Republic of Kosovo and the European Union on the European Union Rule of Law Mission in Kosovo, April 23, 2014.

Law No. 05/L-053 on Specialist Chambers and Specialist Prosecutor's Office, August 3, 2015.

Le Comité de Pilotage du Comité International pour le Jugement Equitable de Hissène Habré. *La condamnation d'Hissène Habré au Tchad n'a aucune incidence sur les obligations du Sénégal*. Communiqué de presse, August 18, 2008.

Le monde. *Le retour annoncé d'Hissène Habré au Tchad provoque la confusion*, July 9, 2011.

Letter of the United Nations Office of High Commissioner for Human Rights to Reed Brody. Reference G/SO 229/31 SENE (1), April 27, 2001.

Lutz, Ellen L., and Caitlin Reiger, eds. *Prosecuting Heads of State*. Cambridge: Cambridge University Press, 2009.

Mari, Jean-Paul. *Le Nouvel Observateur Monde*, July 10–16, 1987.

Mémoire aux fins d'indemnisation, June 10, 2016.

Memorandum of Understanding Between Lebanon and the Special Tribunal for Lebanon Concerning the Office of the Special Tribunal in Lebanon, June 17, 2009.

Moseley, K. P. Zaghawa. In *Ethnic Groups of Africa and the Middle East: An Encyclopedia*, edited by John A. Shoup, 333. Santa Barbara: ABC-CLIO, 2011.

Nguedmbaye, Moussa. Tchad: encore une manifestation des victimes de l'ancien président Habré, Octobre 14, 2019. https://tchadinfos.com/politique/tchad-encore-une-manifestation-des-victimes-de-lancien-president-habre/ (accessed 16 May 2021).

Office of the United Nations High Commissioner for Human Rights. *Rule-of-Law Tools for Post-Conflict States. Truth Commissions.* UN Doc .HR/PUB/06/1, 2006.

Official Website of Hissein Habré. http://hisseinhabre.com/hissein-habre-resume-de-la-biographie-de-l-ancien-chef-de-l-etat-du-tchad.html (accessed 16 May 2021).

ONU info. *L'ONU appelle le Sénégal à revoir sa décision d'extrader Habré au Tchad*, July 10, 2011.

Osiel, Mark. *Mass Atrocity, Collective Memory, and the Law*. New Brunswick, NJ: Transaction Publishers, 1997.

Plainte avec Constitution de Partie Civile. Suleymane Guengueng et al., A Monsieur le Doyen des juges d'instruction près le Tribunal régional hors classe de Dakar, January 2000.

Protocol on Amendments to the Protocol on the Statute of the African Court of Justice and Human Rights, June 27, 2014 (Annex).

Raghavan, Sudarsan. Former Sudanese Ruler Omar Hassan al-Bashir is Convicted of Corruption, Money Laundering. *Washington Post*, December 14, 2019.

Reagan, Ronald. Remarks at a Fundraising Dinner for the Nicaragua Refugee Fund (Speech), April 15, 1985. https://www.reaganlibrary.gov/research/speeches/41585f (accessed 16 May 2021).

Reagan, Ronald. Remarks Following Meetings With President Hissein Habre of Chad, June 19, 1987. https://www.reaganlibrary.gov/research/speeches/061987g (accessed 16 May 2021).

République du Sénégal. Communiqué du Ministère des Affaires étrangères, Novembre 27, 2005. https://www.hrw.org/legacy/french/docs/2005/11/27/chad12130.htm (accessed 16 May 2021).

République du Sénégal. Loi constitutionnelle no. 2008-33 du 7 août 2008.

République du Sénégal. Loi no. 2007-02 du 12 février 2007 modifiant le Code pénal, JO 2007-03-10, n° 6332.

République du Sénégal. Loi no. 2007-05 du 12 février 2007, modifiant le Code de procédure pénale relative à la mise en œuvre du Traité de Rome instituant la Cour pénale internationale.

République du Sénégal. Loi no. 2012-25 du 28 décembre 2012 autorisant le Président de la République à ratifier l'Accord entre le Gouvernement de la République du Sénégal et l'Union africaine sur la création de Chambres africaines extraordinaires au sein des juridictions sénégalaises.

République du Sénégal. Ministère de la justice, Direction de l'administration pénitentiaire. Communiqué de presse, April 6, 2020.

République du Sénégal. Tribunal de Grande Instance Hors Classe de Dakar, Cabinet du juge d'application des peines. Ordonnance accordant une permission de sortir au détenu Hissène Habré, April 6, 2020.

République du Sénégal, Conseil constitutionnel. Affaire no. 1C2015, Décision du 02 mars 2015.

République du Sénégal, Cour d'appel de Dakar (Chambre d'accusation). Arrêt no. 135 du 04-07-2000/Accusation.

République du Sénégal, Cour d'appel de Dakar (Tribunal Régional Hors Classe de Dakar. Cabinet de M. Demba Kandji Juge d'instruction. No. du Parquet: 482, No. de l'instruction: 13/2000), Procès-verbal d'interrogatoire de première comparution, February 3, 2000.

République du Sénégal, Cour de cassation. Souleymane Guengueng et autres c/ Hissène Habré. Arrêt no. 14 du 20-3-2001 Pénal.

RFI Afrique. Tchad: les victimes d'Hissène Habré réclament toujours le versement des indemnisations. February 5, 2020. http://www.rfi.fr/fr/afrique/20200205-tchad-victimes-hiss%C3%A8-habr%C3%A9-r%C3%A9clament-versement-indemnisations (accessed 16 May 2021).

RFI Afrique. Tchad: « sit-in » d'artistes en soutien aux victimes d'Hissène Habré, July 20, 2019. http://www.rfi.f.r/fr/afrique/20190720-tchad-justice-sit-in-artistes-soutien-victimes-hissene-habre (accessed 16 May 2021).

Rich, Jeremy. Idriss Déby Itno. In *Dictionary of African Biography*, edited by Emmanuel Kwaku Akyeampong and Henry Louis Gates, 172–173. New York: Oxford University Press, 2012.

Ridley, Nick. *Terrorism in East and West Africa: The Under-Focused Dimension*. Cheltenham: Edward Elgar Publishing, 2014.

Rohter, Larry. Nicaragua Rebels Accused of Abuses. *New York Times*, March 7, 1985, Section A, Page 1.

Rome Statute of the International Criminal Court. Opened for Signature July 17, 1998. 2187 UNTS 3 (Entered into Force July 1, 2002).

Sada, H. Habré: connais pas. *Jeune Afrique*. No. 1563, December 12–18, 1990.

Sall, Alioune. *L'affaire Habré. Aspects judiciaires nationaux et internationaux*. Paris: L'Harmattan, 2013.

Samb, Moussa. Etat des lieux de la justice. Réflexions sur une justice en crise. In *Senegal (2000–2012). Les institutions et politiques publiques à l'épreuve*, edited by Momar-Coumba Diop, 347–379. Dakar-Paris: CRES-Karthala.

Schotsmans, Martien. Editorial. In *Le procès Habré*, RCN Justice & Démocratie, Le Bulletin n°48. Juillet-Août 2016, 3.

SCSL. *The Prosecutor of the Special Court v. Charles Ghankay Taylor*. No. SCSL-2003-01-T, Transcripts, July 14, 2009.

SCSL. *The Prosecutor v. Charles Ghankay Taylor*. No. SCSL-03-01-T, Judgment, May 18, 2012.

Seck, Cheikh Yérim. Accusé Madické Niang. *Jeune Afrique*, April 21, 2008. https://www.jeuneafrique.com/86140/politique/accus-madick-niang/ (accessed 16 May 2021).

Sénégal, Présidence de la République-Le Ministre Porte-Parole. *Le Sénégal prépare activement le jugement de M. Hissène Habré*. Communiqué, Dakar, November 2, 2006.

Serres, François. Procès Habré: Chroniques d'injustice, Jour 1, September 10, 2015, Online. https://www.dakaractu.com/Proces-Habre-Chroniques-d-injustice-Jour-1_a97175.html (accessed 16 May 2021).

Silberzahn, Claude (avec Jean Guisnel). *Au cœur du secret: 1500 jours aux commandes de la DGSE (1989–1993)*. Paris: Fayard, 1995.

South Africa. *Withdrawal of Notification of Withdrawal*. C.N.121.2017.Treaties-xviii.10, March 7, 2017.

Spartacus, Colonel. *Les documents secrets. Opération Manta. 1983–1984*. Plon, 1985.

Spiga, Valentina. Non-retroactivity of Criminal Law: A New Chapter in the Hissène Habré Saga. *Journal of International Criminal Justice* 9, no. 1 (March 2011): 5–23.

STL. *Akhbar Be/Rut S.A.L. Ibrahim Mohamed Ali Al Amin*. No. Stl-14-06/Pt/Cj, Motifs de la décision Relative à la commission d'office d'un Conseil, June 5, 2014.

Table ronde des donateurs pour le financement du procès d'Hissène Habré. Document final, Dakar, November 24, 2010.

TrustAfrica. *Ministère public contre la défense de Habré, Rapport de l'audience numéro 3 du jeudi 7 septembre 2015*. https://www.trustafrica.org/images/ICJ_reports/fr/CAE%20-%20Audience%20du%207%20septembre%202015.pdf (accessed 28 October 2021).

TV5-Monde. *Tchad: en quoi le procès et la condamnation de Hissène Habré ont été un tournant en Afrique?* August 28, 2021. https://information.tv5monde.com/afrique/tchad-en-quoi-le-proces-et-la-condamnation-de-hissene-habre-ont-ete-un-tournant-en-afrique (accessed 28 October 2021).

UN News. *UN Rights Chief Hails Senegal's Decision Not to Repatriate Former Dictator to Chad*, July 12, 2011.

United Nations News. Chad: UN Rights Office Profoundly Disturbed Over Violence Against Protesters, April 30, 2021. https://news.un.org/en/story/2021/04/1091082 (accessed 16 May 2021).

United Nations Secretary General. *The Rule of Law and Transitional Justice in Conflict and Post-Conflict Societies*. UN Doc. S/2004/616, 2004.

United States Department of State. *Country Reports on Human Rights Practices for 1983*. Submitted to the Committee on Foreign Affairs U.S. House of Representatives and the Committee on Foreign Relations U.S. Senate by the Department of State. Washington, D.C.: Printing Government Office, February 1984.

United States Department of State. *Country Reports on Human Rights Practices for 1984*. Submitted to the Committee on Foreign Relations U.S. Senate and the Committee on Foreign Affairs U.S. House of Representatives by the Department of State. Washington, D.C.: Printing Government Office, February 1985.

United States Department of State. *Country Reports on Human Rights Practices for 1985*. Submitted to the Committee on Foreign Affairs U.S. House of Representatives and the Committee on Foreign Relations U.S. Senate by the Department of State. Washington, D.C.: Printing Government Office, February 1986.

United States Department of State. *Country Reports on Human Rights Practices for 1986*. Submitted to the Committee on Foreign Relations U.S. Senate and the Committee on Foreign Affairs U.S. House of Representatives by the Department of State. Washington, D.C.: Printing Government Office, February 1987.

United States Department of State. *Country Reports on Human Rights Practices for 1987*. Submitted to the Committee on Foreign Affairs U.S. House of Representatives and the Committee on Foreign Relations U.S. Senate by the Department of State. Washington, D.C.: Printing Government Office, February 1988.

United States Department of State. *Country Reports on Human Rights Practices for 1988*. Submitted to the Committee on Foreign Relations U.S. Senate and the Committee on Foreign Affairs U.S. House of Representatives by the Department of State. Washington, D.C.: Printing Government Office, February 1989.

United States Department of State. *Country Reports on Human Rights Practices for 1989*. Submitted to the Committee on Foreign Affairs U.S. House of Representatives and the Committee on Foreign Relations U.S. Senate by the Department of State. Washington, D.C.: Printing Government Office, February 1990.

United States Department of State. *Country Reports on Human Rights Practices for 1990*. Submitted to the Committee on Foreign Relations U.S. Senate and the Committee on Foreign Affairs U.S. House of Representatives by the Department of State. Washington: U.S. Printing Government Office, February 1991.

United States Department of State, Bureau of Public Affairs. *Chad, US Policy*. Washington, D.C.: Bureau of Public Affairs, Department of State, July 1987.

Weddeye, Goukouni. *Combattant, une vie pour le Tchad*. Paris: Espaces & Signes, 2019.

Weill, Sharon, Kim Thuy Seelinger, and Kerstin Bree Carlson. Hissene Habre on Trial: Mapping the Long Road to Justice. In *The President on Trial: Prosecuting Hissene Habré*, edited by Sharon Weill, Kim Thuy Seelinger, and Kerstin Bree Carlson, 1–12. New York: Oxford University Press, 2020.

Wippman, David. The Costs of International Justice. *The American Journal of International Law* 100, no. 4 (2006): 861–881.

Index

About the Author

Emmanuel Guematcha is senior lecturer of international law at the University of French Guiana and lecturer of transitional justice at the University of Paris–Nanterre.

luct-compliance
UK
847